VISUAL QUICKSTART GUIDE

CORELDRAW 11

FOR WINDOWS

Steve Schwartz and Phyllis Davis

Peachpit Press

Visual QuickStart Guide
CorelDraw 11 for Windows
Steve Schwartz and Phyllis Davis

Peachpit Press
1249 Eighth Street
Berkeley, CA 94710
510/524-2178
800/283-9444
510/524-2221 (fax)

Find us on the World Wide Web at: http://www.peachpit.com
To report errors, please send a note to errata@peachpit.com

Peachpit Press is a division of Pearson Education

Copyright © 2003 by Steve Schwartz, Phyllis Davis

Editors: Whitney Walker, Suki Gear
Production Coordinators: Gloria Márquez, Lisa Brazieal
Copyeditor: Steve Schwartz
Compositor: Steve Schwartz
Indexer: Emily Glossbrenner
Cover Design: The Visual Group

ISBN 0-321-13629-2

9 8 7 6 5 4 3 2 1

Printed and bound in the United States of America

About the authors

Steve Schwartz has been a computer industry writer since the days of the early micros. He has written for dozens of major magazines and is the author of more than 40 computer and game books, including these titles in the *Visual QuickStart* series: Microsoft Office v. X, Entourage 2001, Internet Explorer 5, Internet Explorer 3, and Quicken 6. Steve has a Ph.D. in psychology and lives with his sons and faithful pets in the fictional town of Lizard Spit, Arizona. He can be reached via his official Web site at http://www.siliconwasteland.com.

Phyllis Davis is a writer, graphic designer, instructor, and software developer. She wrote the previous editions of the *CorelDraw for Windows: Visual QuickStart Guide*. When she's not busy designing books, fine art posters, and brochures with CorelDraw, Phyllis can be found developing and teaching computer courses, digging in her garden, tap dancing, and playing with her wonderful children.

Special thanks

To Suki Gear, Whitney Walker, Gloria Márquez, Lisa Brazieal, Kate Reber, Emily Glossbrenner, Marjorie Baer, and Nancy Davis of Peachpit Press; Angela Sulpher and Kerry Hodgins of Corel Corporation; and Matt Wagner of Waterside Productions.

TABLE OF CONTENTS

TABLE OF CONTENTS

TABLE OF CONTENTS

INTRODUCTION

Welcome to *CorelDraw 11 for Windows: Visual QuickStart Guide.*

Our purpose in writing this book is to share our collective experience as design and computer professionals. In keeping with the *Visual QuickStart Guide* format, the material is profusely illustrated, presented in easy to follow step-by-step fashion, and designed to take the mystery out of graphic design with CorelDraw.

CorelDraw 11 offers a complete set of tools for creating many kinds of drawings and multipage documents—from birthday cards, logos, brochures, and newsletters to garden designs and World Wide Web pages. CorelDraw has incredible power and loads of features, all incorporated into a sophisticated interface. And yet the program is still easy to use.

If you're new to CorelDraw 11, the program may initially seem complex because its so rich in features. But if you take it one step at a time, you'll soon be creating impressive drawings.

For those of you who are acquainted with previous versions of CorelDraw, you can use this book as a guide to the new features and techniques, as well as a handy reference. This edition has been updated to discuss the new features introduced in CorelDraw 11, as well as many features that were omitted from previous editions.

THE BASICS

In this chapter, you'll be introduced to the essentials of CorelDraw 11, as follows:

◆ A brief explanation of how CorelDraw 11 works and the kinds of drawings you can create with it

◆ A list of the new features in version 11

◆ The important parts of the user interface

◆ Options for viewing your drawings

◆ How to get help when you need it

◆ A glossary of important terms you'll need to understand

Objects vs. Bitmaps

Computer imaging programs are typically designed either to work with objects or with bitmap images. CorelDraw 11 is an *object-oriented* drawing program. Objects are created using drawing tools that make shapes defined by mathematical formulas. Objects are also known as *vectors* or *drawings*.

A vector object has properties that define it, such as color, shape, and size. An object is displayed with smooth lines and continuous colors, whether viewed from far away or up close. Because each object in a drawing (**Figure 1.1**) is independent of every other object, you can easily select, move, resize, alter the color, or change the layer (front to back) of any object. Drawings are *resolution independent;* that is, the printout quality depends only on the resolution of the printer.

Bitmap images (**Figure 1.2**) are made of tiny dots called *pixels.* Although you can create a bitmap image from scratch, the most common sources of such images are digital photos and scans. Corel Photo-Paint and Adobe Photoshop are examples of image-editing programs.

The shape and color of a bitmap image appear smooth from a distance, but—when viewed up close—you can see tiny, individual squares. Because a bitmap image is composed of dots, editing can (and *must*) be done at the dot level. It is more difficult to select items in a bitmap image than it is to select an object in a drawing program because they *are* just dots, rather than selectable objects. The print quality of a bitmap image depends on the resolution at which it was saved; that is, bitmap images are *resolution dependent.*

Figure 1.1 This realistic-looking monitor is actually a drawing composed of 267 separate objects—mainly lines, rectangles, and ellipses.

Figure 1.2 This photograph taken with a digital camera is an example of a bitmap image. To modify this picture, you'd use an image-editing application, such as Corel Photo-Paint.

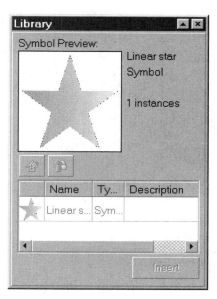

Figure 1.3 Use the Library docker to manage the symbols you've created.

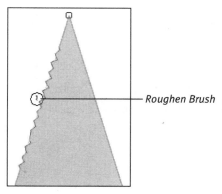

Roughen Brush

Figure 1.4 The Roughen Brush can add irregularities to otherwise smooth lines and curves.

What's New in Version 11?

Here is a brief rundown of the changes introduced in CorelDraw 11:

- ◆ **Saving application defaults.** To make it simpler to set application and document defaults, a Save Settings as Default command has been added to the Tools menu. When you start a new document, the saved settings (such as a new default font) will automatically be used.

- ◆ **Autobackups enhanced.** When an autobackup is in progress, it is indicated in the status bar. You can cancel it by pressing (Esc). Following a crash, you are given an opportunity to open autobackup versions of any files on which you were working.

- ◆ **Library docker.** This new docker (**Figure 1.3**) lets you store and manage *symbols*—reusable objects that you've created.

- ◆ **3 Point Tools.** Rectangles, ellipses, and curves can all be drawn in a new way—by specifying three defining points via clicking and dragging. In support of this feature, three new 3 Point Tools have been added to the toolbox.

- ◆ **New line/curve tools.** A Pen Tool has been added to make it easier for users of other programs to make the transition to CorelDraw. You can use the Polyline Tool to draw both line and curves with one tool.

- ◆ **New brushes.** The new Roughen Brush (**Figure 1.4**) enables you to add jagged imperfections to a line, curve, or text. The Smudge Brush is used to distort or pull out a portion of a curve or bitmap.

CorelDraw 11 in a Nutshell

CorelDraw documents are made up of separate elements called *objects* (**Figure 1.5**). An object's edge is called a *path*. Paths can be *closed* or *open*. An object with a closed path can be filled with color, whereas an object with an open path cannot. The path of an object passes through *nodes* that shape the path.

Some CorelDraw tools automatically create closed path objects. For instance, the Ellipse Tool makes various sized ovals and circles, the Rectangle Tool makes rectangles and squares, and the Polygon Tool makes polygons with three or more sides.

Other tools create closed or open path objects, depending on how they are used. The Freehand Tool can be used to draw a line (an open path) or a squiggly circle (a closed path). The Bézier Tool can be used to draw smooth curving lines or closed, curved shapes.

To modify an object, you must first *select* it. H*andles* appear in a rectangular formation around any selected object (**Figure 1.6**).

Objects can be modified using a variety of program features, such as menu commands, dialog boxes, dockers, and tools. For instance, an object's path can be shaped by moving its nodes and control points with the Shape Tool. An object can be uniformly filled with a spot or process color with one click in the color palette. Objects can be filled with patterns, textures, and fountain fills with the Interactive Fill Tool. Objects can be rotated, skewed, scaled, and mirrored with the Pick Tool. With the Interactive Blend Tool, you can blend one object into another—creating a morph.

CorelDraw lets you be creative with text. Text can be *artistic* or *paragraph*. It can float free on the page as a *text object*, follow the path of an object, or use an object as a container to shape it. Text can also be converted to curves, changing it into a graphic object whose outline can be modified like any other outline.

Figure 1.5 This simple drawing is composed of five separate objects: four colored stars and a text string.

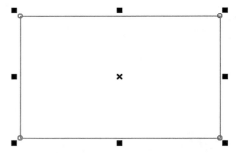

Figure 1.6 You can click and drag any handle to resize an object.

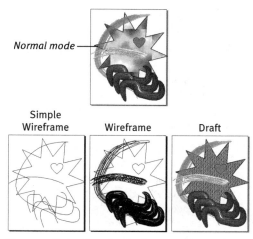

Normal mode

Simple
Wireframe   Wireframe   Draft

Figure 1.7 To improve the display speed for a normal drawing (top), you can view it in any of three reduced detail modes (bottom).

You can change the view of a drawing to make editing easier. You can *zoom in* to get a close look and work with small details or *zoom out* to see the drawing as a whole. You can use the Hand Tool to move the drawing around within the drawing window.

To speed screen redraw, a document can be viewed in any of three reduced-detail modes: simple wireframe, wireframe, or draft (**Figure 1.7**). You can also view a drawing in Enhanced mode or as a Full-Screen Preview.

You can use precision tools such as guidelines, grids, rulers, and the Align and Distribute dialog box to place objects exactly where you want them.

When you finish a drawing, it can be printed or saved to a file for high resolution output or as separations. Prior to printing, you can see what the printed document will look like in Print Preview mode.

CORELDRAW 11 IN A NUTSHELL

The CorelDraw 11 Interface

A program's *interface* refers to the way it looks and to the controls, dialog boxes, and other components that enable you to interact with it. **Figure 1.8** shows the important parts of the CorelDraw 11 interface.

1 **Title bar.** It displays the program name and name/location of the active document.

2 **Menu bar.** Click any menu title (such as File or Edit) to choose commands.

3 **Standard toolbar.** One of many command bars, the Standard toolbar's icons provide quick access to common Windows commands, such as New, Open, Save, and Print.

It also includes CorelDraw commands, such as Import, Export, and Zoom.

4 **Property bar.** This context-sensitive toolbar has icons and drop-down lists that change dynamically, depending on what is selected. This gives you access to the most important commands associated with the selected tool or object.

5 **Rulers.** The mouse pointer's current position is indicated by dotted marks on the vertical and horizontal rulers. Rulers can be moved to where you need them and used to accurately size objects. Double-click either ruler to alter the measurement unit or other ruler properties.

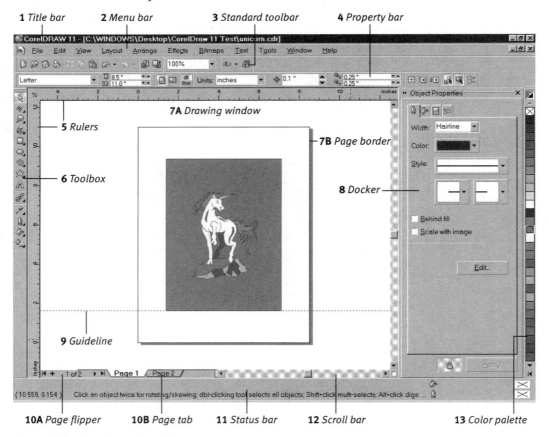

1 *Title bar*   **2** *Menu bar*   **3** *Standard toolbar*   **4** *Property bar*

7A *Drawing window*

5 *Rulers*

7B *Page border*

6 *Toolbox*

8 *Docker*

9 *Guideline*

10A *Page flipper*   **10B** *Page tab*   **11** *Status bar*   **12** *Scroll bar*   **13** *Color palette*

Figure 1.8 The CorelDraw 11 interface.

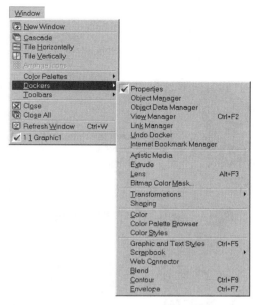

Figure 1.9 To display a docker, choose it from the Window > Dockers submenu.

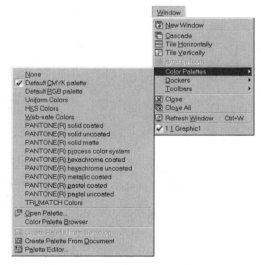

Figure 1.10 To add or remove a color palette, choose it from the Window > Color Palettes submenu. The checked palettes are displayed.

6 Toolbox. The toolbox contains drawing and editing tools. You can drag it onto the drawing window (making it float) or dock it along any edge of the screen (as shown). Click the down-arrow on any icon to display a *flyout* menu of related icons.

7 Drawing Window (A) and Page Border (B). You can draw anywhere you want in the drawing window, but anything drawn outside of the page border won't be printed.

8 Dockers. Each docker (**Figure 1.9**) is related to a specific command or purpose, such as setting object properties, extruding, scaling, or contouring.

9 Guidelines. Use these non-printing, user-placed horizontal, vertical, or slanted guides to align objects. Click and drag from either ruler to create a horizontal or vertical guideline.

10 Page Flipper (A) and Page Tabs (B). Use the page flipper to add pages to a document, switch to another page, or move to the beginning or end of the document. Click any tab to switch to that page.

11 Status Bar. The status bar shows the position of the mouse pointer, lists keyboard shortcuts, and displays object information, such as size, position, and fill color.

12 Scroll Bars. Use the scroll bars to navigate around the drawing window. If you click the down arrow on the vertical scroll bar, the drawing page will move up. If you click the right arrow on the horizontal scroll bar, the page will move to the left.

13 Color Palette. Use a color palette to add fill and outline colors to objects. There are many predefined color systems that can be loaded into the color palette, such as Pantone and TruMatch. There is also a special color palette for creating images for display on the Web (**Figure 1.10**).

CorelDraw 11 Controls

Dialog boxes and toolbars contain many types of controls that you'll use to set options, make choices, and so on. Here are some of the most common controls you'll encounter:

- **Icons.** CorelDraw makes extensive use of tiny icons, as shown in **Figure 1.11**. A selected icon is shown as depressed; an unselected icon is raised. To select an icon (whether it is a single icon or in a set of icons), click it.

- **Flyouts.** A flyout (**Figure 1.12**) is a pop-out icon menu. When you click the tiny down-arrow on any toolbox icon and continue to hold down the mouse button, a flyout menu appears. Click to select an icon from the flyout.

- **Drop-down lists.** Drop-down lists (**Figure 1.13**) present a selection of items from which to choose. To open the list, click the tiny arrow to the right of the list box. Some drop-down lists allow you to enter text if you don't see a choice you like.

- **Text boxes.** Every text box (**Figure 1.14**) is designed to receive either a number or a text string. Those with up and down arrows to the right are meant for numbers. To enter data into a text box, you can type it or select a number by clicking the arrows.

- **Radio buttons.** Radio buttons (**Figure 1.14**) are used to select a single option from a set. Click any radio button to select that option; the selected option is denoted by a black circle.

- **Check boxes.** Click a check box (**Figure 1.14**) to turn an option on or off. A checkmark indicates that the option is on or enabled. Unlike radio buttons, you can normally select multiple check boxes.

Figure 1.11 Here are two pairs of icons; each is a set. The depressed one in each set is selected.

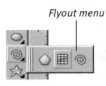

Figure 1.12 To see the flyout menu for any toolbox icon, click the tiny down-arrow.

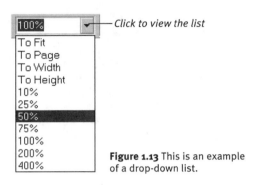

Figure 1.13 This is an example of a drop-down list.

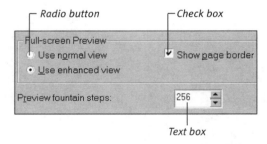

Figure 1.14 This dialog box section employs radio buttons, a text box, and a check box as controls.

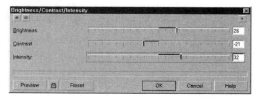

Figure 1.15 You can adjust this style of slider by clicking and dragging the bars or by typing numbers into the text boxes to the right.

Tabs

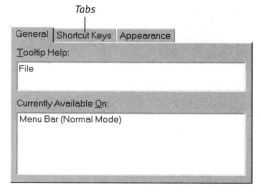

Figure 1.16 To view other sections of a tabbed dialog box, click a tab.

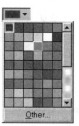

Figure 1.17 This drop-down color palette is a variant of a drop-down list, presenting a palette of colors to choose from rather than words.

Figure 1.18 In a tree view, click the plus or minus signs to expand or to collapse option sets.

◆ **Sliders.** You drag sliders (**Figure 1.15**) to increase or decrease a setting.

◆ **Tabs.** Tabs can be seen in the page flipper at the bottom of the CorelDraw window (see **Figure 1.8**) and in some dialog boxes (**Figure 1.16**). If you click a tab in the page flipper, the document page represented by the tab is displayed. Clicking a tab in a dialog box displays the options that are associated with the tab's name.

◆ **Drop-down palettes.** Rather than a presenting a list, clicking some drop-down buttons displays a graphic palette (such as the one shown in **Figure 1.17**). Make a selection by clicking a color or other graphic item. Click the Other button to view additional choices.

◆ **Tree views.** In a tree view (**Figure 1.18**), options are presented in a hierarchical list. Depending on the list's format, after expanding an item, you can select it (to choose a category from the Options dialog box, for example) or enter a checkmark in a check box.

✔ Tip

■ If you aren't sure what a control does, let the pointer rest over it for a second or so. A pop-up ToolTip will show the control's name and keyboard shortcut (if relevant).

Working with Menus

The menu bar (**Figure 1.19**) has 11 menus. Menus provide access to program commands, submenus, and dialog boxes.

To choose a command from a menu:

1. Click a menu title.

   The menu opens (**Figure 1.20**).

2. Move the mouse down to highlight the item you want.

   A tiny arrow to the right of a command means that it contains a submenu (**Figure 1.21**), which will pop open automatically.

3. Click to select the desired command.

✔ Tips

■ A command followed by an ellipsis (...) indicates that it will open a dialog box.

■ You can also open menus and choose commands using the keyboard. To open a menu, press [Alt]. Then press the underlined letter from the menu (such as **F** for **File**), or press [→] and [←] until you reach the desired menu. If the menu doesn't open automatically, press [Enter] or [↓]. To highlight a menu command, press [↓] and [↑]. (Press [→] to open a selected submenu.) Press [Enter] to execute the chosen command.

■ Some menu commands can be executed by pressing a *keyboard shortcut*—a special key combination, such as [Ctrl][Z]. To use a keyboard shortcut, hold down the *modifier key* or keys (such as [Shift], [Alt], or [Ctrl]), and tap the appropriate letter, number, character, or Function key. To view a list of the available keyboard shortcuts, choose Tools > Customization, click the Commands heading, click the Shortcut Keys tab, and click View All (**Figure 1.22**).

Figure 1.19 The CorelDraw menu bar displays menus.

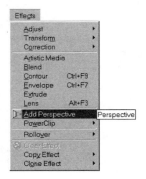

Figure 1.20 The Effects menu.

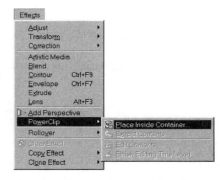

Figure 1.21 Choose a command from the PowerClip submenu.

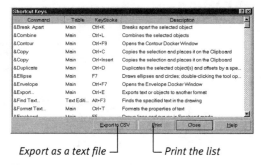

Export as a text file ┘   └ Print the list

Figure 1.22 You can view all available keyboard shortcuts in this dialog box.

Figure 1.23 Click and drag the toolbox ...

Figure 1.24 ... to make it float.

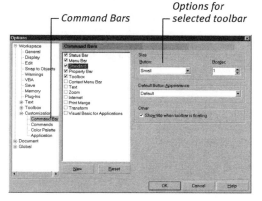

Figure 1.25 You can add or remove toolbars, as well as set options for them, in the Command Bars section of the Options dialog box.

Working with Toolbars

There are a dozen toolbars in CorelDraw 11. They provide easy access to common commands and dialog boxes. Three toolbars are available by default when you first launch the program: the Standard toolbar, the property bar, and the toolbox.

All toolbars can be docked or floating. A *docked* toolbar is locked into position on an edge of the screen; a *floating* toolbar can be freely positioned anywhere onscreen. The toolbox is an example of a docked toolbar. In Figure 1.8, the toolbox is docked on the left side of the screen. To undock the toolbox and make it float, left-click the double gray lines at its top edge (**Figure 1.23**) and drag it into the drawing window (**Figure 1.24**). To dock a floating toolbar, drag it to any edge of the screen: top, bottom, left, or right.

In addition to undocking and docking toolbars, you can display additional toolbars or hide the ones you don't currently need.

To add or remove toolbars:

1. Choose Window > Toolbars > More Toolbars.

   The Options dialog appears with the Customize heading selected.

2. Click the Command Bars heading in the left side of the dialog box.

   The Command Bars section opens (**Figure 1.25**).

3. In the toolbars list, click the check boxes next to the toolbars you want to display. Remove checkmarks from the toolbars you want to hide.

4. *Optional:* You can set display and behavior settings for any toolbar by selecting its name and then choosing options. To restore a toolbar's default behavior, select its name and click the Reset button.

5. Click OK.

The toolbox

The toolbox (**Figure 1.26**) contains dozens of tools for creating, formatting, and editing objects. Each of the currently visible tools in the toolbox can be selected by simply clicking them. However, many are actually a group of related tools. To select any of the other tools in a group, click and hold the tiny black arrow in the corner of the tool icon.

The property bar

The property bar (**Figure 1.27**), normally found beneath the Standard toolbar near the top of the screen, is a context-sensitive command bar. Depending on the tool or object that is selected, it displays different icons and options. For example, when you select the Zoom Tool, the property bar contains only zoom-related controls and icons.

The status bar

The status bar (Figure 1.28) is your guide to what's happening in the drawing window. It gives you information about the position of the pointer and the properties of the selected object, such as its shape, size, and fill and outline colors. The status bar can be one or two lines high. You can change its size by right-clicking the status bar and—from the pop-up menu that appears—choosing Customize > Status Bar > Size, followed by One Line or Two Lines. For more information about customizing the status bar, refer to Chapter 9, "Tools for Precision."

✔ Tips

- Check the status bar for shortcuts on how to perform common tasks that are relevant to the currently selected tool.

- You can learn what each icon and control does by letting the cursor rest over it for a moment. A pop-up ToolTip will appear.

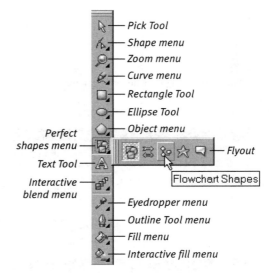

Figure 1.26 You select drawing tools by clicking icons in the toolbox.

Figure 1.27 The options in the property bar change to match the currently selected tool or object.

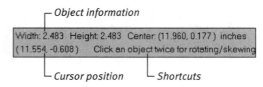

Figure 1.28 The status bar shows cursor and object positions, keyboard shortcuts, and many other types of useful information.

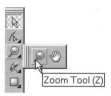

Figure 1.29 Select the Zoom Tool from the toolbox.

Zoom levels

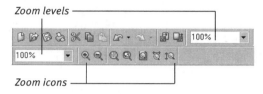

Zoom icons

Figure 1.30 For precision zooming, you can click icons and choose or set percentages on the property bar.

Setting a View Quality

The View menu provides commands for setting the view quality. *View quality* refers to the amount of detail displayed in the drawing window. To set a view quality, choose one of the following commands from the View menu.

- ◆ **Simple Wireframe.** Hides fills, extrusions, contours, and intermediate blend objects; shows only simple outlines and monochromatic bitmaps.

- ◆ **Wireframe.** Hides fills and displays monochromatic bitmaps, extrusions, contours, and intermediate blend objects.

- ◆ **Draft.** Shows some fills and only low-resolution bitmaps.

- ◆ **Normal.** The default view; shows all fills, objects, and high-resolution bitmaps.

- ◆ **Enhanced.** Uses over-sampling to enhance view quality.

Using the Zoom Tool

You use the Zoom Tool to magnify or reduce your view of a drawing. You can *zoom in* to see detail or *zoom out* to view the entire drawing. The property bar works in concert with the Zoom Tool. When the Zoom Tool is selected, the property bar displays zoom-related icons.

To zoom in (magnify):

1. Select the Zoom Tool from the toolbox or press [Z] (**Figure 1.29**).

2. Left-click the area you want to magnify or click the Zoom In icon on the property bar (**Figure 1.30**).

   The magnification will double.

To zoom out (reduce):

1. Select the Zoom Tool from the toolbox or press [Z].

2. Right-click the area you want to reduce or click the Zoom Out icon on the property bar (**Figure 1.30**).

   The magnification will be halved.

✔ Tips

- Zooming has no effect on the drawing, only on your view of it.

- You can also press [F3] to zoom out and [F4] to zoom in on all objects in a drawing. Press [Shift][F2] to zoom in on (fill the window with) a selected object.

- To zoom to a *preset* magnification, click the arrow on a zoom level box and select a magnification. To zoom to a *specific* magnification, type a number in a zoom level box and press [Enter].

- With the Zoom Tool selected, you can quickly achieve a variety of zoom effects by clicking the appropriate icon on the property bar (see **Figure 1.30**).

- You can view a drawing in Full-Screen Preview mode by pressing [F9].

13

Using the Hand Tool

You use the Hand Tool (or Pan Tool) to move the drawing within the drawing window.

To use the Hand Tool:

1. If the Hand Tool isn't visible in the toolbox, click the small arrow at the bottom right of the Zoom Tool to open the flyout menu (see **Figure 1.29**).

2. Click the Hand Tool icon (the open hand) to select it.

   The Hand Tool icon takes the place of the Zoom Tool in the toolbox. The pointer changes to a hand.

3. Position the Hand Tool over the drawing.

4. Left-click and drag in the desired direction (**Figure 1.31**). Drag up to move the drawing page up; drag down to move the page down.

5. Release the mouse button when the drawing page is in the desired position onscreen.

✔ Tip

■ You can quickly select the Hand Tool by pressing Ⓗ.

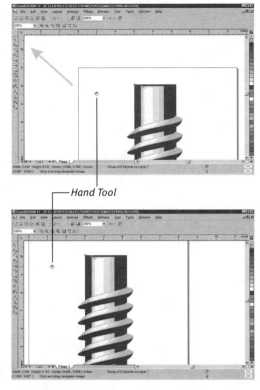

— Hand Tool

Figure 1.31 This pair of screen shots illustrates the process of using the Hand Tool to drag the drawing window up and to the left.

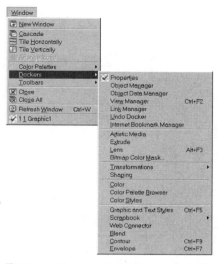

Figure 1.32 Choose a docker to open from the Window > Dockers submenu.

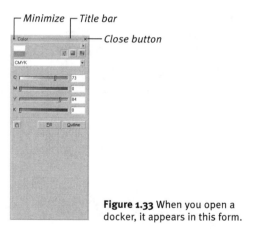

Figure 1.33 When you open a docker, it appears in this form.

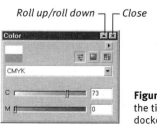

Figure 1.34 Double-click the title bar to undock a docker.

Working with Dockers

A *docker* is a tool palette/dialog box. Unlike most dialog boxes, dockers remain onscreen after changes are applied, letting you continue to work without having to reopen the docker. When you aren't using a docker, you can minimize it, leaving only the name tab visible. You can also undock any docker and move it to a more convenient screen position.

To open a docker:

1. Choose Window > Dockers.

A large submenu appears (**Figure 1.32**).

2. Choose a docker from the submenu.

The chosen docker opens and is docked (**Figure 1.33**).

To undock a docker:

◆ Double-click the docker's title bar (**Figure 1.34**).

◆ Click the double lines at the top of the docker and drag it onto the desktop.

To minimize a docked docker, click the double arrows in its title bar. To expand a minimized docker, click its name tab.

To close a docker (whether it is docked or undocked), click its Close button (**Figures 1.33** and **1.34**).

✔ Tips

■ You can have multiple dockers open. To switch from one to another, click the name tab of the docker you want to use.

■ Dockers can be docked at the right, left, top, or bottom of the drawing window.

■ When a docker is undocked, you can roll it up to save space by clicking the arrow in its title bar (**Figure 1.34**). To unroll the docker, click the arrow again. To redock a floating docker, double-click its title bar.

Getting Help

CorelDraw 11 includes a comprehensive help system with multiple components.

◆ **CorelDraw 11 User Guide.** This paper manual ships with CorelDraw.

◆ **Help Topics.** This Windows-style Help system has three sections: Contents, Index, and Search. To view this help information (**Figure 1.35**), choose Help > Help Topics.

◆ **CorelTutor.** The browser-based Tutor gives step-by-step instructions for completing tasks. Choose Help > CorelTutor.

◆ **What's New?** Choose Help > What's New? to get an overview of the new features.

◆ **Technical Support.** If you're having trouble getting CorelDraw to work, choose Help > Technical Support. Help Topics opens to the appropriate page.

◆ **Corel on the Web.** Choose links from the Help > Corel on the Web submenu (**Figure 1.36**). You can get more online help by clicking the Corel Online icon on the standard toolbar. The Web Connector docker opens with links to Corel's Web site.

◆ **ToolTips.** Pop-up balloons appear when you rest the pointer over an icon or other CorelDraw element (**Figure 1.37**).

✔ Tips

■ You can get help in many dialog boxes by clicking the Help button.

■ If you need to contact Corel's Technical Support or are just curious about your computer, choose Help > About CorelDraw. Click the System Info button in the dialog box that appears to view (and optionally save) an extraordinary amount of useful information about your PC (**Figure 1.38**).

View Help Topics table of contents
View the Index
Perform a free-form search

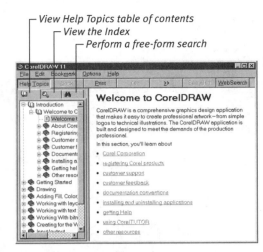

Figure 1.35 When you need help, you can turn to the CorelDraw 11 Help system.

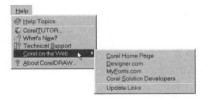

Figure 1.36 Choose a command to visit a helpful Corel Web page.

Figure 1.37 This is an example of a ToolTip.

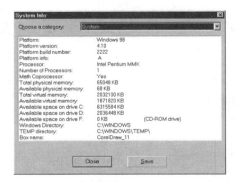

Figure 1.38 You can view and save detailed information about your computer hardware.

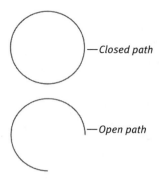

—Closed path

—Open path

Figure 1.39 Every object has either a closed or an open path.

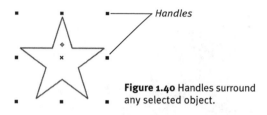

Handles

Figure 1.40 Handles surround any selected object.

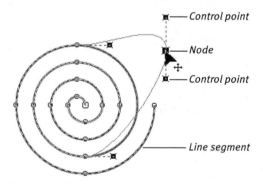

Control point

Node

Control point

Line segment

Figure 1.41 Elongating a line segment of a spiral.

Terms You Should Know

Following are some basic—yet essential—terms you will need to know as you use CorelDraw 11.

- **Object.** An object is an independent element that you can modify. Everything you draw in CorelDraw is an object.

- **Path.** A path is the outside perimeter of an object. Paths can either be open or closed (**Figure 1.39**). Paths pass through nodes.

- **Properties.** Properties are an object's attributes, such as fill color, size, and shape.

- **Handles.** These are the eight black squares that appear around any selected object (**Figure 1.40**). You use handles to change an object's dimensions or shape.

- **Nodes.** Nodes are the squares through which paths pass (**Figure 1.41**). Nodes can be manipulated with the Shape Tool.

- **Line segment.** This is the portion of a path between two nodes (**Figure 1.41**).

- **Control points.** These are the handles that you use to shape a line segment (**Figure 1.41**).

- **Select.** To select objects, click them with the Pick Tool. To select nodes, click them with the Shape Tool.

- **Multiple select.** Press (Shift) while clicking to select multiple objects or nodes.

- **Marquee select.** Using the Pick or Shape Tool, you can click and drag to create a dashed rectangle surrounding (and selecting) a group of objects or nodes.

- **Outline.** This line represents the path. An outline can be colored or invisible.

- **Fill.** A fill is a color, pattern, texture, or fountain added to the inside of an object.

- **Fountain fill.** A fountain fill is a gradual blend from one color to another or a cascade of different colors added to the inside of an object.

- **Guidelines.** Use these non-printing lines to precisely position and align objects.

- **Layer.** This is the transparent plane on which objects in a drawing are placed.

- **Stacking order.** This is the sequence in which objects are drawn (**Figure 1.42**). The first object drawn is at the bottom of the stack, while the last is on top.

- **Group.** A group is a set of combined objects that can be moved or modified as a single object (**Figure 1.43**).

- **Nested group.** A nested group is a grouping of two or more groups that behaves as a single object.

- **Ungroup.** Use the Ungroup command to restore a previously grouped set of objects to the original, individual objects.

Figure 1.42 These three objects are stacked one above the other.

Figure 1.43 When grouped, these objects can be moved and otherwise treated as a single object.

START-UP AND FILE HANDLING

2

It's time to get started! In this chapter, you'll learn about launching and exiting CorelDraw, as well as these important file-handling tasks:

◆ Creating, opening, saving, and closing CorelDraw documents

◆ Making backups of your drawings

◆ Importing and exporting graphics and text

◆ Managing document windows by moving, resizing, minimizing, maximizing, and arranging them onscreen

Launching CorelDraw

Like any other Windows program, you must launch (or *run*) CorelDraw in order to create, view, or edit documents. There are several ways you can do this.

To launch CorelDraw 11:

◆ Click the Start button on the Windows taskbar, and choose Programs > Corel Graphics Suite 11 > CorelDraw 11.

◆ Double-click a CorelDraw 11 shortcut that you've placed on the Windows desktop, in a folder, or in the Quick Launch toolbar (**Figure 2.1**). Depending on how you've configured Windows, you'll either need to double-click or click the shortcut.

◆ Double-click (or click) a CorelDraw file icon or any other type of graphic file that you've associated with CorelDraw. The program launches and opens the file.

When you launch CorelDraw 11 for the first time, you'll see the Welcome screen (**Figure 2.2**). The Welcome screen provides convenient access to six common commands: start a new graphic, open the last file you worked on, open an existing CorelDraw graphic, use a template as the basis for a new graphic, run CorelTutor, or learn about in the program's new features. Click an icon or click the close box to dismiss the Welcome screen.

If you don't want the Welcome screen to appear at start-up, remove the check from the check box at the bottom of the screen (**Figure 2.2**). In the future, CorelDraw will open to a blank screen. (This is the same as clicking the Welcome screen's close box or setting Nothing as the start-up action.) To later restore the Welcome screen or to set a different start-up action, choose Tools > Options (or press Ctrl J), select General, and choose an option from the pop-up list (**Figure 2.3**).

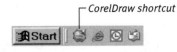

CorelDraw shortcut

Figure 2.1 You can drag your favorite shortcuts into the Quick Launch toolbar.

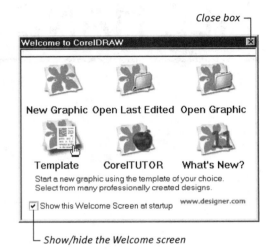

Close box

Show/hide the Welcome screen

Figure 2.2 Pick an option from the Welcome screen.

Figure 2.3 You can choose a start-up action from this pop-up list at the bottom of the Options dialog box.

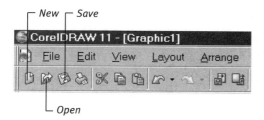

Figure 2.4 By clicking an icon, you can create a new file, open an existing file, or save your changes.

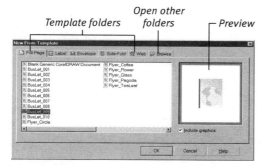

Figure 2.5 To open a CorelDraw template, select its file name and click OK.

Templates vs. Originals

One major advantage of using a template is that when you create a new document that is based on a template, you're always working with a *copy* of the template. You don't have to worry about inadvertently altering the original.

Creating a New Document

If you want to create a new, blank document, choose File > New, click the New toolbar icon (**Figure 2.4**), or press Ctrl N.

A new document can also be based on a template. CorelDraw *templates* are files that help you quickly create professional-looking documents, such as brochures, flyers, labels, and Web pages. Templates include settings for page size and orientation, grids, and guidelines. They often include graphics and placeholders for text. You can use the provided templates or ones you've saved as CorelDraw templates.

To start a new graphic from a template:

1. Choose File > New From Template.
   The New From Template dialog box appears (**Figure 2.5**).

2. Click the tab for the type of template you'd like to use: Full Page, Label, Envelope, Side-Fold, or Web. CorelDraw 11 includes several dozen templates stored in the folders represented by these tabs.

   or

   Click the Browse tab to view templates in other folders or disks. (You can use Browse to load templates from the Corel Graphics Suite 11 CDs, for example.)

3. Select a template, using the preview pane to see what it looks like.

4. Check the Include graphics check box to create a document that includes the displayed design elements. (If you remove the checkmark, only the layout settings will be used.)

5. Click OK.
   A new document is created from the template, ready for your modifications.

Opening Documents

In addition to creating new documents, you will also want to open existing drawings (in CorelDraw or other formats) to view, edit, or print them.

To open an existing document:

1. Choose File > Open, press Ctrl O, or click the Open toolbar icon.

   The Open Drawing dialog box appears (**Figure 2.6**).

2. Navigate to the folder where the document is stored.

3. Select a file, and click the Open button.

   The drawing opens in a new window.

✔ Tips

- When CorelDraw is running, you can also open additional documents by double-clicking their file icons (found on the desktop or in a folder).

- As shown in **Figure 2.6**, the Open Drawing dialog box has two pop-up lists that can help simplify the task of finding the drawing you want to open:

  ▲ To open a file you've recently worked on, click the down arrow at the end of the File name text box.

  ▲ To restrict displayed files to only those of a particular type of illustration (such as CorelDraw, CorelDraw templates, or Adobe Illustrator files), select a type from the Files of type list.

- You don't have to close the current document before you create or open another. In fact, the only limitation on the number of open documents is the amount of memory allocated to CorelDraw. To change the memory setting, choose Tools > Options, click the Memory heading, and specify a new percentage in the Maximum text box (**Figure 2.7**).

— Restrict to a file type
— Recently opened files

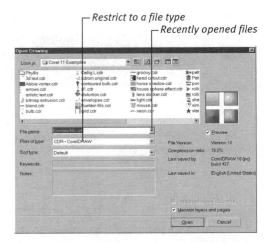

Figure 2.6 Select a file to open from this dialog box.

— Set memory allocation percent

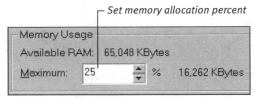

Figure 2.7 The new memory setting will be in effect the next time you launch CorelDraw.

Setting File Associations

When you installed CorelDraw, it claimed the Windows file association for certain types of drawing files. You can associate CorelDraw with additional file types by choosing Tools > Options and selecting the Global > Filters > Associate heading. Click check boxes to add or remove the desired file associations, and then click OK. You'll now be able to open these file types from the Open Drawing dialog box, as well as by double-clicking their desktop icons.

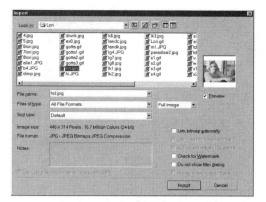

Figure 2.8 Select an image or text file to import.

Figure 2.9 You can crop an image (left) by dragging handles or entering specific location and size numbers. You can also resize or change an imported image's resolution (right).

Adding Scans or Photos

If you have a scan or photo that you want to incorporate into the current drawing, you can use the Import command. You can also scan directly into a drawing or transfer pictures from your digital camera into a drawing. Choose File > Acquire Image > Select Source, choose your connected digital camera or scanner from the list that appears, and click Select. Then choose the File > Acquire Image > Acquire command.

Importing Graphics and Text

You can import many types of files (such as CorelDraw clip art, text, graphics, and so on) into a drawing. While the Open command can open most draw-type files, you must use Import to open a text file or any other type of graphic (such as a scan or photo).

To import a file into a drawing:

1. Choose File > Import or press Ctrl I.
   The Import dialog box appears (**Figure 2.8**).

2. Navigate to the folder where the file you want to import is stored. Select the file.
   To see a preview of the image, check the Preview check box. Additional information about the file is displayed beneath the text boxes.

3. From the pop-up list on the right, indicate whether you want to import the entire file (Full Image), a selected part of the image (Crop), or the image at a different size or resolution (Resample).

4. Review and set options in the bottom-right area of the dialog box. (The listed options vary with the type of file selected.)

5. Click the Import button.

6. If you chose Crop or Resample in Step 3, a new dialog box appears (**Figure 2.9**). Make the desired changes and click OK.

7. An import cursor appears, showing the file name of the image to be imported. Move the cursor to where you'd like the image to be placed, and then click to complete the import process.

✔ Tip

■ To make it easier to locate a file, you can restrict the file list so it displays only one file type. Select a file format from the Files of type list.

Saving Drawings

Until you've saved a newly-created drawing, it only exists in the computer's memory. The same is true of edited documents. If you want edits to be permanent, you must save them.

To save a new drawing:

1. Choose File > Save (Ctrl S), choose File > Save As (Shift Ctrl S), or click the Save toolbar icon.

   The Save Drawing dialog box appears (**Figure 2.10**).

2. Navigate to the folder in which you want to save the drawing.

3. Enter a name for the drawing in the File name text box.

4. *Optional:* The default file type is CorelDraw (denoted by the .cdr extension). To save the drawing in another file format, choose a format from the Save as type list.

5. *Optional:* To later help identify the drawing, you can enter keywords and notes.

6. *Optional:* To change file compression and other settings, click the Advanced button.

   The Options dialog box appears, open to the Save section (**Figure 2.11**). Make any necessary changes and click OK.

7. Click the Save button.

To resave a previously saved drawing:

◆ To save the drawing using its original name, location, and file type, choose File > Save, press Ctrl S, or click the Save toolbar icon. No dialog box appears; the edited file overwrites the original file.

◆ To save the file with a new name, as a different file type, or to a different location on disk, choose File > Save As (Shift Ctrl S). The Save Drawing dialog box appears. Set options as explained in the previous step list and click Save.

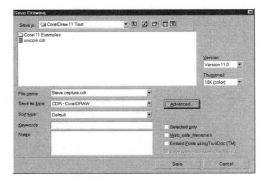

Figure 2.10 Navigate to the desired folder, name the drawing, choose a file type, and click Save.

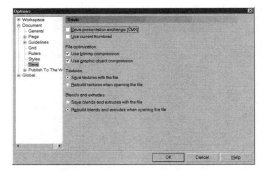

Figure 2.11 You can view or change compression and other drawing settings in the Document Save section of the Options dialog box.

More Save Options

Although CorelDraw 11 includes dozens of useful templates, you can create reusable templates from your own drawings, too. In the Save Drawing dialog box, choose CDT-CorelDraw Template as the file type.

If you've created a complex illustration, you can elect to save any part of the drawing as a separate file. To do this, select the part (or parts) and then click the Selected only check box at the bottom of the Save Drawing dialog box.

SAVING DRAWINGS

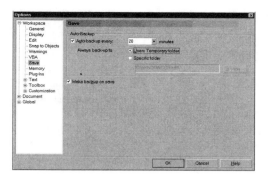

Figure 2.12 You can set global backup settings in the Workspace > Save section of the Options dialog box.

Backup from Save   Original

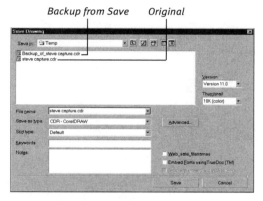

Figure 2.13 File names for backups are generated by adding an auto_backup_of_ or backup_of_ prefix to the original file name.

There's Always a Way Out

If you find yourself in a dialog box that you didn't mean to use, don't panic. Just click the Cancel button. The dialog box will close, and you'll return to the drawing window with nothing changed.

Making Backup Files

Because you've invested time in your drawings, CorelDraw provides ways for you to protect them from computer disasters, such as crashes, inadvertent deletions, and corrupted files. By setting the appropriate backup options, you can make automatic backups at regular intervals, as well as make a backup on each save. Either method enables you to restore the previous version of a drawing.

To set backup options:

1. Choose Tools > Options or press Ctrl J. The Options dialog box appears.

2. Click the Save heading (**Figure 2.12**).

3. To automatically create a backup of any open document at preset intervals, check Auto-backup every and specify the time interval (in minutes).

4. Click a radio button to indicate where the auto-backup files will be stored. Such backups are named auto_backup_of_ *file name*.

5. To create a backup file whenever you perform a Save, click the check box to Make backup on save.

    These backups are automatically stored in the same folder as the original drawing and are named backup_of_*file name*.

6. Click OK to dismiss the dialog box.

✔ Tips

- Backup and auto-backup settings are applied to *all* CorelDraw documents, not just the one that is active when you open the Options dialog box.

- To restore a backup file, open it with the File > Open command (**Figure 2.13**). You'll also probably want to save the file again using the File > Save As command and give it a new name.

Exporting Drawings

You can export your drawings in a format that enables them to be read by another program or used on a Web page. Just create the drawing and export it in the desired file format, such as TIFF, PICT, JPEG, or GIF.

To export a drawing:

1. Open the drawing you want to export.

2. Choose File > Export or press [Ctrl] [E]. The Export dialog box appears (**Figure 2.14**).

3. Navigate to the folder where you want store the exported drawing, and then enter a name in the File name text box.

4. Choose a file type for the exported drawing by clicking the down arrow beside the Save as type drop-down list.

5. *Optional:* If you pre-selected part of the drawing, you can export just those objects by clicking the Selected only check box.

6. If you've selected a compressable file format (such as TIFF), choose a compression algorithm from the drop-down menu.

7. Click the Export button.

8. *Optional:* If you chose a bitmap file type (such as JPEG or TIFF) as the export format, the Bitmap Export dialog appears (**Figure 2.15**).

   In this dialog box, you can set the number of colors for the exported graphic, the image size, and the resolution. Make any necessary changes, and click OK to export the file to the chosen format.

✔ Tip

- If a complex drawing doesn't export properly, try grouping all objects and then repeating the Export procedure. (Choose Edit > Select All > Objects, followed by Arrange > Group.)

Figure 2.14 Using options in the Export dialog box, you can export a CorelDraw drawing or selected objects from the drawing.

Figure 2.15 When exporting a drawing as a bitmap file, you can change the image's size, colors, and resolution.

Exporting Drawings as Bitmaps

Remember that the higher the bitmap settings (colors, image size, and resolution), the larger the resulting file will be. And large files take longer to display and print.

Always try to use the fewest colors and lowest resolution you need—especially when exporting a drawing for use on the Web. You might have to export the image a few times until you get the desired effect, but smaller images can mean real time savings when loading or printing.

Title bars *Close* — *Maximize/Restore* — *Minimize* —

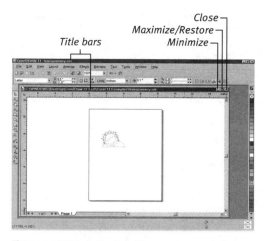

Figure 2.16 This is the CorelDraw program window.

Minimized application on the Windows taskbar

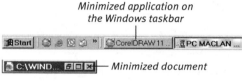

Minimized document

Figure 2.17 The CorelDraw program (top) and documents (bottom) can both be minimized.

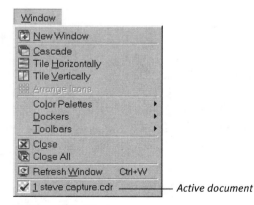

Active document

Figure 2.18 The Window menu has commands for arranging, closing, and choosing windows.

Window Management

As in most Windows programs, you can move, resize, minimize, or maximize the main window or individual document windows. In addition, several other useful window-related commands can be found in the Window menu.

◆ To move the CorelDraw window or a document window, click the window's title bar (**Figure 2.16**) and drag.

◆ To change the size of the CorelDraw window or a document window, click and drag any window corner or edge.

Resizing can only be accomplished when a window isn't maximized. If it is, it may be necessary to first click the restore box in the window's upper-right corner.

◆ Minimizing CorelDraw shrinks it to a button on the Windows taskbar (**Figure 2.17**). Minimizing a document window shrinks it to an icon at the bottom of the CorelDraw desktop (**Figure 2.17**). To minimize the main window or a document window, click its minimize box.

◆ Maximizing CorelDraw causes it to fill the entire screen; maximizing a document causes it to fill the CorelDraw desktop. To maximize the main window or a document window, click the maximize box.

◆ If you have multiple documents open, you can make a different one active by choosing its name from the Window menu (**Figure 2.18**) or by clicking any part of the window to which you want to switch.

◆ You can arrange open windows in various configurations by choosing commands from the Window menu (**Figure 2.18**).

◆ You can make another copy of the active document by choosing Window > New Window. Doing so enables you to simultaneously view the document at two different magnifications, for example.

WINDOW MANAGEMENT

Closing Documents

When you're done working with a document or want to free up memory so you can open other documents, you can close any or all document windows.

To close a document:

1. Switch to the document that you wish to close (making it the *active* document).

2. *Do one of the following:*
   ▲ Choose File > Close.
   ▲ Choose Window > Close.
   ▲ Press Ctrl F4 .
   ▲ Click the close box in the upper-right corner of the document (see **Figure 2.16**).

3. If the document has been changed since the most recent Save, CorelDraw will automatically ask whether you want to save it (**Figure 2.19**).

✔ Tips

■ To simultaneously close all CorelDraw document windows, choose Window > Close All. As an alternative, you may wish to just quit the program by choosing File > Exit. Quitting automatically closes all open windows, yet gives you an opportunity to save any changed documents.

■ If you're working on several documents and need to move one out of the way, you don't have to close it. Click the minimize box in the upper-right corner of the document window. Minimized documents drop to the bottom-left corner of the CorelDraw desktop. To restore a minimized document, select its name from the Window menu or click its maximize box.

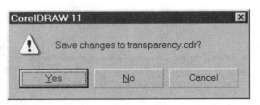

Figure 2.19 Choose Yes to save the document before closing it, No to close the window without saving, or Cancel if you've changed your mind about closing.

About File Extensions

Extensions are the three letters that end every Windows file name. For instance, boxshapes.cdr has a .cdr extension. An extension tells Windows—and you—the kind of file it is and how to interpret it.

CorelDraw uses several native extensions:
CDR. The native CorelDraw file extension that is appended to document names when you save them
CDT. CorelDraw Template
CDX. CorelDraw Compressed
CMX. Corel Presentation Exchange

Some other file extensions that you may see while using CorelDraw 11 include:
CPT. Corel Photo-Paint
CLK. Corel R.A.V.E.
BMP. Windows bitmap
EPS. Encapsulated PostScript
TIF. Tagged Image File Format bitmap

These formats are used for Web graphics:
GIF. CompuServe (Graphics Interchange Format) bitmap
JPG. Joint Photographic Experts Group (JPEG) bitmap

For more information about the GIF and JPEG file formats, see Chapter 17.

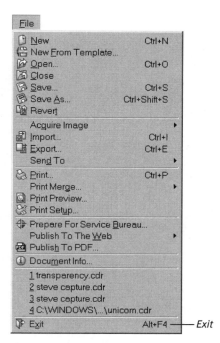

Figure 2.20 To quit CorelDraw, choose File > Exit.

Quitting CorelDraw

When you've finished working on your drawings, you can quit CorelDraw to free up memory for other applications and the system software.

To quit CorelDraw:

◆ Choose File > Exit (**Figure 2.20**).

◆ Press Alt F4.

  or

◆ Click the close box in the upper-right corner of the main CorelDraw window.

✔ Tip

■ When you quit CorelDraw, all open files are closed. If changes have been made to any open file since it was last saved, CorelDraw will automatically ask whether you want to save it (see Figure 2.19).

Viewing File Extensions

To see file extensions in folders and dialog boxes, open any folder and choose View > Folder Options. The Folder Options dialog box appears. Click the View tab. If you have Windows 95, the option to "Hide MS-DOS file extensions for file types that are registered" should not be checked. If you have Windows 98 or NT, the option to "Hide file extensions for known file types" should not be checked. The option's wording in later versions of Windows should be similar.

RECTANGLES AND ELLIPSES

This chapter will get you started on the road to designing fantastic graphics in CorelDraw 11. The simple shapes you'll create here are the basis for every drawing. Many complex illustrations are composed almost entirely of basic shapes, such as rectangles and ellipses.

Everything you create using the tools in CorelDraw 11—whether it's a line, a triangle, or a circle—has a *path*. Paths can be either *open* or *closed*. The beginning and end of an open path do not connect. For example, a line is an open path. A closed path has no distinct beginning or end, just as a circle or rectangle has no beginning or end. In other words, a closed path is a *shape*.

In CorelDraw, a line or shape is also known as an *object*. The outside perimeter of an object is a path. In addition, every object has *properties* that you can set. These properties include such elements as the object's size, shape, position, and color.

In this chapter, you'll learn to draw rectangles and round their corners, as well as how to draw ellipses, pie shapes, and arcs. You'll also learn to use the new rectangle and ellipse tools introduced in CorelDraw 11: the 3 Point Rectangle Tool and the 3 Point Ellipse Tool. These two tools provide alternate ways of creating rectangles and ellipses. In some cases, you'll find them preferable to using the original Rectangle and Ellipse Tools.

Working with Rectangles

A *rectangle* is a four-sided, two-dimensional object with a right angle in each corner. A *square* is a rectangle with four sides that are of equal length. Using the Rectangle or the 3 Point Rectangle Tool, you can create perfect rectangles and squares, as well as *rounded rectangles* (rectangles with rounded corners).

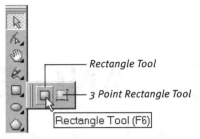

Figure 3.1 Select the Rectangle Tool from the toolbox.

To draw a rectangle with the Rectangle Tool:

1. Select the Rectangle Tool icon in the toolbox (**Figure 3.1**) or press [F6].

   The pointer changes to a cross-hair with a tiny rectangle attached to it.

2. Press the left mouse button and drag diagonally. As you drag, the rectangle takes shape.

3. To complete the rectangle, release the mouse button.

   The rectangle will be selected, showing four nodes—one per corner—and a set of eight outer handles (**Figure 3.2**). You can click and drag a handle to change the rectangle's dimensions. Nodes are discussed later in this section, as well as in Chapter 6, "Nodes and Paths."

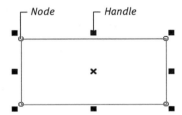

Figure 3.2 A selected rectangle has four nodes and eight handles.

✔ Tips

- To draw a square, hold down [Ctrl] as you drag. Be sure to release the mouse button before [Ctrl]; otherwise, the object will spring back to a non-symmetrical shape.

- To draw a rectangle that fills the drawing page, double-click the Rectangle Tool icon in the toolbox.

- You can change the outline color or fill of any closed-path object, such as a rectangle or square. For information on fills and outlines, see Chapter 11, " Working with Text."

Drawing an Object from the Center

In addition to drawing an object from its edge or corner, you can also draw from its center. To draw a rectangle or ellipse from its center, hold down [Shift] while dragging. When the object is the desired size, release the mouse button before you release the [Shift] key; otherwise, the object will be created from its edge.

To draw a perfectly symmetrical object (such as a circle or square) from its center, hold down [Ctrl] and [Shift] while dragging. Release the mouse button before releasing the modifier keys.

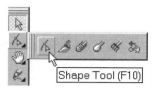

Figure 3.3 Select the Shape Tool icon from the Shape Tool flyout.

Figure 3.4 When selected with the Shape Tool, a rectangle initially has four nodes—one in each corner.

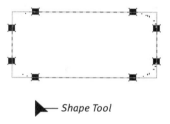

Figure 3.5 To round the corners, click a node and drag. The number of nodes doubles to eight.

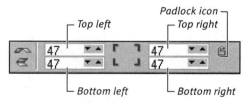

Figure 3.6 To set the rounding for a specific corner, unlock the padlock icon, and then type a value or click the arrows for that corner.

To draw a rectangle with the 3 Point Rectangle Tool:

1. Select the 3 Point Rectangle Tool icon in the toolbox (see Figure 3.1).

2. Click and drag to draw the first side. When it's the desired length and angle, release the mouse button. (To restrict the angle to a 15-degree increment, press Ctrl as you drag.)

3. Drag to complete the rectangle. (To draw a square, press Ctrl as you drag.) When the rectangle is the desired size, click once.

Creating a rounded rectangle

After drawing a rectangle, you can round its corners. You can round all corners at once or choose specific ones to round.

To round the corners of a rectangle:

1. In the toolbox, select the Shape Tool icon from the Shape Tool flyout (**Figure 3.3**) or press F10.

2. Select the rectangle you wish to round.

    Four black nodes appear around the rectangle (**Figure 3.4**). Unselected nodes—if any—are displayed as circles.

3. To round all corners equally (**Figure 3.5**), make sure that all nodes are selected (black) and then drag any node.

    or

    To round individual corners, click to select a node (or Shift-click to select multiple nodes) and then drag any selected node.

✔ Tips

- Double-click the Shape Tool to select all nodes.

- You can also set rounding values in the Corner Roundness text boxes (**Figure 3.6**) on the property bar. Larger values result in rounder corners. When the padlock icon is locked, rounding is set for all corners. When it is unlocked, you can set the rounding for individual corners.

WORKING WITH RECTANGLES

Working with Ellipses

Using the Ellipse Tool or 3 Point Ellipse Tool, you can create ovals, circles, arcs, and pies, as described in the following sections.

To draw a closed oval or circle with the Ellipse Tool:

1. Select the Ellipse Tool icon from the tool-box (**Figure 3.7**) or press F7.

   The pointer changes to a cross-hair with a tiny ellipse attached to it.

2. Press the left mouse button and drag diagonally. As you drag, the ellipse takes shape.

3. To complete the ellipse, release the mouse button.

   The ellipse will be selected, displaying a single node at its top and eight handles (**Figure 3.8**).

✔ Tip

- To draw a circle, press Ctrl as you drag. When you're done dragging, release the mouse button before releasing Ctrl.

To draw a closed oval or circle with the 3 Point Ellipse Tool:

1. Select the 3 Point Ellipse Tool icon from the toolbox (**Figure 3.7**).

2. Click and drag to draw the radius. When it's the desired length and angle, release the mouse button. (To restrict the angle to a 15-degree increment, press Ctrl as you drag.)

3. Drag to complete the ellipse. (To draw a circle, press Ctrl as you drag.) When the ellipse is the desired size, click once.

   The ellipse will be selected, displaying a single node and eight handles (**Figure 3.8**).

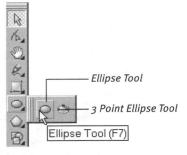

Ellipse Tool

3 Point Ellipse Tool

Ellipse Tool (F7)

Figure 3.7 Select the Ellipse Tool from the toolbox.

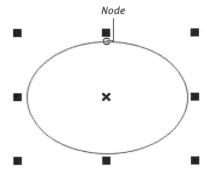

Node

Figure 3.8 A selected ellipse has one node and eight outer handles.

There's an X in My Object!

Every time you draw a new object, an X appears inside it. The X is there to make it easier for you to move the object with your mouse. For instructions on moving objects, see Chapter 4, "Select, Move, Copy, and Size."

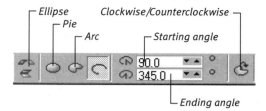

Figure 3.9 On the property bar, you can change a selected ellipse into a pie or arc, enter a specific starting or ending angle, or reverse the visible angle.

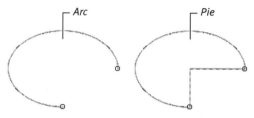

Figure 3.10 An arc (left) is an open shape, while a pie (right) is a closed shape.

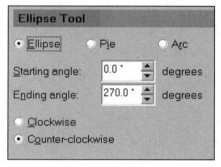

Figure 3.11 You can specify the default ellipse shape, angle, and direction in the Ellipse Tool section of the Options dialog box.

Directly Drawing Pies and Arcs

If you only occasionally want to draw a pie or arc, another way to do so is to select the Ellipse Tool, click the Pie or Arc icon on the property bar, and then draw.

Creating an arc or pie shape

After you've drawn an ellipse, you can change it into an arc or pie shape.

To change an ellipse into an arc or pie:

1. In the toolbox, select the Shape Tool or the Pick Tool.

2. Click to select the ellipse (if it isn't already selected).

3. To change the ellipse into a pie shape, click the Pie icon on the property bar (**Figure 3.9**). The ellipse becomes a pie, as shown in **Figure 3.10**.

   or

   To change the ellipse into an arc, click the Arc icon on the property bar.

✔ Tips

■ To change an arc or pie back into its original ellipse, select the arc or pie, and click the Ellipse icon on the property bar.

■ You can also create an arc or pie by clicking the ellipse's node with the Shape or Pick Tool and dragging. To create an arc, drag outside the ellipse; to create a pie, drag inside the ellipse. To restrict movements to 15-degree increments, press [Ctrl] as you drag.

■ You can flip the angle of an arc or pie by 180 degrees, effectively reversing it—changing a pie into a wedge, for example. Select the arc or pie, and then click the Clockwise/Counterclockwise icon on the property bar.

■ In CorelDraw 9, you could set the Ellipse Tool's properties so it drew pies or arcs, rather than ellipses. This feature has been restored in CorelDraw 11. Choose Tools > Options and then select the Toolbox > Ellipse Tool heading in the Options dialog box (**Figure 3.11**).

WORKING WITH ELLIPSES

SELECT, MOVE, COPY, AND SIZE

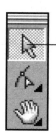

— *Pick Tool*

Figure 4.1 The Pick Tool can be found at the top of the toolbox.

In Chapter 3, you learned to draw simple shapes. In this chapter, you'll learn to select, move, copy, duplicate, clone, resize, and delete objects. You'll use the Pick Tool (**Figure 4.1**) to accomplish these tasks.

✔ Tip

- You can also use many other tools (such as the Rectangle Tool and the Ellipse Tool) to select objects.

Selecting Objects

Before you can change the size, fill, or other properties of an object, you must first *select* it. You use the Pick Tool to select objects and to manipulate an object's handles. *Handles* are the black squares that appear around a selected object (**Figure 4.2**). They are used to change the dimensions of an object.

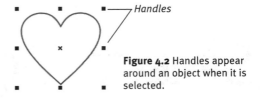

Figure 4.2 Handles appear around an object when it is selected.

To select an object:

1. Select the Pick Tool from the toolbox.

2. Click the object you wish to select.

   Black handles appear around the object to show that it is selected (**Figure 4.2**).

To select multiple objects by clicking:

1. Select the Pick Tool from the toolbox.

2. Hold down ⇧Shift while clicking each object you want to select.

   As you select additional objects, the set of handles expands to surround all selected objects (**Figure 4.3**).

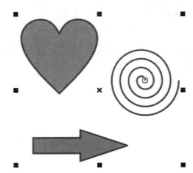

Figure 4.3 When you select multiple objects, the handle formation expands to surround all selected objects.

To select multiple objects by dragging:

1. Using the Pick Tool, click near—but outside of—the objects you wish to select.

2. Drag to select the objects.

   As you drag, a dashed blue rectangle (or *marquee*) appears, showing the selection area (**Figure 4.4**).

3. Release the mouse button when the marquee encompasses the objects.

   The items will be selected as a group with a single set of handles.

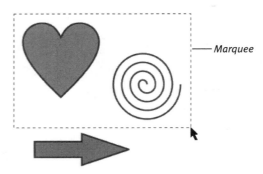

Figure 4.4 As you drag to select multiple objects, a marquee appears around them.

To select all objects on a page:

◆ Choose Edit > Select All > Objects.

◆ Press Ctrl A.

◆ Double-click the Pick Tool's toolbox icon.

Deselecting Objects

To deselect all selected objects, click outside of the objects with the Pick Tool or press Esc. To deselect one object within a multi-object selection, hold down ⇧Shift and click the object you wish to deselect.

Pointer becomes a cross

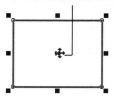

Figure 4.5 When dragging with any tool other than the Pick Tool, you must position the pointer over the *x* in the object's center and then drag.

Horizontal (X)
Vertical (Y)

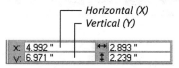

Figure 4.6 To precisely position an object, enter X and Y coordinates in these two boxes on the property bar.

Figure 4.7 You can set the nudge, micro nudge, and super nudge distances in the Rulers section of the Options dialog box.

Double-Headed Arrows?

If you click on a *selected object* (one whose handles are already visible), the handles change to double-headed arrows. These arrows are used to skew and rotate the object. To get the black handles back, click the object again.

Moving Objects

There are three basic ways to reposition an object: dragging, *nudging* (pressing the arrow keys), or entering page coordinates.

To move an object by dragging:

◆ With the Pick Tool selected, click anywhere within the object and drag it to its new location. (It isn't necessary to select the object before you start dragging.)

◆ With another tool selected (such as the Rectangle Tool), click to select the object and then—with the pointer over the *x* in the center of the object (**Figure 4.5**)—click and drag it to its new location.

To move an object by nudging:

1. Select the object with the Pick Tool or another tool.

2. Press ←, →, ↑, or ↓ to move the object the preset nudge distance.

   To move the object a *fraction* of the nudge distance, press Ctrl in combination with an arrow key. To move the object a *multiple* of the nudge distance, press Shift in combination with an arrow key.

To move an object using coordinates:

1. Select the object with the Pick Tool or another tool.

2. On the property bar (**Figure 4.6**), enter values for the X (horizontal) and/or Y (vertical) coordinates and press Enter. The values refer to the object's center.

✔ Tips

■ You can modify the default nudge distances in the Rulers section of the Options dialog box (**Figure 4.7**).

■ To move an object between pages, drag it onto the destination page tab and then release it when it's in the desired position.

Moving objects via drag-and-drop

While the object moves discussed on the previous page were made within a drawing, you can also move objects *between* documents. CorelDraw 11 is *drag-and-drop enabled.* That is, you can move an object from one document to another using a drag-and-drop operation.

To move an object between documents:

1. Open two CorelDraw documents.

2. Choose Window > Tile Vertically or Window > Tile Horizontally.

3. Using the Pick Tool, drag an object from one document to the other (**Figure 4.8**).

4. Release the mouse button when the object is in the proper position.

✔ Tips

■ You can also use the Copy and Paste commands to copy objects in one CorelDraw 11 document and paste them into another.

■ Moving an object between documents is a destructive procedure, similar to a Cut. Rather than *move* the object, you may prefer to perform a drag-and-drop *copy.* Right-click the object and drag it from one document into the other. When the mouse button is released, a pop-up menu appears (**Figure 4.9**). Choose Copy Here.

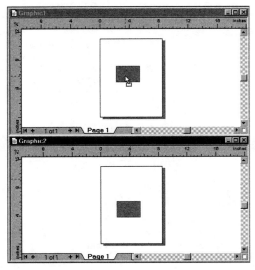

Figure 4.8 You can drag an object from the drawing in the bottom window to the one in the top window.

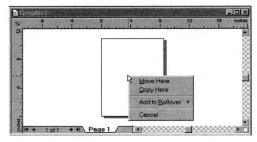

Figure 4.9 If you right-click and then drag an object between documents, you can elect to move or copy the object.

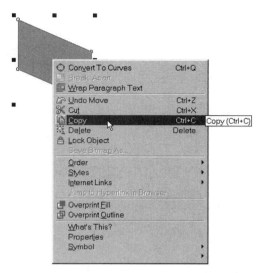

Figure 4.10 You can choose a variety of object-related commands (such as Copy and Delete) by right-clicking an object.

Figure 4.11 Choose Copy Here to create the copy.

Selecting with the Tab Key

When working with several objects that are close together or on top of each other, it can be difficult to click the object you want to select. You can use the keyboard to pick the correct object. Begin by selecting any object and then repeatedly press [Tab] until the desired object is selected. (As you press [Tab], watch the status bar. It gives information about the location and type of object that is currently selected.)

Copying Objects

There are two ways to copy an object: *copy* it to the Windows Clipboard (and then paste it into the document) or *duplicate* it. The result is the same, but the amount of computing power used for the two procedures is different.

If you copy an object to the Clipboard, you can then paste it into the current page or other pages in your CorelDraw document. It will also be available for pasting into other Windows programs. For example, you could paste a rectangle or star copied from CorelDraw into a Microsoft Word document. However, copying and pasting an object—especially a complex one—can tie up your computer.

CorelDraw's Duplicate command bypasses the Clipboard, making it a faster operation. In addition, you can specify exactly where the duplicate will appear in relation to the original, whereas a copy will always appear on top of the original.

To copy an object using the Clipboard:

1. Select the object you want to copy.

2. Choose Edit > Copy, press [Ctrl][C], or right-click the object and choose Copy from the pop-up menu that appears (**Figure 4.10**). The object is copied to the Clipboard.

3. Choose Edit > Paste or press [Ctrl][V]. A copy of the object appears, directly on top of the original.

4. Drag the copy to the desired position.

To copy an object by dragging:

1. Using the Pick Tool (or another tool), right-click the object you want to copy and drag it to the desired position.

2. Release the mouse button.

3. Choose Copy Here from the pop-up menu that appears (**Figure 4.11**).

To duplicate an object:

1. Select the object to be duplicated.

2. Choose Edit > Duplicate or press Ctrl D.
   The duplicate appears slightly to the right
   and above the original (**Figure 4.12**).

Smart duplication helps you create a series of
evenly spaced duplicate objects.

To create a series of objects using smart duplication:

1. Select the object you want to duplicate.

2. Choose Edit > Duplicate or press Ctrl D.
   A selected duplicate of the original appears.

3. Using the Pick Tool, move the duplicate
   object to the desired position in the series
   (**Figure 4.13**). Be sure to leave the duplicate object selected.

4. To duplicate the repositioned duplicate
   object, choose Edit > Duplicate or press
   Ctrl D again.
   A second duplicate appears, positioned the
   same distance and direction away.

5. Continue choosing Edit > Duplicate or
   pressing Ctrl D until there are as many
   evenly spaced duplicates as you need
   (**Figure 4.14**).

✔ Tips

- Another quick way to copy a selected
  object is to press + on your numeric keypad. This places a copy of the object on top
  of the original.

- Remember that if you're dragging an object
  with any tool other than the Pick Tool, you
  must first select the object and drag from
  the *x* in its center.

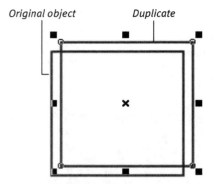

Original object   Duplicate

Figure 4.12 A duplicate is automatically offset
from the original and selected.

Figure 4.13 Reposition the
first duplicate so it's the
desired distance and direction from the original.

Figure 4.14 Continue making duplicates until you've
completed the series.

COPYING OBJECTS

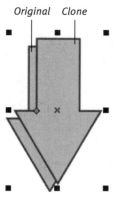

Original   Clone

Figure 4.15 The clone appears, above and offset from the original.

Figure 4.16 Use the Revert to Master dialog box to undo changes to a clone.

Cloning objects

Like duplication, cloning bypasses the Clipboard to quickly create a copy of the original. However, unlike duplication, cloning creates a *link* between the original and the copy. Any changes made to the original also affect the clone. This is handy, for example, if you have 100 cloned circles in a drawing and want to change all of their fill colors from red to blue. All you'd have to do is select the original circle and fill it with blue.

To clone an object:

1. Select an object with the Pick Tool.

2. Choose Edit > Clone.

A clone appears (**Figure 4.15**).

3. To make additional clones of the same object, repeat Steps 1 and 2. (Note that you must make each clone from the original object; you cannot clone a clone.)

✔ Tips

■ The link between a clone and the original goes only one way. If you alter the original, all clones are changed, too. But if you alter a clone, the original is unaffected.

■ Once you've altered a specific attribute of a given clone (its color, for example), that attribute is no longer linked to the original. However, all *other* attributes (shape and size, for example) continue to be linked to the original. To restore a clone's attributes so that it matches the original again, right-click the clone and choose Revert to Master from the pop-up menu that appears. In the Revert to Master dialog box (**Figure 4.16**), enter checkmarks for the attributes to be restored and then click OK.

■ You can distinguish a clone from the original by checking the status bar. If a clone is selected, the description will include the word "Clone." If the original is selected, the description will include the word "Control."

COPYING OBJECTS

Resizing Objects

Handles appear in a rectangular formation around an object when it is selected (**Figure 4.17**). These handles have various functions:

◆ The handles that appear to the right and left center of the object affect the object's *horizontal scale* by making it wider or narrower.

◆ The handles that appear at the top and bottom center of an object affect the object's *vertical scale* by making it taller or shorter.

◆ The handles that appear at the corners affect the object's *proportional scale* by simultaneously changing its horizontal and vertical size.

To change an object's size:

1. Select the object with the Pick Tool.

2. *Do one of the following:*

   ▲ To change an object's width, click the left or right center handle and drag horizontally.

   ▲ To change an object's height, click the top or bottom center handle and drag vertically.

   ▲ To proportionately change an object's size, click any corner handle and drag diagonally.

3. Release the mouse button when the object is the desired size.

✔ Tips

■ Another way to resize an object is by typing new dimensions into the appropriate property bar text boxes and then pressing Enter, as shown in **Figure 4.18**.

■ You can also change an object's size by *scaling* it, as explained in Chapter 14, "Object Arrangement."

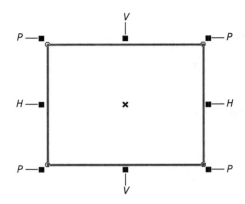

Figure 4.17 You can manually alter an object's size horizontally (H), vertically (V), or proportionately (P) by clicking and dragging a handle.

Width — Height

Figure 4.18 To set an object's exact width or height, enter the dimensions in these property bar boxes.

More About Dragging Handles

◆ To scale an object from its center, hold down Shift while dragging a handle.

◆ To resize an object in 100 percent increments, press Ctrl while dragging any handle.

RESIZING OBJECTS

Deleting Objects

Rather than reshape, resize, or edit a flawed object, sometimes the preferable action is simply to *delete* the object.

To delete an object:

1. Select the object with the Pick Tool or another tool.

2. Choose Edit > Delete, press Del or Delete, or right-click the object and choose Delete from the pop-up menu that appears (see Figure 4.10).

✔ Tips

- If you press Backspace instead of Del or Delete, nothing will happen.

- A mistakenly deleted object can be restored by immediately choosing Edit > Undo Delete or by pressing Ctrl Z. Other deletions can be restored by stepping through the previously executed commands in the Undo docker.

- You can delete several objects at the same time, if you wish. Just select them all prior to performing the deletion.

COMPLEX SHAPES

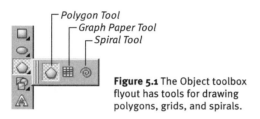

Figure 5.1 The Object toolbox flyout has tools for drawing polygons, grids, and spirals.

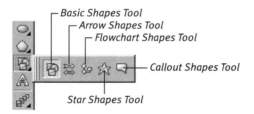

Figure 5.2 Select a tool from the Perfect Shapes flyout to draw teardrops, arrows, stars, flowchart symbols, and other complex shapes.

In CorelDraw 11, it's easy to draw many kinds of complex objects. You don't have to construct them by painstakingly combining individual objects. All you have to do is select a tool from the Object flyout (**Figure 5.1**) or Perfect Shapes flyout (**Figure 5.2**) and then click-and-drag to draw the object.

The techniques you'll learn in this chapter will enable you to add a variety of professional-quality objects to your drawings. Not only will you learn how to create polygons, spirals, stars, arrows, and flowchart symbols, but you'll also discover how to create grids with the Graph Paper Tool, text balloons with the Callout Shapes Tool, and smiley faces, teardrops, hearts, and lightning bolts with the Basic Shapes Tool.

Polygons and Stars

A *polygon* is a multisided closed figure. The simplest form of polygon is a triangle: a three-sided object. CorelDraw 11 enables you to create polygons with as many as 500 sides. A *star* is just a special instance of a polygon. Once you've drawn a polygon, you can easily change it into a star and vice versa.

To create a polygon:

1. Select the Polygon Tool from the Object flyout in the toolbox (see Figure 5.1) or press [Y].

   The pointer changes to a cross-hair with a tiny polygon attached to it.

2. On the property bar, click the Polygon icon and specify the desired number of sides in the Number of Points on Polygon text box (**Figure 5.3**).

3. To create the polygon, click and drag diagonally.

   When you release the mouse button, nodes appear around the object's perimeter and the object is selected (**Figure 5.4**).

To create a star:

1. Select the Polygon Tool from the Object flyout in the toolbox (see Figure 5.1) or press [Y].

   The pointer changes to a cross-hair with a tiny polygon attached to it.

2. On the property bar, click the Star icon and specify the number of sides in the Number of Points on Polygon text box (**Figure 5.3**).

3. To create the star, click and drag diagonally.

   When you release the mouse button, nodes appear around the object's perimeter and the object is selected (**Figure 5.5**).

Polygon — *Star*

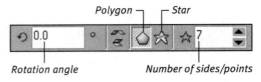

Rotation angle   *Number of sides/points*

Figure 5.3 Before or after drawing a polygon or star, you can set or change its options on the property bar.

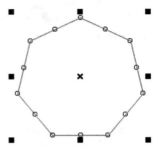

Figure 5.4 This is a selected polygon with seven sides.

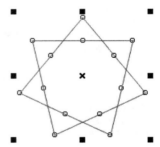

Figure 5.5 This is a selected star with seven points.

Preview window

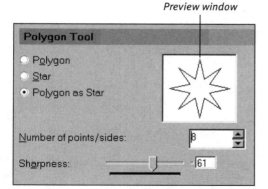

Figure 5.6 Click the Polygon as Star radio button, set options, and then click OK to dismiss the dialog box.

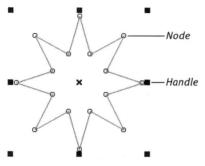

Node

Handle

Figure 5.7 Drag a handle to resize a polygon as star or a node to change its angularity.

Polygon as Star

Using the Polygon Tool, you can create another type of star called *polygon as star*. Unlike the star you just created, a polygon as star is an outline that is easily filled with a color, texture, or pattern.

To create a polygon as star:

1. Double-click the Polygon Tool.

   The Options dialog box appears open to the Polygon Tool section (**Figure 5.6**).

2. Click the Polygon as Star radio button.

3. Specify the number of points for the star and adjust the Sharpness slider bar.

   As you change settings, the prospective star is shown in the preview window.

4. Click OK.

   The drawing window reappears.

5. Click and drag to create a polygon as star (**Figure 5.7**).

   Release the mouse button and the object is selected.

✔ Tips

- When drawing a polygon as star, all you are really doing is creating a special instance of a polygon. To later convert a polygon as star into a normal star, select the object and click the star toolbar icon. Similarly, to change a normal star into a polygon as star, select the object and then click the Polygon toolbar icon.

- You can create several types of predefined stars by drawing with the Star Shapes Tool, as described in "Drawing Perfect Shapes," later in this chapter.

POLYGONS AND STARS

Modifying a polygon or star

After drawing a polygon or star, you can alter it in any of the following ways:

◆ Change a selected polygon into a star or a star into a polygon by clicking the Star or Polygon icon on the property bar.

◆ Change the number of sides by choosing or entering a different number in the text box on the property bar.

◆ Rotate the object by typing a number in the Angle of Rotation text box on the property bar or by clicking its center and dragging a rotation arrow (**Figure 5.8**).

◆ Alter the sharpness (**Figure 5.9**) of any star with seven or more points by moving the Sharpness slider on the property bar.

◆ Change a polygon or star's line thickness, outline color, or fill.

◆ Change the object's size by clicking and dragging a handle.

◆ Reshape the object by clicking nodes with the Shape Tool and then dragging.

✔ Tips

■ The default settings for the Polygon Tool—not the settings on the property bar—determine whether you'll draw a polygon or a star, its number of sides, and its sharpness. To set new defaults (see Figure 5.6), double-click the Polygon Tool icon or set polygon options on the property bar when no object is selected.

■ When you change the setting in the Number of Points On Polygon text box (see Figure 5.3), it only affects new polygons or any polygon that is currently selected.

■ You can draw a polygon or star with equal-length sides by pressing Ctrl as you draw. If you press Shift as you draw, the object will be drawn from its center.

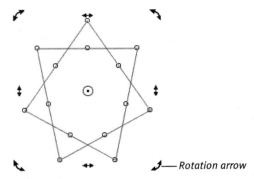

Figure 5.8 Click and drag any rotation arrow to rotate the object.

Rotation arrow

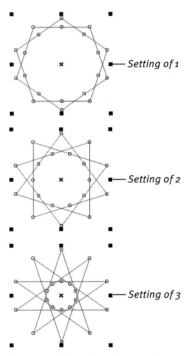

Setting of 1

Setting of 2

Setting of 3

Figure 5.9 These three images show the sharpness settings (1–3) for a 10-sided star. The more sides a star has, the more sharpness settings from which you can choose.

Figure 5.10 You can draw two kinds of spirals: symmetrical (left) and logarithmic (right). Press Ctrl as you drag to create a concentric/perfect spiral.

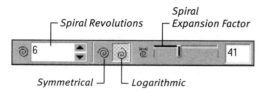

Figure 5.11 Prior to drawing a spiral, choose the desired settings from the property bar.

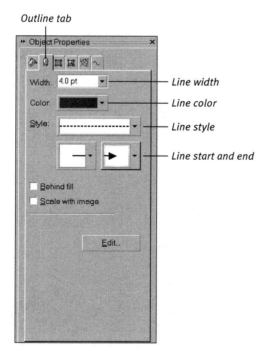

Figure 5.12 You can also alter a drawn spiral by setting options in the Object Properties docker.

Creating Spirals

You can create two types of spirals: symmetrical and logarithmic (**Figure 5.10**). The space between revolutions of a *symmetrical spiral* is constant, while the spacing in a *logarithmic spiral* increases with each new revolution.

To create a spiral:

1. Select the Spiral Tool from the Object fly-out in the toolbox (see Figure 5.1) or press Ⓐ. The pointer changes to a cross-hair with a tiny spiral attached to it.

2. Select a symmetrical or logarithmic spiral by clicking the appropriate button on the property bar (**Figure 5.11**).

3. Indicate the desired number of revolutions by entering a number in the Spiral Revolutions text box.

4. If you've chosen a logarithmic spiral, set a revolution expansion factor by dragging the slider or by entering a number in the Spiral Expansion Factor text box.

5. To create the spiral, left-click and drag diagonally. Release the mouse button when the spiral is the desired size.

✔ Tips

- Unlike drawing polygons and stars, you must specify spiral settings on the property bar *before* you draw. Settings changed afterward won't modify a selected spiral; they apply to the *next* spiral drawn.

- The manner in which a spiral is displayed depends on the diagonal direction that you drag. Try all four possibilities.

- To set a different line width, type, color, or end effect (such as arrows), select the previously drawn spiral, choose Edit > Properties, and click the Outline tab of the Object Properties docker (**Figure 5.12**).

Drawing Grids

If you want to create an object that looks something like graph paper or a spreadsheet grid, you can use the new Graph Paper Tool.

1. Select the Graph Paper Tool from the Object toolbox flyout (**Figure 5.13**) or press D.

   The pointer changes to a cross-hair with a tiny grid attached to it.

2. In the property bar text boxes, specify the number of columns and rows for the grid (**Figure 5.14**).

3. To draw the grid, click and drag.

   Release the mouse button when the grid is completed. The grid is selected (**Figure 5.15**).

✔ Tips

- To draw a grid with a square outline, press Ctrl as you drag.

- A grid is actually composed of a series of grouped rectangles. If you want to modify any of the individual grid cells (to remove a cell or selectively color it, for example), you must first ungroup the grid. Select the grid, and then choose Arrange > Ungroup (or press Ctrl U).

- You can also ungroup a grid by selecting it with the Pick Tool and then clicking the Ungroup button on the property bar.

- You must specify the number of grid rows and columns *before* drawing. Settings changed afterward won't modify a selected grid; they apply to the *next* grid drawn.

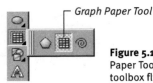

Graph Paper Tool

Figure 5.13 Select the Graph Paper Tool from the Object toolbox flyout.

Columns

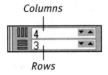

Rows

Figure 5.14 Set the number of columns and rows in these property bar text boxes.

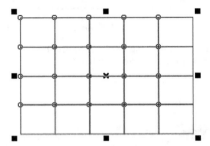

Figure 5.15 This is a finished, selected grid with five columns and four rows.

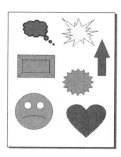

Figure 5.16 These are just a few of the available Perfect Shapes.

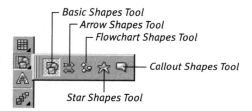

Figure 5.17 Select a tool from the Perfect Shapes flyout in the toolbox.

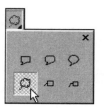

Figure 5.18 Click the Perfect Shapes property bar icon and choose a shape from the ones presented.

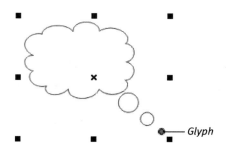

Figure 5.19 You can drag a glyph to change an aspect of the object, such as the angle of these bubbles.

Drawing Perfect Shapes

Perfect Shapes (**Figure 5.16**) are predefined, familiar objects that you can create as easily as drawing rectangles and ellipses.

1. Select a tool from the Perfect Shapes flyout in the toolbox (**Figure 5.17**).

   The pointer changes to a cross-hair with a tiny Perfect Shapes icon attached to it.

2. From the Perfect Shapes icon on the property bar (**Figure 5.18**), choose the type of object you wish to draw.

3. Click and drag to draw the perfect shape. Release the mouse button to complete the drawing.

   The new object is selected.

✔ Tips

- You can change the line width and style for the completed object by choosing options from the property bar.

- Many of the Perfect Shape objects contain a diamond-shaped *glyph* you can drag to alter an aspect of the object (**Figure 5.19**). On the smiley face, for example, you can drag the glyph to change its expression.

- Some of the Perfect Shape objects (such as the smiley face) are automatically drawn symmetrically. To *force* a Perfect Shape object to be drawn symmetrically, press Ctrl as you draw.

- To draw a Perfect Shape object from its center, press Shift as you draw.

- To get additional effects when drawing Perfect Shapes, remember that you don't always have to drag diagonally down and to the right. Try dragging in other directions, too.

NODES AND PATHS

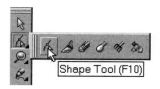

Figure 6.1 Select the Shape Tool from the Shape Edit flyout or press F10.

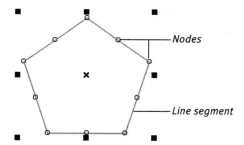

Figure 6.2 Nodes appear on an object's path when it's selected.

Control point

Figure 6.3 When you select a node with the Shape Tool, its control points (if any) become visible.

You use the Shape Tool (**Figure 6.1**) to manipulate an object's nodes. *Nodes* are the small, hollow squares that appear on an object's path immediately after the object is drawn or when it has been selected with the Shape Tool (**Figure 6.2**). A *line segment* is the line that connects a pair of nodes.

Nodes may appear to be of no consequence, but, in fact, they are very powerful. You use the nodes to manipulate specific line segments of an object's path, enabling you to make intricate changes to the object's shape. For coarser changes, you can manipulate the line segments directly.

When you select the Shape Tool, the pointer changes to a black arrowhead. When you use the Shape Tool to select a node, two things happen: the node changes from hollow to black, and—in the case of a curved line or object—one or two control points attached to the node become visible (**Figure 6.3**). *Control points* determine the curvature of the segments of a path.

In order for a path segment to be bent, it must have control points. If a path segment is not bordered on either side by a control point, the path segment is straight. A node can have 0, 1, or 2 control points.

Three Types of Nodes

CorelDraw provides three types of nodes:

◆ A *smooth node* is used to create a seamless curve. The control points of a smooth node are always directly opposite each other. If you move one control point, the opposite control point moves, too. The distance between control points can vary (**Figure 6.4**). This means that the path on one side of a node can be curved differently than the path on the other side of the node.

◆ A *symmetrical node* is similar to a smooth node. Its control points are always opposite each other. If you move a control point, the opposite control point moves, too. What's different is that the control points are always the same distance from each other (**Figure 6.5**). This results in an even shape on both sides of the node.

◆ A *cusp node* is used to create sharp corners on a path. The cusp node's control points move independently of one another; thus, a curve that passes through a cusp node can bend at a sharp angle (**Figure 6.6**).

To change any type of node to another type, right-click it with the Shape Tool and choose a node type from the pop-up menu that appears (**Figure 6.7**). The type of node you choose will depend on how you want to shape the surrounding line segments.

Figure 6.4 The control points for a smooth node are locked into alignment, but the connecting lines can be different lengths.

Figure 6.5 The control points for a symmetrical node are also locked into alignment, but the connecting lines are the same length.

Figure 6.6 A cusp node's control points move independently of one another, and the connecting lines can be different lengths.

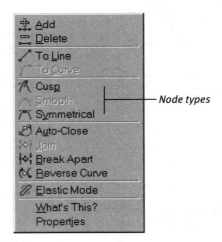

Figure 6.7 You can freely change a node's type.

Figure 6.8 Use the Convert to Curves command or icon to change a defined object to one composed of curves.

Converting an Object to Curves

If you draw a shape such as a circle or a rectangle, you won't be able to edit its nodes until you convert the object to curves. (Only spirals, freehand lines, and Bézier lines are initially created as curved objects.)

To convert an object to curves:

1. Select the object using the Pick Tool.

2. Choose Arrange > Convert To Curves, press [Ctrl][Q], or click the Convert To Curves icon on the property bar (**Figure 6.8**).

✔ Tip

■ Check the status bar to see if an object already has curves or if it is a defined shape, such as an oval. If an object is a defined shape, the status bar will say something like "Ellipse on Layer 1" or "Symmetrical Polygon with 10 sides on Layer 1." If an object has curves (whether it was drawn that way initially or has been converted to curves), the status bar will display something like "Curve on Layer 1" and also state the number of nodes. (Note that the wording of the status bar text depends on whether you select the shape with the Pick Tool or the Shape Tool.)

Working with Nodes

To modify a curve, you select and manipulate its nodes. Here are some of the things you can do with nodes:

♦ Add control points to a node

♦ Make straight lines curved or curved lines straight

♦ Move nodes to different positions and manipulate their control points

♦ Add or delete nodes

♦ Break nodes apart

♦ Join two nodes into one

Selecting nodes

Of course, in order to work with nodes, you must first select them.

To select a node:

1. Select a curve object (or one that has been converted to a curve object) with the Shape Tool.

   The object's nodes appear on the shape's path. (Check the status bar to make sure that the object is a curve.)

2. Click a node with the Shape Tool to select it (**Figure 6.9**).

To select multiple nodes:

1. Select a curve object with the Shape Tool.

2. Hold down (Shift) while clicking the nodes you wish to select.

   or

   Drag a marquee around the nodes you wish to select (**Figure 6.10**).

✔ Tip

■ To select all nodes, choose Edit > Select All > Nodes. To unselect all selected nodes, click any open area in the drawing window.

WORKING WITH NODES

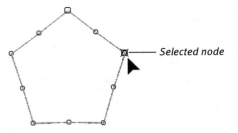

Figure 6.9 Use the Shape Tool to select a node on a curve object or one converted to a curve object.

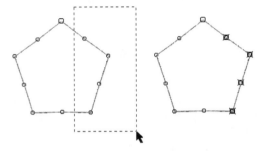

Figure 6.10 You can use the marquee selection technique (left) to drag-select several nodes at once. In this example, four nodes have been selected (right).

Switching Between Tools

You can quickly switch between the tool you are using and the Pick Tool by pressing (Spacebar). To switch back to the other tool, press (Spacebar) again.

Figure 6.11 The selected node has no control points, indicating that the line is straight.

Convert Line To Curve

Figure 6.12 Click this icon to convert a straight line to a curve.

Figure 6.13 After converting the straight line to a curve, control points border the line segment.

Figure 6.14 Use the Shape Tool to select the node you want to convert into a straight line.

Convert Curve To Line

Figure 6.15 Click the Convert Curve To Line icon.

Figure 6.16 The previously curved line is converted to a straight line.

Node and path properties

You can use property bar icons to change the properties of nodes and paths. For example, suppose there are two lines that you want to connect. You could use the property bar to join the nodes at the end of each line. You can also click icons to change a straight line into a curve or a curved line into a straight line, as explained in the following sections.

Making a straight line into a curve

Sometimes you'll encounter a node with no control points (**Figure 6.11**). This is because a straight line segment is passing through the node. To add control points to such a node, you must convert the line to curves.

To add control points to a node (or make a straight line curved):

1. Use the Shape Tool to select a node that has no control points (**Figure 6.11**).
2. Click the Convert Line To Curve property bar icon (**Figure 6.12**).

   Control points appear, bordering each side of the line segment (**Figure 6.13**)—one on the selected node and the other on the node located in a counterclockwise position from the selected node.

Making a curved line straight

To make a curved line segment straight, you do the opposite of converting a line to curves.

To make a curved line straight:

1. Use the Shape Tool to select the node you want to convert (**Figure 6.14**).
2. Click the Convert Curve To Line property bar icon (**Figure 6.15**).

   The control points disappear and the line becomes straight (**Figure 6.16**).

Reshaping an object

Of course, the main purpose of nodes is that you can use them to modify line segments and change an object's shape. To change the shape of an object, you can drag nodes, control points, or line segments.

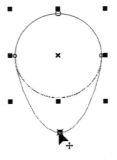

Figure 6.17 You can click and drag a node to change an object's shape—adding an elongated curve to this circle, for example.

To move a node:

1. Select the object with the Shape Tool.

2. Click the node and drag until you're satisfied with the resulting shape (**Figure 6.17**).

3. Release the mouse button.

To manipulate a control point:

1. Select a node with the Shape Tool.

2. Click and drag a control point until you achieve the desired curve (**Figure 6.18**).

To alter a line segment:

1. Select the object with the Shape Tool.

2. Place the pointer of the Shape Tool on the object's path.

   A small squiggle appears, attached to the Shape Tool's pointer.

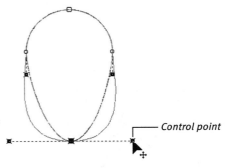

Control point

Figure 6.18 You can further modify a curve by dragging the node's control points.

3. Drag a line segment with the Shape Tool (**Figures 6.19** and **6.20**).

   As you drag, you'll note that stretching the line segment also affects the rest of the object; the nodes remain stationary while the line segments stretch and curve according to the type of node they pass through.

4. When you are satisfied with the shape, release the mouse button.

Figure 6.19 You can also use the Shape Tool to drag a line segment.

Figure 6.20 The object's nodes remain stationery, while the affected path segments change.

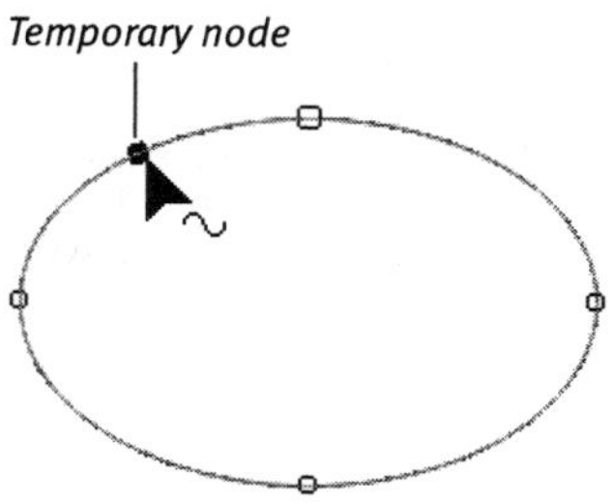

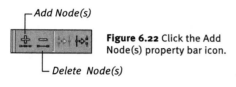

Figure 6.21 Click the point on the path where you want to create a new node.

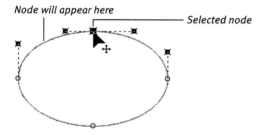

Figure 6.22 Click the Add Node(s) property bar icon.

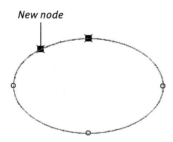

Figure 6.23 Select the node clockwise from the line segment on which you want to add a node.

Figure 6.24 The new node appears in the middle of the line segment.

Adding nodes to a path

To help you shape a path, you can add more nodes wherever they're needed. Nodes can be added *manually* (by clicking the desired location on a line segment) or *automatically* (placed in the exact middle of a line segment).

To manually add a node to a path:

1. Select the object with the Shape Tool.

2. Click on the path where you want to add the node.

   A circular, temporary node appears on the line segment (**Figure 6.21**).

3. *Do one of the following:*

   ▲ Right-click the temporary node and select Add from the pop-up menu that appears (see Figure 6.7).

   ▲ Press the ⊞ key on the numeric keypad.

   ▲ Click the Add Node(s) icon on the property bar (**Figure 6.22**).

✔ Tip

■ The fastest way to add a new node is to double-click the desired spot on the path.

To automatically add a node to a line segment:

1. Using the Shape Tool, select the node whose position is clockwise to the line segment you want to edit (**Figure 6.23**).

   The property bar displays node editing icons.

2. Click the Add Node(s) icon on the property bar (**Figure 6.22**).

   A new node appears that divides the path into two segments (**Figure 6.24**).

Deleting nodes

You can also delete nodes, if necessary.

To delete a node from a path:

- ◆ Double-click the node.

- ◆ Select the node with the Shape Tool, and press [Del] or press [−] on the numeric keypad.

- ◆ Select the node with the Shape Tool, and click the Delete Node(s) icon on the property bar (see Figure 6.22).

- ◆ Right-click the node, and choose Delete from the pop-up menu that appears (see Figure 6.7).

✔ Tip

- ■ You can delete several nodes at once by selecting multiple nodes and using any of these deletion techniques.

Breaking a curve

Using the Break Apart command, you can change a closed-path curve into an open path.

To break a curve apart:

1. With the Shape Tool, right-click the node where you want to break the curve and choose Break Apart from the pop-up menu that appears (see Figure 6.7).

   or

   Select the node with the Shape Tool (**Figure 6.25**) and click the Break Curve icon on the property bar.

2. Use the Shape Tool to move the new node off the original node (**Figure 6.26**).

✔ Tip

- ■ If you break the path of a filled closed object, its color, pattern, or texture will be removed (because the path is now open).

Figure 6.25 Using the Shape Tool, select the node where you want to break the curve apart.

Figure 6.26 After choosing the Break Apart command, drag the node to a new location to complete the break.

A Rule of Thumb for Nodes

When you make changes to a node, the changes will always affect the line segment located in a *counterclockwise* position from the selected node.

Figure 6.27 Select two nodes that you wish to join together.

Join Two Nodes

Figure 6.28 Click the Join Two Nodes icon.

Figure 6.29 Choose Join from the pop-up menu.

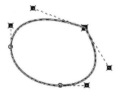

Figure 6.30 The line segments attached to the two nodes move together.

Extend Curve to Close

Figure 6.31 Click the Extend Curve to Close icon on the property bar.

Figure 6.32 The two nodes are joined together by a straight line.

Joining two nodes

To create a closed path, you can join a pair of nodes. There are two ways to do this:

◆ Change two nodes into a single node

◆ Connect the two nodes with a straight line

To join two nodes into one:

1. Select the first node with the Shape Tool. The property bar displays node editing icons.

2. Press Shift and click the second node that you want to join to the first (**Figure 6.27**).

3. Click the Join Two Nodes icon on the property bar (**Figure 6.28**).

   or

   Right-click either of the selected nodes, and choose Join from the pop-up menu that appears (**Figure 6.29**).

   The two nodes move together and become one (**Figure 6.30**).

To join two nodes with a straight line:

1. Select the two nodes you want to join (**Figure 6.27**).

   The property bar displays node editing icons.

2. Click the Extend Curve to Close icon on the property bar (**Figure 6.31**).

   A straight line appears, joining the nodes (**Figure 6.32**).

LINES AND CURVES

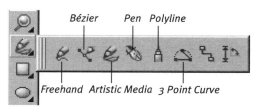

Bézier   Pen Polyline

Freehand Artistic Media 3 Point Curve

Figure 7.1 All tools for drawing lines and curves can be found on the Curve flyout.

CorelDraw 10 had three tools for drawing lines and curves: the Freehand, Bézier, and Artistic Media Tools. In CorelDraw 11, three additional tools have been added: the Pen, Polyline, and 3 Point Curve Tool. You'll find all six tools on the Curve flyout (**Figure 7.1**).

Briefly, here's how they work:

- *Freehand Tool:* Works like a pencil on paper. As you drag, it creates curves and lines, mirroring the motions of the mouse.

- *Bézier Tool:* You place nodes and then shape the line segments between them, creating smooth curves.

- *Pen Tool:* Duplicates the functions of the Bézier Tool, making the transition to CorelDraw easier for people who previously used another illustration program.

- *Polyline Tool:* Enables you to draw straight lines and freehand-style curves with a single tool.

- *3 Point Curve Tool:* Draw smooth curves by defining three points on the curve.

- *Artistic Media Tool:* Drag to draw lines of varying thicknesses and shapes, paint with a brush or sprayer, and draw calligraphic lines. However, instead of creating a single, thick outline as the Freehand Tool does, it creates closed-path objects.

Using the Freehand Tool

The Freehand Tool will probably feel familiar to you immediately, since it's so much like drawing with a pen or pencil. At first, your lines may be rough, but you can refine them with the Shape Tool. The more that you use the Freehand Tool, the more natural it will become.

To draw a straight line:

1. Select the Freehand Tool (see Figure 7.1).

   The pointer changes to a cross-hair with a tiny squiggle attached to it.

2. Click where you want the line to begin.

3. Click where you want the line to end (**Figure 7.2**).

To constrain (force) a straight line to an angle:

1. With the Freehand Tool, click where you want the line to start.

2. Press and hold down Ctrl.

3. Move the mouse to where you want the line to end.

   As you move the mouse up or down, the line moves in 15-degree increments.

4. Click where you want the line to end, and then release Ctrl.

✔ Tip

■ Watch the status bar as you draw the line. It shows the current angle.

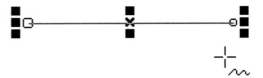

Figure 7.2 To create a straight line, click to start the line and click where you want it to end.

Figure 7.3 Click and drag to draw the desired shape.

Figure 7.4 When you're finished drawing, release the mouse button. Nodes automatically appear along the drawn path.

Figure 7.5 The Close Path submenu offers additional options for closing a path.

Why Are There More Nodes on One End of the Curve?

As you draw a curve with the Freehand Tool, CorelDraw automatically places nodes along the curve. The faster you move the mouse, the fewer nodes that appear along the curve. If you slow down while drawing, CorelDraw adds extra nodes. It assumes you are trying to emphasize that part of the curve. (Remember that if there are too many nodes on a curve section, you can later delete them using the Shape Tool.)

To draw a curved line:

1. Select the Freehand Tool (see Figure 7.1).
2. Click and drag (as you would when drawing with a pencil on paper) to create the curve (**Figure 7.3**).
3. Release the mouse button when you're finished.

   CorelDraw smooths the curve. Several nodes appear along the path (**Figure 7.4**).

To erase part of a line as you draw:

1. Without releasing the mouse button, press and hold down [Shift].
2. Drag the Freehand Tool backwards along the line that you've drawn.

   As you drag backwards, the line is erased.
3. Release [Shift] when you're done erasing (but don't release the mouse button).
4. Resume drawing the line.

To create a closed object:

◆ Use the Freehand Tool to create the desired shape, but make sure that the line segments begin and end at the same point.

✔ Tip

■ You can also close a path by clicking the Auto-Close Curve icon on the property bar or by choosing a more specific command from the Arrange > Close Path submenu (**Figure 7.5**).

USING THE FREEHAND TOOL

Using the Bézier Tool

Use the Bézier Tool to precisely draw smooth curves, node-by-node. As each node is created, you can control the curvature of the line by manipulating the node's control points.

To draw a straight line:

1. Select the Bézier Tool from the Curve fly-out (see Figure 7.1).

   The pointer changes to a cross-hair with a tiny curve connected to it.

2. Click to position the first node.

3. Click to place the next node.

   A straight line segment appears between the two nodes (**Figure 7.6**).

4. To draw additional connected straight lines, repeat Step 3.

5. When you are done drawing, double-click, press (Spacebar), or select another tool.

To create a curve:

1. Select the Bézier Tool.

2. Position the Bézier Tool where you want to start the curve, and then click and drag.

   A node appears with two control points that stretch in opposite positions as you drag (**Figure 7.7**).

3. Release the mouse when the control points are the desired distance from the node.

4. Move the mouse to where you want to place the next node.

5. Click and drag to create another node with two control points.

   A curved line segment appears between the two nodes (**Figure 7.8**).

6. To add another node to continue the curve, repeat Steps 4 and 5. If you are done drawing, double-click, press (Spacebar), or select another tool.

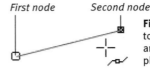

Figure 7.6 Click once to place the first node and a second time to place the next node.

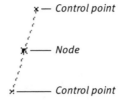

Figure 7.7 Click and drag to create a node with two control points.

Figure 7.8 Click and drag again to add a second node and create the curve.

Who Was Bézier?

The *Bézier curve* (the curve representation used most frequently in computer graphics) is named for Pierre Bézier, a French engineer who worked for Renault, the car manufacturer. While he was drawing car parts in the 1960s, he developed the mathematical equations to geometrically represent a curve.

✔ Tips

- To create a closed object with the Bézier Tool, make sure that the final click is directly on top of the first node that you placed.

- The distance between a node and its control points determines how curved the line segment will be. The farther away the control points are from the node, the deeper the curve will be.

- As you draw your object with the Bézier Tool, you can go back and edit any of the curves and lines by clicking their nodes. You can also change the type of any node by right-clicking it and choosing a new type from the pop-up menu that appears.

- Using the Shape Tool, you can also perform any of these edits *after* the object has been drawn.

Using the Pen Tool

Think of the Pen Tool (**Figure 7.9**) as simply a variation of the Bézier Tool. It can be used to draw straight lines and curves using the procedures described previously for the Bézier Tool. However, you'll probably notice one difference—a visual one. As you draw with the Pen Tool (**Figure 7.10**), lines and curves are always visible; with the Bézier Tool, the lines appear after you click.

The Pen Tool provides additional options if you hold down a modifier key as you draw, as follows:

◆ If you hold down Shift as you draw, new lines are constrained to specific angles.

◆ If you hold down Control or Alt, the Pen Tool switches to edit mode. You can modify the current object without worrying about accidentally adding new lines or curves. Release the modifier key when you're ready to continue drawing.

✔ Tips

■ The lines are always visible as you draw with the Pen Tool because the default setting for the Preview Mode icon on the property bar is depressed/enabled. If you want the Pen Tool to work just like the Bézier Tool, disable Preview Mode.

■ You can use the Pen Tool to add nodes to any existing curve. Select the object or line with the Pick Tool, select the Pen Tool, and then click between any two existing nodes to create a new node.

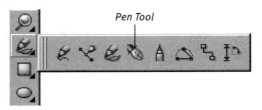

Figure 7.9 Select the Pen Tool from the Curve flyout.

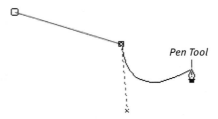

Figure 7.10 You can use the Pen Tool to draw lines or curves, and to add nodes to existing objects.

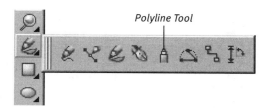

Polyline Tool

Figure 7.11 Select the Polyline Tool from the Curve flyout.

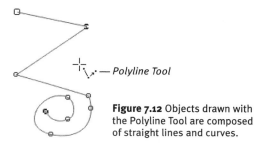

— *Polyline Tool*

Figure 7.12 Objects drawn with the Polyline Tool are composed of straight lines and curves.

Using the Polyline Tool

Consider using the new Polyline Tool when you want to create lines that combine straight and Freehand Tool-style segments.

To draw with the Polyline Tool:

1. Select the Polyline Tool from the Curve flyout (**Figure 7.11**).

2. *Do one of the following:*
   ▲ To draw a straight line segment, click to set the start of the line and click again to set the line's endpoint.
   ▲ To draw a freehand/curved line, hold down the mouse button and drag in the drawing area. Release the mouse button to complete the segment.

3. To create additional straight or freehand segments that continue from the last segment, repeat Step 2.

4. When the line or object is completed, double-click to set the endpoint.

   The lines and curves are automatically smoothed (**Figure 7.12**).

✔ Tip

■ After you've set the endpoint for a polyline object (by double-clicking), you can edit the object with the Polyline Tool, too. When the Polyline Tool pointer moves over a node, it changes to the Shape Tool. You can click and drag any node to change the shape of the curve.

USING THE POLYLINE TOOL

The 3 Point Curve Tool

If you find manipulating control points cumbersome, you'll appreciate the elegant way that the 3 Point Curve Tool works.

To create a curve with the 3 Point Curve Tool:

1. Select the 3 Point Curve Tool from the Curve flyout (**Figure 7.13**).

2. Click to set the starting point of the curve, and then drag to set the width/size.

3. Release the mouse button when the line is the desired size.

4. Move the mouse to create the curve.

5. Click once to complete the curve (**Figure 7.14**).

✔ Tips

■ To add an additional curve to an endpoint, move the 3 Point Curve Tool's cursor over the endpoint. The tiny icon attached to the cursor changes to a curve with an arrowhead. Click the endpoint and repeat Steps 2 through 5 to create the additional curve.

■ If you've used the 3 Point Curve Tool to create a line or object with multiple curves, you can modify the curves by clicking any node.

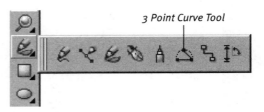

Figure 7.13 Select the 3 Point Curve Tool from the Curve flyout.

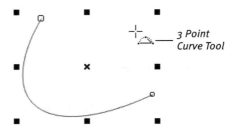

Figure 7.14 The completed curve and its endpoints are selected.

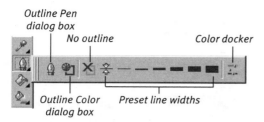

Figure 7.15 In the Outline flyout, you can set a line width for an object or open an Outline dialog box.

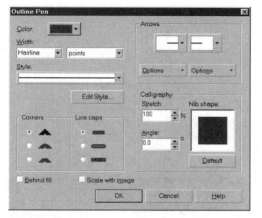

Figure 7.16 Use the Outline Pen dialog box when you want to change several line/outline properties at the same time.

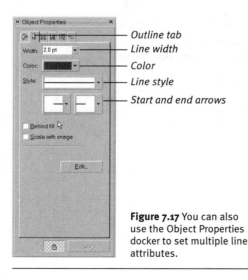

Figure 7.17 You can also use the Object Properties docker to set multiple line attributes.

Setting Line Properties

Creating lines and curves is just the beginning. Using the Outline flyout (**Figure 7.15**) and the Outline Pen dialog box (**Figure 7.16**), you can make lines thicker, change the style from solid to dashed or dotted, pick a new color, add arrowheads, or make them look like they were drawn with a calligraphy pen.

The Outline flyout

You may have already noticed that the last four icons in the toolbox are separated from the rest by a line. This is because these four icons—the Eyedropper and Paintbucket Tools, the Outline Tool, the Fill Tool, and the Interactive Fill Tool—work differently from their neighbors. Instead of being used for drawing, the icons represent tools that change the appearance of a drawing. The Fill, Eyedropper, and Paintbucket Tools are discussed in Chapter 10, "Color and Fills." In this section, you'll learn about the Outline Tool and options on the Outline flyout.

The Outline Pen dialog box

The Outline Pen dialog box (**Figure 7.16**) is used to change the properties of lines. When you need to make multiple changes to a line's properties, the Outline Pen dialog box is very useful. For simple changes, however, it's faster to choose new settings from the property bar.

✔ Tip

■ You can also set line width, style, color, and arrowheads in the Outline tab of the Object Properties docker (**Figure 7.17**). To open the docker, right-click an object and choose Properties from the pop-up menu, or choose Window > Dockers > Properties.

To change a line's width:

1. Select a previously drawn object or line.

2. *Do one of the following:*

   ▲ Open the Outline Tool flyout, and choose one of the preset line width icons (see Figure 7.15).

   ▲ Choose a line width from the Outline Width drop-down list on the property bar (**Figure 7.18**).

   ▲ Select the Outline Pen dialog box from the Outline flyout or press F12. Choose a line thickness from the Width drop-down list (see Figure 7.16). Click OK.

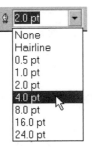

Figure 7.18 You can choose a new line or outline width from this drop-down list on the property bar.

To change a line's style:

1. Select a previously drawn object or line.

2. Choose a line style from the Outline Style Selector drop-down list on the property bar (**Figure 7.19**).

   or

   Select the Outline Pen dialog box from the Outline flyout or press F12. Choose a new line style from the Style drop-down list (see Figure 7.16). Click OK.

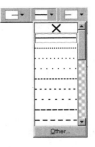

Figure 7.19 Choose a line or outline style from this drop-down list on the property bar. (To eliminate an object's outline, choose the X.)

To set a line's color:

1. Select a previously drawn object or line.

2. *Do one of the following:*

   ▲ Right-click a color in any open color palette.

   ▲ Select the Outline Pen dialog box from the Outline flyout or press F12. Choose a new color style from the Color drop-down list (see Figure 7.16). Click OK.

   ▲ Select the Outline Color dialog box from the Outline flyout or press Shift F12. On the Models tab (**Figure 7.20**), choose a color by clicking in the colored area, dragging the slider, choosing from the Name list, and/or entering numbers in the text boxes. Click OK.

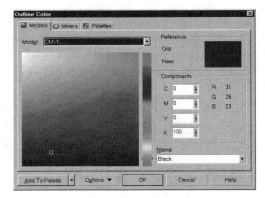

Figure 7.20 For more precise color requirements, click the Models tab of the Outline Color dialog box and specify a line or outline color.

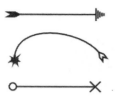

Figure 7.21 You can turn any line into an arrow by picking starting and ending styles.

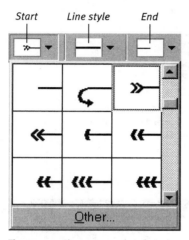

Figure 7.22 Choose arrowhead start and end styles from the drop-down lists on the property bar or in the Outline Pen dialog box.

Figure 7.23 Select a symbol, letter, or shape in the drawing window.

Figure 7.24 You can add the custom arrowhead to either end of a line.

Adding Arrowheads

You can embellish any line or curve by adding a starting and/or ending arrowhead to it (**Figure 7.21**). And if you don't like the predefined arrowhead styles, you can design your own.

To add arrowheads to a line:

1. Select a line with the Pick Tool.

2. Choose line start and end styles from the drop-down lists on the property bar (**Figure 7.22**).

   or

   Select the Outline Pen dialog box from the Outline flyout or press F12. Choose line start and end styles from the drop-down lists in the Arrows section of the dialog box (see Figure 7.16). Click OK.

Creating custom arrowheads

You can create custom arrowheads from any shape, letter, or symbol.

To create a custom arrowhead:

1. Using the Pick Tool, select a letter, symbol, or shape in the drawing window that will become the arrowhead (**Figure 7.23**).

2. Choose Tools > Create >Arrow.

   The Create Arrow dialog box appears asking if you want to create an arrowhead from the selected object.

3. Click OK.

   The letter, symbol, or shape is added as a new arrowhead at the bottom of the Start and End drop-down lists.

4. Use the Pick Tool to select the line to which you want to add the arrowhead.

5. From the Start and/or End lists in the property bar or the Outline Pen dialog box, select the new arrowhead.

   The custom arrowhead appears attached to the selected line (**Figure 7.24**).

Reshaping or sizing arrowheads

Like other objects, you are free to change the shape and size of existing arrowheads, as well as those of the custom arrowheads you've created. (You'll note that custom arrowheads are often very tiny. Using the following procedure, you can enlarge them.)

To change an arrowhead's shape and/or size:

1. Add the arrowhead to a line in the drawing window, and then select the line.

2. On the property bar, open the start or end drop-down list that displays the arrowhead and click the Other button.

    or

    In the Arrows area of the Outline Pen dialog box, click the Options button beneath the displayed arrowhead and choose Edit (**Figure 7.25**).

    The Edit Arrowhead dialog box appears (**Figure 7.26**).

3. Drag handles to change the arrowhead's size and/or shape. (Drag a corner handle to resize proportionately.)

4. Click OK when you are done editing. (If the Outline Pen dialog box is open, click OK to close it, too.)

✔ Tip

- You're limited to 100 arrowheads. To delete one you don't need, choose it in the Outline Pen dialog box, click Options, and choose Delete (**Figure 7.25**).

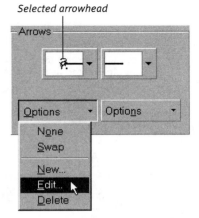

Selected arrowhead

Figure 7.25 Click the Options button beneath the arrowhead you want to modify, and choose Edit.

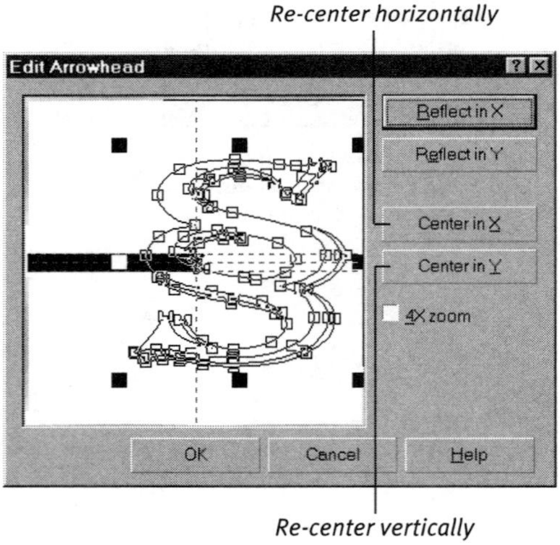

Re-center horizontally

Figure 7.26 Use this dialog box to change the size and/or shape of the arrowhead.

Re-center vertically

Figure 7.27 Select a line to which you want to add a calligraphy effect.

Nib shape   Stretch percentage   Preview

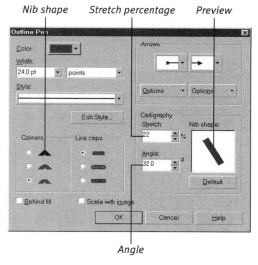

Angle

Figure 7.28 Select a corner (nib) shape, specify a stretch percentage, and set an angle.

Figure 7.29 When you close the dialog box, the line is transformed.

Calligraphic Lines

By setting options in the Outline Pen dialog box, you can edit an existing line to make it look like it was drawn with a calligraphy pen.

To give a line the appearance of calligraphy:

1. Select an existing line with the Pick Tool (**Figure 7.27**).

2. Select the Outline Pen dialog box from the Outline flyout or press F12.

   The Outline Pen dialog box opens (**Figure 7.28**).

3. Select a corner style for the nib shape.

   The top and bottom styles create a square nib. The middle style creates a round nib. (A *nib* is the point of a calligraphy pen.)

4. In the Calligraphy area, set the nib's Stretch and Angle.

   The Stretch setting determines how square or round the nib will be. The lower the setting, the thinner the nib and the more variation there will be in line thickness.

5. Click OK.

   The line is redrawn to look like it was drawn with a calligraphy pen (**Figure 7.29**). Note the variations in line thickness.

Cutting Objects Apart

The Knife Tool (**Figure 7.30**) cuts away a portion of an object's path while adding new paths. It works like the Freehand Tool. You can make straight cuts or freehand cuts.

Figure 7.30 Select the Knife Tool from the Shape Tool flyout.

To make a straight cut:

1. Select the Knife Tool from the Shape Tool flyout.

   The cursor changes to an angled knife.

2. Move the knife cursor over the object's path where you want to start cutting.

   When the cursor is over the path, it snaps upright—indicating that it's ready to cut.

3. Click to start the cut.

4. Move the cursor to the spot on the path where you want to complete the cut.

   CorelDraw previews the cut (**Figure 7.31**).

5. To complete the cut, click a second time.

   A straight line appears, splitting the object in two. If you switch to the Pick Tool, you'll see that you can drag the pieces apart (**Figure 7.32**).

To make a freehand cut:

1. Select the Knife Tool.

2. Move the knife cursor over the object's path where you want to start cutting.

   When the cursor is over the path, it snaps upright—indicating that it's ready to cut.

3. Click and drag as if you were drawing with the Freehand Tool (**Figure 7.33**).

4. Release the mouse button when the cursor reaches the spot on the object's path where you want to stop cutting.

   The freehand cut splits the object. If you switch to the Pick Tool, you'll see that you can drag the pieces apart.

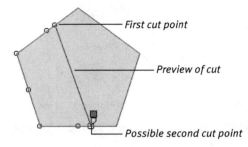

Figure 7.31 When the Knife Tool touches the path again, you'll be shown a cut preview.

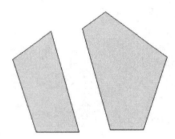

Figure 7.32 After the cut, you can drag the two objects apart.

Figure 7.33 To illustrate a broken heart, you can make a freehand cut.

Figure 7.34 You can also make series of straight cuts.

✔ Tips

■ The beginning and final cut *must* be over the object's path/outline. If you find that you aren't allowed to make a particular cut, be sure that you're over the path when you click.

■ When you use the Knife Tool to split an object, the object is automatically converted to curves.

■ If you want to make a series of perfectly straight freehand cuts (**Figure 7.34**), hold down ⟨Shift⟩ and click at every new cut point (rather than dragging to cut). To make smooth curved cuts, hold down ⟨Shift⟩ and drag.

Using the Eraser Tool

One way to remove part of an object is to use the Shape Tool to cut or delete nodes. Another is to use the Eraser Tool. With a swipe of the Eraser Tool, you can selectively erase parts of an object—just as you can when editing a bitmap photo in an image-editing program.

To erase part of an object:

1. Select the Eraser Tool from the Shape Tool flyout (**Figure 7.35**) or press X.

    The cursor changes to a circle. The circle indicates the area that will be erased.

2. Select the object you want to work on by clicking it with the Eraser Tool.

3. *Do one of the following:*

    ▲ Double-click to erase the area beneath the circle.

    ▲ Click and drag to remove an irregular portion of the object.

    ▲ For a straight erasure (**Figure 7.36**), click once to set the starting point for the erasure and click a second time to indicate the end point.

    CorelDraw modifies the object's path to account for the erasure (**Figure 7.36**).

✔ Tips

■ If you erase too much, you can undo the erasure by choosing Edit > Undo Erase or by pressing Ctrl Z.

■ You can change the eraser's size or shape by setting options on the property bar (**Figure 7.37**). Click the Circle/Square button to select a circular or square eraser. To change the eraser's size, enter a new number in the Eraser Thickness text box and press Enter. (The default size is 0.25".)

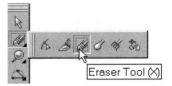

Figure 7.35 Select the Eraser Tool from the Shape Tool flyout.

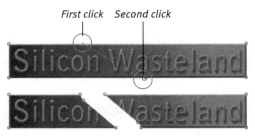

Figure 7.36 To erase in a straight line, click for the start point and click again for the end point (top). The result is a straight erasure (bottom).

Figure 7.37 Use these property bar controls to change the size or shape of the eraser.

USING THE ERASER TOOL

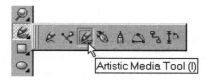

Figure 7.38 Select the Artistic Media Tool from the Curve flyout.

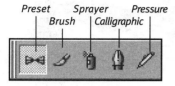

Figure 7.39 Click an icon on the property bar to set the Artistic Media Tool's mode.

The Artistic Media Tool

Using the Artistic Media Tool, you can draw lines of varying thicknesses and shapes, paint with a brush or sprayer, or draw calligraphic lines. The tool has five drawing modes: Preset, Brush, Sprayer, Calligraphic, and Pressure.

You can use the Artistic Media Tool in two ways:

◆ Draw with it as you do the Freehand Tool, clicking and dragging to create lines.

◆ Select an existing object, such as a line or circle, and apply one of the Artistic Media Tool strokes to it.

To set the Artistic Media Tool's mode:

1. Select the Artistic Media Tool from the Curve flyout (**Figure 7.38**) or press ⓘ.

2. Click one of the five mode icons on the property bar (**Figure 7.39**). Each Artistic Media Tool mode produces a different effect:

   ▲ *Preset mode:* Draws outline brush strokes that can be filled with a color, pattern, or texture.

   ▲ *Brush mode:* Uses artistic brushes to transform lines into images.

   ▲ *Sprayer mode:* Replaces lines with image patterns.

   ▲ *Calligraphic mode:* Produces lines of varying thicknesses that look as though they were drawn with a calligraphy pen.

   ▲ *Pressure mode:* Uses a drawing tablet or cursor keys to create lines whose darkness is proportional to the pressure exerted.

THE ARTISTIC MEDIA TOOL

Using Preset mode

The Preset mode of the Artistic Media Tool draws curves using preset strokes that you select from the property bar.

To draw a Preset curve:

1. Select the Artistic Media Tool from the Curve flyout (see Figure 7.38).

2. Click the Preset mode icon on the property bar (see Figure 7.39).

3. Set the curve's width in the Artistic Media Tool Width text box (**Figure 7.40**).

4. Select a stroke shape from the drop-down list of preset strokes (**Figure 7.40**).

5. Click and drag to create the desired shape (**Figure 7.41**).

   When you release the mouse button, the curve redraws as an outline—ready to be filled with a color, texture, or pattern (**Figure 7.42**).

✔ Tip

■ You can alter the stroke width or shape of a previously drawn preset object by selecting it with the Artistic Medial Tool and choosing new options from the property bar.

Artistic Media Tool Width *Preset Stroke List*

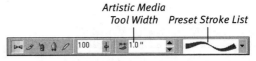

Figure 7.40 Set the Artistic Media Tool mode and options using these property bar controls.

Figure 7.41 Click and drag to draw the desired shape.

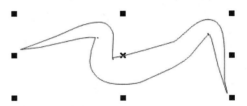

Figure 7.42 When you release the mouse button, the shape is redrawn to match the tool's settings.

Browse

Figure 7.43 Select a brush stroke from this drop-down list on the property bar.

Figure 7.44 Click and drag to create the brush stroke.

Figure 7.45 When you release the mouse button, the shape is redrawn to match the tool's settings.

Using Brush mode

Use Brush mode to apply predefined brush strokes to curves. It works just like Preset mode. All you have to do is select a brush stroke from the property bar, and then click and drag.

To draw a Brush curve:

1. Select the Artistic Media Tool from the Curve flyout (see Figure 7.38).

2. Click the Brush mode icon on the property bar (see Figure 7.39).

3. Set the curve's width in the Artistic Media Tool Width text box (see Figure 7.40).

4. Select a brush stroke from the Brush Stroke List on the property bar (**Figure 7.43**).

5. Click and drag to create the desired shape (**Figure 7.44**).

   When you release the mouse button, the curve redraws using the chosen brush style (**Figure 7.45**).

✔ Tips

■ You aren't restricted to the brush strokes shown in the Brush Stroke List. If you have others stored on disk, click the Browse icon to the left of the Brush Stroke List.

■ To change the shape of an existing curve, select the curve with the Shape Tool and manipulate the curve's nodes and handles. For more information about nodes and handles, see Chapter 6, "Nodes and Paths."

THE ARTISTIC MEDIA TOOL

Using Sprayer mode

Sprayer mode lets you add a series of objects—such as ghosts, bats, flowers, or pebbles—to the curves you draw.

To draw a Sprayer curve:

1. Select the Artistic Media Tool from the Curve flyout (see Figure 7.38).

2. Click the Sprayer mode icon on the property bar (see Figure 7.39).

3. Select a stroke style from the Spraylist File List on the property bar (**Figure 7.46**).

4. Click and drag to create the desired curve. (You'll note that the curve is a nice, thin line rather than the blobs generated when you draw in Preset or Brush mode.)

   When you release the mouse button, the curve redraws, displaying the sprayer objects you selected (**Figure 7.47**).

✔ Tips

■ To make the objects smaller or larger, enter new percentages in the Size of Objects to be Sprayed text boxes on the property bar. If you want the new size to be proportional to the original size, be sure that the tiny padlock icon is closed (depressed).

■ To space the objects differently, enter new numbers in the Dabs/Spacing of Object(s) to be Sprayed text boxes on the property bar (**Figure 7.48**). The number in the top box represents the number of objects that will appear at each spacing point. The number in the bottom sets the distance between spacing points.

Figure 7.46 Pick a stroke style from the Spraylist File List.

Figure 7.47 When you release the mouse button, the shape is redrawn to match the chosen spray pattern.

— *Number of objects*
— *Object spacing*

Figure 7.48 You can change the number and spacing of objects in the spray pattern.

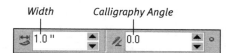

Width   *Calligraphy Angle*

Figure 7.49 Set the pen's width and drawing angle in these text boxes on the property bar.

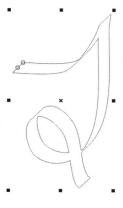

Figure 7.50 Release the mouse when you're done drawing to reveal the calligraphic outline.

Figure 7.51 You can fill the object with a color, pattern, or texture, such as this grayscale fountain fill.

Using Calligraphy mode

You use Calligraphy mode to create curves that look as though they were drawn with a calligraphy pen. All you have to do is set the width of the curve and the nib angle.

To draw a Calligraphy curve:

1. Select the Artistic Media Tool from the Curve flyout (see Figure 7.38).

2. Click the Calligraphy mode icon on the property bar (see Figure 7.39).

3. Set the curve's width in the Artistic Media Tool Width text box (**Figure 7.49**).

4. Set the angle of the tool's nib in the Calligraphy Angle text box (**Figure 7.49**).

5. Click and drag to create the desired curve. When you release the mouse button, the curve redraws, displaying the outline of the calligraphy curve (**Figure 7.50**).

✔ Tips

- You can use the Shape Tool to manipulate the curve's nodes and handles, changing the shape or size of the calligraphy curve. For details, see Chapter 6.

- As was the case with Preset mode curves, you can fill a calligraphy outline with a color, texture, or pattern (**Figure 7.51**). For instructions, refer to Chapter 10.

Using Pressure mode

In Pressure mode, the harder you press, the wider the stroke. To work in this mode, you either need a pressure-sensitive pen or you can simulate one by pressing the ⬆ and ⬇ keys as you drag with the mouse.

To draw using the Pressure mode:

1. Select the Artistic Media Tool from the Curve flyout (see Figure 7.38).

2. Click the Pressure mode icon on the property bar (see Figure 7.39).

3. Set the curve's maximum width in the Artistic Media Tool Width text box on the property bar.

4. Click and drag to draw. Press ⬆ to apply more pressure, making the line thicker. Press ⬇ to make the line thinner.

   If you are using a pressure pen or stylus, the line will get thicker as you press harder.

5. When you release the mouse button, the curve redraws, displaying its outline (**Figure 7.52**).

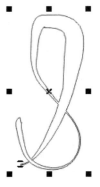

Figure 7.52 In Pressure mode, you can vary the thickness of your strokes as you draw.

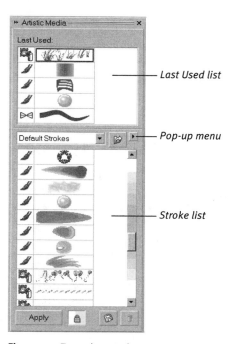

Last Used list

Pop-up menu

Stroke list

Figure 7.53 To apply a stroke to a selected curve, pick one from the scrolling list.

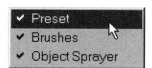

Figure 7.54 To limit the list to only certain types of strokes, remove checkmarks from this pop-up menu.

Applying a mode to a curve

You can also apply the Preset, Brush, or Sprayer modes to a curve that has already been drawn.

To apply a mode to an existing curve:

1. Open the Artistic Media docker (**Figure 7.53**) by choosing Window > Dockers > Artistic Media.

2. Using the Artistic Media Tool, select the curve you want to change.

3. Select a new Preset, Brush, or Sprayer stroke in the Artistic Media docker.

   The curve assumes the selected stroke.

✔ Tips

- If you don't like the effect of a selected stroke, you don't have to choose the Undo command—just select a different stroke.

- At the top of the docker is the Last Used list: a record of the most recently applied strokes. To reapply a recent stroke, you can choose it from this list rather than hunting through the main stroke list.

- By default, the main list in the Artistic Media docker includes Preset, Brush, and Sprayer strokes. You can limit the list to fewer categories by clicking the right arrow on the side of the docker and removing checkmarks from the pop-up menu that appears (**Figure 7.54**).

PAGE AND DOCUMENT SETUP

Besides being a versatile drawing tool, CorelDraw 11 has impressive desktop publishing capabilities. This means that you can use it to design many types of multi-page publications, such as brochures, flyers, and catalogs. In addition, you can create documents for any paper size that is used anywhere in the world.

In this chapter, you'll learn how to accomplish the following tasks:

- ◆ Set page size and orientation
- ◆ Set an optional document background
- ◆ Add, delete, rearrange, and name document pages
- ◆ Navigate among document pages
- ◆ View a document's information

✔ Tip

- ■ Selecting a paper size, orientation, and other page/document options is often just a preparatory step one performs prior to printing. To learn about printing your CorelDraw masterpieces, see Chapter 18, "Printing."

Setting Page Size and Orientation

When creating a drawing, it's important to design with a paper size and orientation in mind. You can use either of the following procedures to specify these settings.

To set a page size and orientation using the property bar:

1. With nothing selected on the drawing page, choose the Pick Tool from the toolbox.

2. On the property bar, click the down arrow beside the Paper Type/Size drop-down list and choose a paper (**Figure 8.1**).

   The chosen paper's dimensions are displayed in the Width and Height text boxes.

3. Click the Portrait (vertical) or Landscape (horizontal) icon to set a page orientation.

To set a page size and orientation using the Options dialog box:

1. Choose Layout > Page Setup.

   The Options dialog box appears (**Figure 8.2**), open to the Size section.

2. Click the Normal Paper radio button.

3. Choose a paper size from the Paper drop-down list.

4. Click the Portrait or Landscape radio button to set the page orientation.

5. *Optional:* To set a paper size for only the currently selected page, click the check box marked Resize current page only.

6. *Optional:* To set the page orientation to match the orientation set for your printer in the Print Setup dialog box (displayed by choosing File > Print Setup), click the Set From Printer button.

7. Click OK to accept the settings.

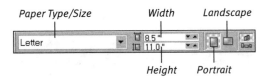

Figure 8.1 You can set page size and orientation for a document by choosing options from the property bar.

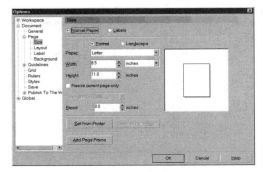

Figure 8.2 Standard and advanced page options can be set in the Options dialog box.

Custom Paper Sizes

Although CorelDraw supports most common paper sizes, you can also define and use custom paper sizes. Choose Custom from the drop-down Paper list and specify the paper dimensions. If you want to be able to reuse this custom size for other documents, click the Save Custom Page button and enter a name for the paper in the dialog box that appears.

SETTING PAGE SIZE AND ORIENTATION

Set for all pages

Set for current page only

Figure 8.3 To set options for all document pages, click the top button. To set options for the current page only, click the bottom button.

Selected page

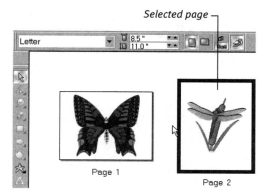

Page 1

Page 2

Figure 8.4 Choosing page settings is very convenient in Page Sorter View.

Label styles

Labels radio button

Label preview

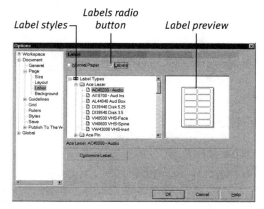

Figure 8.5 CorelDraw 11 supports dozens of label styles and layouts.

✔ Tips

- To set a new paper size for this page only, switch to the appropriate document page before beginning the second step list.

- You can add a hairline frame around the page by clicking the Add Page Frame button in the Options dialog box.

- Another way to set the orientation for only the current page is to click the bottom button of the Set Default or Current Page and Orientation pair on the property bar (**Figure 8.3**) and then click an orientation button. You can also use this technique to set a different paper size for only the current page.

- To simultaneously set the orientation or paper size for *all* pages in a document, click the top button of the Set Default or Current Page and Orientation pair on the property bar (**Figure 8.3**). Then select a paper size or orientation.

- This pair of property bar buttons can also be used to set orientation or paper size in Page Sorter View (choose View > Page Sorter View), as shown in **Figure 8.4**. To alter the settings for an individual page, select the page's thumbnail and click the bottom button of the Set Default or Current Page and Orientation pair.

- You can also design and print pages of labels with CorelDraw 11. In the Size section of the Options dialog box, click the Labels radio button. A list of common label manufacturers and their supported labels appears (**Figure 8.5**). Select a label style and then click OK. (If you can't make the label list appear, return to this dialog box after creating a new document.)

Setting a Page Background

You can add a background color or picture to any document. Backgrounds are commonly used on party invitations, brochures, and Web pages, for example. (Note that when you set a background, it is applied to *all* pages in the document.)

To add a document background:

1. Choose Layout > Page Background.

   The Options dialog box appears, open to the Background section (**Figure 8.6**).

2. Select one of these options:

   ▲ To remove an unwanted background, click the No Background radio button.

   ▲ To set a single-color background, click the Solid radio button and select a color from the drop-down palette to the right (**Figure 8.7**).

   ▲ To use a bitmap image (such as a JPEG file) as the background, click the Bitmap radio button, click Browse to display the Import dialog box (**Figure 8.8**), and select a picture file.

   From the drop-down list, choose Full Image to display the image as-is, choose Crop to use only a selected part of the image, or choose Resample to change the image's dimensions and resolution. Click the Open button.

3. *Bitmaps only:* In the Source section of the dialog box (**Figure 8.9**), click the Embedded radio button to add the background as a static entity. Click the Linked radio button to maintain a link to the bitmap file, enabling it to automatically update if you edit the bitmap.

   To change the size of the bitmap, click the Custom Size radio button in the Bitmap Size section and enter new horizontal (H) and vertical (V) dimensions.

4. Click OK.

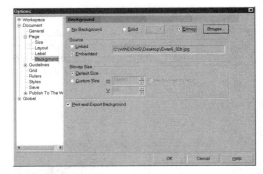

Figure 8.6 Choose a background color or picture in the Background section of the Options dialog box.

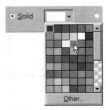

Figure 8.7 Pick a background color. Click Other to choose a color that isn't displayed.

Figure 8.8 You can select a bitmap image to use as a background for the current document.

Figure 8.9 You can set other options for bitmap backgrounds.

Add page to end of document   *Current page*

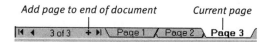

Figure 8.10 You can use the Document Navigator to add a page to the beginning or end of the document.

Number of pages to add

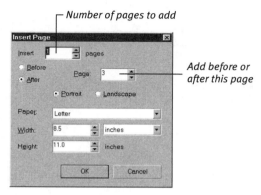

Add before or after this page

Figure 8.11 You can insert one or more consecutive new pages using the Insert Page dialog box.

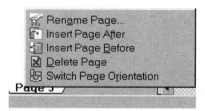

Figure 8.12 You can access most page-related commands by right-clicking a page tab in the Document Navigator.

Adding Pages

You can use either of the following procedures to add new pages to a document.

To add pages to the beginning or end of a document:

1. Locate the Document Navigator (**Figure 8.10**) in the lower-left corner of the screen.

2. To insert a new page at the beginning of the document, click the tab for the current first page and click the left plus (+) icon.

   or

   To insert a new page at the end of the document, click the tab for the current last page and click the right plus (+) icon.

To add pages anywhere in a document:

1. Choose Layout > Insert Page.

   The Insert Page dialog box appears (**Figure 8.11**).

2. In the Insert text box, enter or select the number of pages you wish to add.

3. In the Page text box, enter the page number that the new page(s) will be inserted before or after.

4. Click the Before or After radio button.

5. *Optional:* Specify a new orientation or paper size for the inserted page(s).

6. Click OK.

✔ Tips

- A document can contain up to 999 pages.

- You can also insert a page by right-clicking a page tab in the Document Navigator and choosing Insert Page After or Insert Page Before (**Figure 8.12**).

- You can also summon the Insert Page dialog box by pressing (Page Up) when on the first page or (Page Down) when on the last page.

Deleting Pages

If you decide that a page is no longer needed, you are free to delete it.

To delete one or more pages:

1. Choose Layout > Delete Page.

   The Delete Page dialog box appears, showing the currently selected page (**Figure 8.13**).

2. You can delete an individual page or a consecutive range of pages:

   ▲ To delete one page, enter its page number in the Delete page text box.

   ▲ To delete a range of pages, enter the number of the first page in the Delete page text box. Click the Through to page check box and enter the number of the last page in the second text box.

3. Click OK.

   The page or range of pages is deleted. The remaining pages are renumbered.

✔ Tips

■ When deleting pages, you are allowed to delete all but one. Thus, if a document contains only a single page, you cannot execute the Delete Page command. Similarly, if a document has two pages, you cannot delete a page range.

■ You can also delete an individual page by right-clicking its page tab in the Document Navigator and choosing Delete Page from the pop-up menu that appears (see Figure 8.12).

■ If you delete a page by mistake, you can restore the page by immediately choosing Edit > Undo Delete Page or by pressing Ctrl Z. If necessary, you can also restore a deleted page by stepping back through the Undo docker.

First page to delete

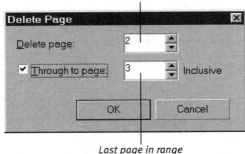

Last page in range

Figure 8.13 You can delete a single page or a consecutive range of pages.

Naming and Renaming Pages

CorelDraw automatically names each page according to its position in the document (Page 1, Page 2, and so on). You may find it beneficial to assign *real* names to some pages, identifying a page by its contents, for instance.

To name or rename a page, switch to that page, choose Layout > Rename Page, enter a name, and click OK. Alternately, you can right-click a page tab and choose Rename Page. The renamed page is designated by its number and name, such as *2: Logo*.

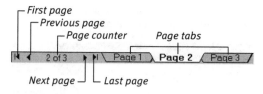

Figure 8.14 The page tabs at the bottom of the screen let you switch from one page to another.

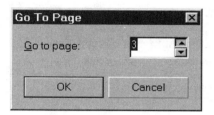

Figure 8.15 Use the Go To Page dialog box to jump directly to any page in a multi-page drawing.

Reorganizing Pages

As you add and remove pages, it isn't unusual to find that they're out of order. You can use either of the following procedures to reorganize the document pages.

♦ In the Document Navigator, drag page tabs left or right to a new position (**Figure 8.14**).

♦ Switch to Page Sorter View by choosing View > Page Sorter View. Click to select the page you want to move and then drag it to a new position.

Document Navigation

When working on a multi-page document such as a brochure, you can easily switch from one page to the next or jump to a specific page.

To switch to another page:

♦ Click a page tab at the bottom of the CorelDraw window (**Figure 8.14**).

♦ Click the left or right arrows on either side of the page counter.

The standard arrows move one page in the chosen direction; arrows with a vertical bar move to the first or last page in the document.

♦ Choose Layout > Go To Page.

The Go To Page dialog box appears (**Figure 8.15**). Type the page number you want to move to and click OK.

♦ Choose View > Page Sorter View.

A page appears that contains thumbnail representations of the document pages. Double-click any thumbnail to go to the page it represents.

✔ Tips

■ The Go To Page dialog box is particularly useful when you're working with a large document. It lets you jump to a specific page. Another way to summon the Go To Page dialog box is to click the page counter at the bottom of the screen (**Figure 8.14**).

■ You can also press (Page Up) to go to the previous page or (Page Down) to go to the next page.

DOCUMENT NAVIGATION

Viewing Document Info

With CorelDraw 11, it's easy to learn just about anything you want to know about the contents of a document (known as the *document info*). For example, you can see how many objects are in the document, what fonts have been used, the page size and orientation, when the document was created and last modified, and where on disk the file is stored.

To view document information:

◆ Choose File > Document Info.

The Document Information dialog box appears (**Figure 8.16**). Scroll to view the information.

◆ To generate a printout of the document info, click the Print button.

◆ To save a copy of the document info as a text file (as an archival reference, for example), click the Save As button, name the text file in the dialog box that appears, and click Save.

✔ Tips

■ To specify the document information you want to view, add or remove checkmarks on the right side of the Document Information dialog box.

■ If you double-click a saved document info file, it will normally open in Notepad, as shown in **Figure 8.17**. However, you can also open the file from within any text editor or word processor by choosing the program's File > Open command.

Save info as a text file —
Check/uncheck to set display options —

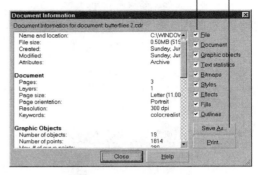

Figure 8.16 The Document Information dialog box displays a wealth of useful information about the current drawing.

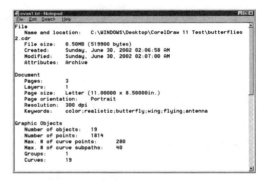

Figure 8.17 After saving a document's info as a text file, you can open it in Notepad.

TOOLS FOR PRECISION

CorelDraw 11 includes several tools to help you make your drawings more precise. In this chapter, you'll learn to do the following:

◆ Use the horizontal and vertical rulers, change the rulers' zero point, and set the default unit of measurement

◆ Use guidelines (dashed, non-printing lines) to shape and align objects

◆ Use grids (regularly spaced, non-printing dots or lines) to accurately position objects

◆ Use the Dimension Tool to determine and display the dimensions of drawn objects

◆ Customize the status bar

◆ Align objects to a common edge

Working with the Rulers

The horizontal ruler is located below the property bar and the vertical ruler is on the left side of the screen beside the toolbox (**Figure 9.1**). The two rulers meet at a small square in the upper-left corner of the screen called the *ruler intersection point*. The rulers show the location of the pointer by displaying horizontal and vertical *tracking lines*.

All measurements are made from the *zero point* (the point where both the vertical and horizontal rulers show a value of 0). By default, the zero point is located at the bottom-left corner of the page. This is the standard way that the printing industry measures a page. However, you might find it easier to measure a page from the top down, for example.

To move the rulers' zero point:

1. Click the ruler intersection and drag to the position where you would like the zero point to be. As you drag, two intersecting lines appear (**Figure 9.2**).

   For example, if you want the zero point at the top-left corner of the page, align the dashed lines there.

2. Release the mouse button.

   The rulers redraw and show the new zero point. To later reset the zero point to the bottom-left corner of the page, double-click the ruler intersection point.

✔ Tips

- The View > Rulers command works as a toggle. When checked, the rulers are shown; when unchecked, they're hidden.

- You can move the rulers closer to or into the drawing area, making it easier to view the tracking lines as you draw. Press (Shift), click a ruler, and drag it to a new position. To move both rulers back to the default positions, press (Shift) and double-click either ruler.

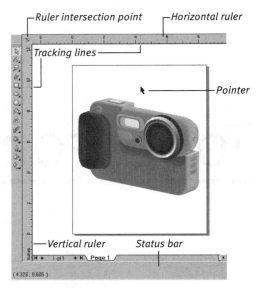

Figure 9.1 The rulers and status bar surround the workspace.

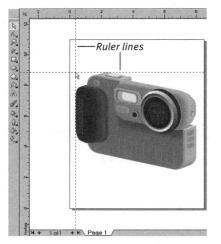

Figure 9.2 Drag the lines to set a new zero point for the rulers.

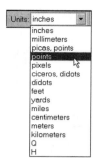

Setting the Unit of Measure

The default unit of measure for CorelDraw is inches. However, there are more than a dozen units of measure from which you can choose, such as millimeters, points, pixels, and miles. You can change the unit of measure for the current document or set a new default unit of measure for all future documents.

Figure 9.3 You can freely switch units of measure by choosing a new one from the property bar.

Figure 9.4 You can also set a new default unit of measure for the rulers in the Options dialog box.

To set the unit of measure for the current document:

◆ On the property bar, click the Units drop-down list (**Figure 9.3**) and choose a unit of measure.

The unit is applied to both rulers.

To set the default unit of measure:

1. Open the Options dialog box by double-clicking a ruler or by right-clicking a ruler and choosing Ruler Setup from the pop-up menu that appears.

   The Rulers section of the Options dialog box appears.

2. In the Units area of the dialog box (**Figure 9.4**), choose a new unit of measure from the Horizontal drop-down list.

3. *Optional:* If you want to set the unit of measure separately for the horizontal and vertical rulers, remove the checkmark from Same units for Horizontal and Vertical rulers. Then choose a separate unit of measure from the Vertical drop-down list.

4. Click OK.

   The dialog box closes and the new measurement system is applied. On all future documents, the chosen measurement system will be used.

Using Guidelines

Guidelines are non-printing extensions of rulers that can be positioned anywhere in the drawing window (**Figure 9.5**). They are very useful for setting up the areas where you are going to draw and for helping to align objects. Guidelines can be vertical, horizontal, or angled.

To add guidelines to a page:

1. To create a horizontal guideline, click the horizontal ruler and drag down. To create a vertical guideline, click the vertical ruler and drag across.

2. When the guideline is in the proper position, release the mouse button.

To move a guideline:

1. Select the Pick Tool and move the pointer over the guideline.

   The pointer changes to a double-headed arrow (**Figure 9.6**).

2. Click and drag the guideline to a new position in the drawing window.

To remove a guideline:

1. Using the Pick Tool, click to select the guideline you want to remove.

   The guideline changes color to show that it is selected.

2. Choose Edit > Delete or press Del.

To remove all guidelines:

1. Choose Edit > Select All > Guidelines.
   The guidelines change color to show they are selected.

2. Choose Edit > Delete or press Del.

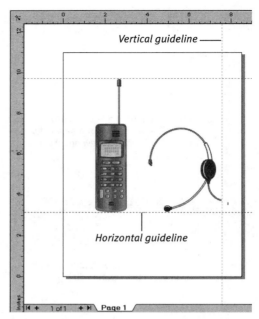

Figure 9.5 This is an example of guidelines. Note that you can add as many as you need.

Figure 9.6 When you move the pointer over a guideline, it changes to this shape.

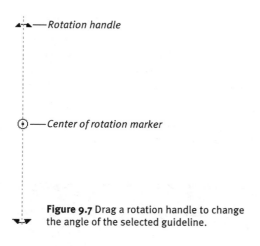

—— Rotation handle

—— Center of rotation marker

Figure 9.7 Drag a rotation handle to change the angle of the selected guideline.

Node   Node

Figure 9.8 To change the guideline's angle, click and drag a node with the Shape Tool.

Figure 9.9 Type a rotation angle into this text box on the property bar.

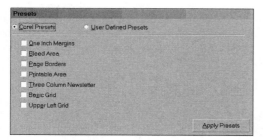

Figure 9.10 You can specify common guideline arrays by selecting them from the Presets list.

To create an angled guideline:

Do one of the following:

- ◆ Using the Pick Tool, click to select a guideline. When you click the guideline a second time, a *center of rotation marker* and *rotation handles* appear (**Figure 9.7**). Drag a rotation handle until the guideline is at the desired angle and release the mouse button.

- ◆ Select a guideline with the Shape Tool. Two nodes will appear on it (**Figure 9.8**). Click a node and then drag until the guideline is the desired angle.

- ◆ Select a guideline. Enter an angle in the Angle of Rotation text box on the property bar (**Figure 9.9**) and press (Enter).

✔ Tips

- ■ You can use the Options dialog box to add, edit, and delete guidelines. To open the Options dialog box to the Vertical or Horizontal section of the Guidelines topic, double-click a guideline.

- ■ CorelDraw 11 comes with several guideline *presets* that quickly set up guidelines in specific locations. Double-click any guideline and then select the Document > Guidelines > Presets heading (**Figure 9.10**) in the Options dialog box. Click the Corel Presets radio button, enter checkmarks for the desired presets, click Apply Presets, and then click OK.

- ■ Using the same section of the Options dialog box (**Figure 9.10**), you can create your own complex guideline arrays. Click the User Defined Presets radio button, and then enter the necessary settings for margins, columns, and/or grids.

Setting Snap To Guidelines

One of the most useful guideline features is Snap To Guidelines. When enabled, this feature makes it easy to align objects by letting them snap to a guideline—as though they were magnetically drawn to it.

To turn on Snap To Guidelines:

1. Add some guidelines to a document.

2. *Do one of the following:*

   ▲ Choose View > Snap To Guidelines.

   ▲ Select a guideline and then click the Snap To Guidelines button on the property bar (**Figure 9.11**).

   ▲ Open the Options dialog box, select the Document > Guidelines heading, and enter a checkmark in the box for Snap To Guidelines. Click OK.

3. To test the Snap To Guidelines feature, draw a rectangle near a guideline. As you draw, the rectangle's edges will "snap" to the guideline. Similarly, if you move any object close to a guideline, it will automatically be attracted to it.

✔ Tips

■ Snap To Guidelines is a toggle command. When enabled, the command is preceded in the View menu by a checkmark. Choose the command again to reverse its state.

■ Another way to reach the Guidelines section of the Options dialog box is to choose View > Guidelines Setup. (You can also right-click a ruler and choose Guidelines Setup.)

■ To view or edit the settings for *all* guidelines (whether they're horizontal, vertical, or angled), open the Options dialog box and select the Document > Guidelines > Guides heading (**Figure 9.12**).

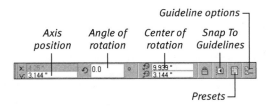

Figure 9.11 When you select a guideline, several guideline-related controls appear on the property bar.

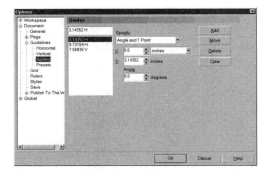

Figure 9.12 You can view the settings for all guidelines in the Guides section of the Options dialog box.

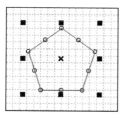

Figure 9.13 Here is a line grid with 1/4 inch spacing.

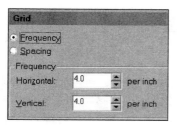

Figure 9.14 You can create a grid by setting the number of grid dots per measurement unit (Frequency).

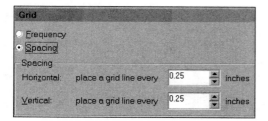

Figure 9.15 Or you can specify the distance between grid dots (Spacing).

Figure 9.16 These are the additional grid options.

Using Grids

Grids (**Figure 9.13**) are extremely useful for creating precise drawings, such as flowcharts, office layouts, blueprints, and anything else that requires straight lines, uniform shapes, and exact alignment. The grid dots or lines are non-printing.

To set up a grid:

1. Choose View > Grid and Ruler Setup.

   or

   Right-click a ruler and choose Grid Setup from the pop-up menu that appears.

   The Grid section of the Options dialog box appears.

2. There are two ways to create a grid. Click the appropriate radio button and then set options, as follows:

   ▲ *Frequency:* Specify the number of horizontal and vertical dots per unit of measurement (**Figure 9.14**).

   ▲ *Spacing:* Specify the distance between grid lines (**Figure 9.15**).

3. Check the Show grid check box (**Figure 9.16**).

4. Click a radio button to display the grid as lines or as dots.

5. Click OK.

   The specified grid appears.

✔ Tip

■ Set Snap to grid if you want the points and sides of new objects to automatically align to the nearest grid intersection or line. This also restricts the size of every new object to multiples of the grid increment.

Using the Dimension Tool

Using the new Dimension Tool, you can accurately determine and display the dimensions of objects in the same manner as you might see them in an architectural blueprint or a schematic (**Figure 9.17**).

To draw a dimension line:

1. From the Curve flyout on the toolbox, select the Dimension Tool (**Figure 9.18**).

2. Click a property bar icon (**Figure 9.19**) to indicate whether you want to draw a vertical, horizontal, or slanted dimension line.

3. As desired, specify other settings for the dimension line by choosing options from the property bar.

4. Click to set one end of the dimension line and then click to set the opposite end.

5. Drag to indicate the direction and size of the lines marking the end points, and then click to complete the dimension line.
   The dimension measurement appears.

✔ Tips

- To change any of the options for a previously drawn dimension line, select the dimension line with the Pick Tool and choose new settings from the property bar. (Be sure to select the dimension line—not just the dimension text.)

- To change the font, size, or style of the dimension text, select the text block with the Pick Tool and then choose font settings from the property bar.

- If you prefer to use a docker to modify a dimension line, double-click any dimension line with the Pick Tool. The Linear Dimensions docker appears (**Figure 9.20**). Select new settings and click the Apply button.

Figure 9.17 You can use dimension lines to display the horizontal, vertical, and slanted dimensions of an object.

Figure 9.18 Select the Dimension Tool from the Curve flyout on the toolbox.

Figure 9.19 Use property bar controls to set or alter the properties of a dimension line.

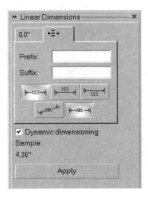

Figure 9.20 You can also use the Linear Dimensions docker to set properties.

USING THE DIMENSION TOOL

Figure 9.21 The status bar at the bottom of the screen gives detailed information about selected objects.

Status Bar ──┐ ┌─Commands ┌─Currently Available On

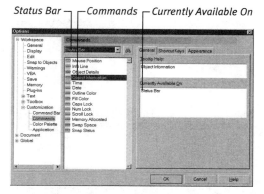

Figure 9.22 Select available commands from the list and drag them onto the status bar.

Using the Status Bar

The *status bar* (**Figure 9.21**) gives information about everything you do in CorelDraw: the position of the cursor, the Snap To constraints that are enabled, and the object that is selected and its details (such as size and color).

The status bar can be one or two lines high. The smaller setting saves screen space, but hides information. If you like, you can change the status bar's height, as well as change the information it displays.

To change the status bar information:

1. To open the Options dialog box, choose Tools > Customization.

2. Select the Customization > Commands heading.

3. From the drop-down list at the top of the dialog box, choose Status Bar.

   A list of available commands appears (**Figure 9.22**).

4. Click to select any information item.

   If the item is already in use, "Status Bar" will display in the Currently Available On list box.

5. To add an unused item to the status bar, drag it into the desired position on the status bar and release the mouse button.

6. To remove an information item from the status bar, drag it off the status bar.

7. When you are done modifying the status bar, click OK to close the dialog box.

To change the status bar's height:

Do one of the following:

◆ Move the pointer over the status bar's upper edge. When it changes to a double-headed arrow, click and drag up or down.

◆ Right-click the status bar. Choose Customize > Status Bar > Size, followed by One Line or Two Lines (**Figure 9.23**).

◆ Choose Tools > Customization to open the Options dialog box, select the Command Bars heading, and highlight the Status Bar choice. In the Status Bar Properties section of the dialog box (**Figure 9.24**), specify 1 or 2 as the Number of lines when docked.

✔ Tip

■ If you really need some additional screen space, you can hide the status bar by choosing Window > Toolbars > Status Bar. Choose the command a second time to display the status bar.

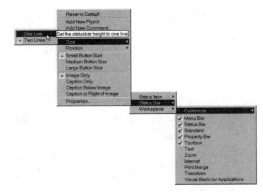

Figure 9.23 You can change the status bar's height or docked position by choosing commands from this menu.

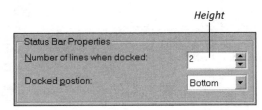

Figure 9.24 Click the arrow buttons to set a new height for the status bar.

Figure 9.25 Select two or more objects that you want to align.

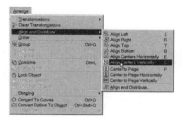

Figure 9.26 You can align selected objects by choosing a command.

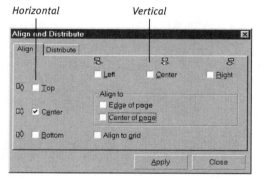

Figure 9.27 Check the horizontal and/or vertical alignment options that you want to apply.

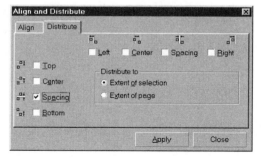

Figure 9.28 Check the distribution options that you want to apply.

Aligning Objects

When selected, every object has handles that surround it. The handles also serve another purpose. They make an invisible rectangular boundary around objects. This boundary is used when aligning objects. When objects are aligned, they are lined up using a common boundary or page edge. For instance, if two objects are aligned on the left, the objects are aligned using each invisible left boundary.

To align objects:

1. Select two or more objects (**Figure 9.25**).

2. Choose Arrange > Align and Distribute, followed by an alignment command (**Figure 9.26**). The command is executed immediately.

   or

   For more extensive alignment requirements, click the Align and Distribute button at the right end of the property bar or choose Arrange > Align and Distribute > Align and Distribute. The Align and Distribute dialog box appears (**Figure 9.27**), open to the Align tab.

3. Select the type of alignment you want: horizontal and/or vertical. You can align the objects in two dimensions simultaneously or in just one dimension. Click Apply.

4. *Optional:* To change the spacing between objects, click the Distribute tab (**Figure 9.28**). Select the desired horizontal and/or vertical distribution options. Click Apply.

5. When you're satisfied with the alignment and distribution of the selected objects, click Close to dismiss the dialog box.

   continues on next page

ALIGNING OBJECTS

✔ Tips

- In CorelDraw 10, the Align and Distribute dialog box sported handy Preview and Reset buttons. Since they're gone in CorelDraw 11, you may wish to open the Undo docker so you can easily correct alignment mistakes.

- If you select multiple objects by holding down [Shift] and clicking them, the last object selected will be the target object for the alignment. For example, when aligning the right edges, the objects will align to the right edge of the last object selected.

- If you marquee-select objects, on the other hand, the last object *created* will be used as the target object for the alignment.

ALIGNING OBJECTS

10

COLOR AND FILLS

In this chapter, you'll learn how to fill closed objects with uniform (solid) colors, fountain fills (gradients), patterns, and textures; change outline colors; and sample a color from one object and apply it to a different object. You will use the color palette, Fill Tool, Interactive Fill Tool, Interactive Mesh Fill Tool, Eyedropper Tool, and Paintbucket Tool.

Solid Color Fills and Outlines

Color can bring a drawing to life. Filling an object with a solid color (called a *uniform fill*) is just a point-and-click procedure. However, before an object can be filled with color, it must have a closed path.

To ensure a freehand object has a closed path:

1. Select a freehand object with the Pick Tool.

   If the Auto-Close Curve icon is visible on the property bar (**Figure 10.1**), the curve is open; if not, the curve is closed.

2. To close the curve, click the icon.

To fill objects with a solid color:

1. Select one or more closed objects.

2. Click a color in any open color palette (**Figure 10.2**).

✔ Tips

■ Normal shapes, such as an arc, cannot be closed using the Auto-Close Curve icon.

■ To view additional available colors on a color palette, click the up and down arrows.

■ To view an entire color palette (**Figure 10.3**) by expanding it horizontally, click the left-arrow at the bottom of the palette. To make it float (**Figure 10.4**), double-click in a blank area of the palette or drag it into the workspace.

■ To replace an object's current color fill with another, select the object and click a different color. To remove a color fill from an object, select the object and then click the color square with the X in it.

■ To change the outline color of a selected object, right-click a color in the color palette. To remove an outline color, right-click the color square with the X in it.

Auto-Close Curve

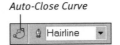

Figure 10.1 You can close paths manually or click the Auto-Close Curve icon.

Normal palette

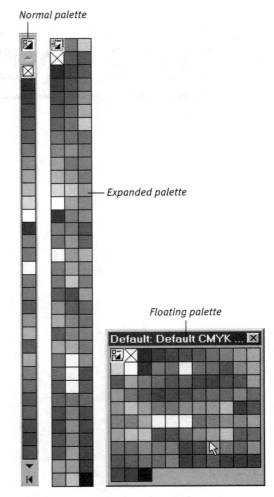

Expanded palette

Floating palette

Figures 10.2–10.4 A color palette in three states: normal, expanded, and floating. To shrink an expanded palette, click the gray bar at the bottom. To dock the floating palette, double-click its title bar.

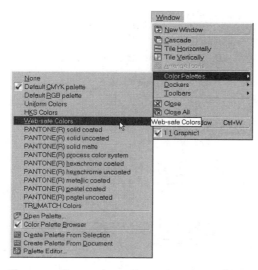

Figure 10.5 You can choose the most common palettes from the Color Palettes submenu.

Figure 10.6 The entire set of color palettes is available in the Color Palette Browser.

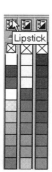

Figure 10.7 You can have several color palettes open at the same time.

Using Color Palettes

Although one color palette always appears when you run CorelDraw 11, there are more than 100 color sets and matching systems that you can display in the color palette. If you like, multiple color palettes can be used together. To open one of the more popular palettes (such as Web-safe Colors), choose Window > Color Palettes, followed by the name of the palette (**Figure 10.5**).

To open any of the provided CorelDraw color palettes:

1. Choose Window > Dockers > Color Palette Browser.

   The Color Palette Browser docker opens, displaying a tree view with hundreds of different color palettes (**Figure 10.6**).

2. Expand the palette folders until you find the color palette you want to use.

3. Click the check box beside the palette you want to use.

   The chosen palette appears to the left of the other palette(s) (**Figure 10.7**).

To close a color palette:

Do one of the following:

- Choose Window > Color Palettes, followed by the palette you want to close (**Figure 10.5**). Choosing a checked palette from this submenu removes its checkmark and closes the palette.

- In the Color Palette Browser, uncheck the palette's check box.

✔ Tip

- For an explanation of how to collapse or expand a color palette, as well as how to make it float, see the instructions on the previous page.

Using the Eyedropper and Paintbucket

The Eyedropper and Paintbucket tools work together to make adding color fills quick and easy. You use the Eyedropper Tool to sample or pick up the desired color, fountain, pattern, or texture from an object that's already filled. Then use the Paintbucket Tool to apply the color, pattern, or texture to fill a different object.

To sample a color:

1. Select the Eyedropper Tool from the Eyedropper flyout on the toolbox (**Figure 10.8**).

   The pointer changes to a small eyedropper. The property bar displays Eyedropper Tool icons (**Figure 10.9**).

2. Click one of the following icons on the property bar to set the sampling method:

   ▲ **Fill/Outline.** Click to sample the entire fill or outline of an object. For example, if the fill is composed of a pattern or texture, the entire pattern or texture is sampled. If the fill is a solid color, the sample will be that color.

   ▲ **Size.** Click to sample an area of a specific size in pixels (1x1, 3x3, or 5x5) and then combine the sampled colors.

   ▲ **Selection.** Marquee select an area using the Eyedropper Tool, combining the sampled colors.

3. On the document page, click the fill or outline in the object you want to sample.

   The color, fountain, pattern, or texture is displayed in the Fill box on the right side of the status bar (**Figure 10.10**).

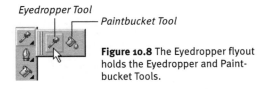

Eyedropper Tool — Paintbucket Tool

Figure 10.8 The Eyedropper flyout holds the Eyedropper and Paintbucket Tools.

Fill/Outline   Selection
1X1 3X3 5X5

Figure 10.9 Choose a mode for the Eyedropper Tool from these property bar icons.

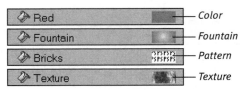

Red — Color
Fountain — Fountain
Bricks — Pattern
Texture — Texture

Figure 10.10 The sampled color, fountain, pattern, or texture is shown on the status bar.

Filling Open-Path Objects

Although it makes sense that only closed-path objects can be filled with a color, texture, or pattern, you *can* also fill open-path objects. Open the Options dialog box by choosing Tools > Options, select the Document > General heading, and then click the Fill Open Curves check box.

Ineligible   *Eligible*

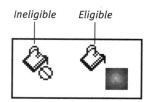

Figure 10.11 The Paintbucket Tool's cursor changes to show whether it's over a fillable object.

Figure 10.12 As shown here, you can fill any object—including text—with a color, pattern, or texture.

The Pop-up Color Palette

Depending on the color palette you are using, you may find that a shade of a given color is close, but not quite close enough. You can use the *pop-up color palette* to find the right shade. Left-click a color well on the color palette that is close to the color you want and hold the mouse button down until the pop-up color palette appears. Click a color to select it.

To fill an object with the Paintbucket:

1. Make sure the object you want to fill has a closed path.

2. Select a color or pattern with the Eyedropper Tool.

3. Select the Paintbucket Tool from the toolbox (see Figure 10.8).

   The pointer changes to a tiny paint bucket. When the pointer is over a fillable object, it displays a sample of the pattern or color (**Figure 10.11**).

4. Click the object to fill it with the sampled color, pattern, or texture (**Figure 10.12**).

To set an outline with the Paintbucket:

1. Select a solid color with the Eyedropper Tool.

2. Select the Paintbucket Tool from the toolbox (see Figure 10.8).

   The pointer changes to a tiny paint bucket. When the pointer is over an eligible object, it shows a sample of the color (**Figure 10.11**).

3. Click the outline you want to color.

✔ Tips

- You can press (Shift) to toggle between the Eyedropper Tool and the Paintbucket Tool.

- Choose Fill/Outline mode to sample a solid color, pattern, or texture. The other modes are appropriate when you wish to combine the colors from the sampled area.

- The Fill/Outline mode Eyedropper can also be used to sample PostScript fills and fountain (gradient) fills.

- If you've added a custom color to the current drawing (as explained in "The Uniform Fill Dialog Box" in the next section) but didn't add it to a palette, you can reapply the color elsewhere using the Eyedropper and Paintbucket Tools.

The Uniform Fill Dialog Box

In addition to choosing fill colors from open color palettes, you can use the Uniform Fill dialog box to choose more precise colors and create custom colors.

To use the Uniform Fill dialog box to fill an object with a color:

1. Select the object you want to fill with color.

2. From the Fill flyout in the toolbox, select the Fill Color Dialog icon (**Figure 10.13**) or press Shift F11.

   The Uniform Fill dialog box opens to the Models tab (**Figure 10.14**).

3. Select a color model from the Model drop-down list. (For example, RGB and CMYK are commonly used color models.)

4. In the color selector, choose a color by performing any combination of the following actions:

   ▲ Drag the vertical slider so the desired shade of color is displayed in the large colored area, and then click to choose a color.

   ▲ Enter numeric values for the desired color in the text boxes.

   ▲ Choose the name of a specific color (such as Red) from the Name drop-down list (**Figure 10.15**).

   The selected color is shown as New in the Reference area.

5. Click OK.

   The dialog box closes, and the object fills with the selected color.

Figure 10.13 Select the Fill Color Dialog icon from the Fill flyout.

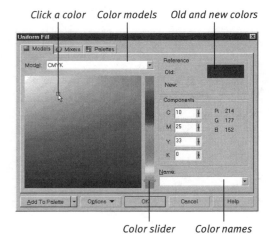

Figure 10.14 Select a fill color from the Models tab of the Uniform Fill dialog box.

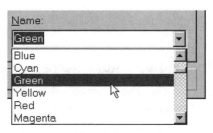

Figure 10.15 You can also choose a basic color by its name.

Drag to choose colors

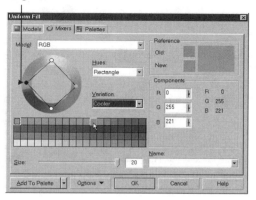

Figure 10.16 Using the Mixers tab, you can choose complementary or harmonious colors.

Color grid   Choose a variation   Grid size slider

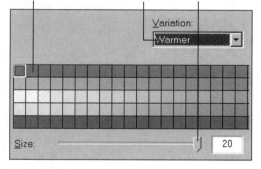

Figure 10.17 You can expand the color grid to show more variations of the chosen colors.

Color Models

A color model breaks colors down into base or primary colors. If you are familiar with a color wheel, you know that red, yellow, and blue are the primary colors that can be mixed to create all the colors our eyes can see. Printers use a different group of primary colors: cyan, magenta, yellow, and black. These four colors represent the CMYK color model. Other color models include HSB (Hue, Saturation, and Brightness) and RGB (Red, Green, Blue).

To create a custom color:

1. Perform Steps 1 and 2 from the previous step list.

2. Click the Mixers tab (**Figure 10.16**).

3. Select a color model from the Model list.

4. Select an option from the Hues drop-down list to set the relationships of the colors on the grid below the color wheel.

   For instance, Complement displays two dots directly across from one another on the color wheel. When you select a color on the color wheel, the chosen and the complementary color are both displayed in the color grid.

5. To choose a color, drag the black dot on the color wheel until the color you want is shown beside New in the Reference area.

   or

   Click a colored rectangle in the color grid.

6. *Optional:* If you think you'll also want to use the color in other objects, you can add it to any open color palette. Click the down arrow beside the Add To Palette button, choose a color palette, and then click Add To Palette.

7. Click OK.

   The dialog box closes, and the selected object is filled with the custom color.

✔ Tips

■ To view variations of the chosen color, select an option from the Variation drop-down list (**Figure 10.17**). Drag the Size slider to specify the number of variations displayed.

■ You can also use these procedures to choose or create a custom *outline* color. Choose the Outline Color Dialog icon from the Outline Tool flyout. For information about this dialog box, see Chapter 7, "Lines and Curves."

THE UNIFORM FILL DIALOG BOX

Color Management

If you're creating professional illustrations, it's critical that the colors you see onscreen precisely represent what you'll see when you get the prints back from your service bureau. In fact, color management is all about matching colors on all devices involved in creating your drawings, such as a scanner, digital camera, monitor, desktop printer, and/or the service bureau's output device. Because color printing errors are costly, CorelDraw provides color management tools to help you avoid them.

To use the Color Management tool:

1. Choose Tools > Color Management.

   The Color Management dialog box appears (**Figure 10.18**).

2. Solid arrows indicate device combinations that will be profile-driven. Click the arrows, as necessary.

3. Click the down triangle beside the device you wish to configure.

   A drop-down list appears.

4. *Do one of the following:*

   ▲ If your device is listed, choose it.

   ▲ To check the CorelDraw software for the device's profile, insert the appropriate Corel CD into your CD-ROM drive and choose Get profile from disk. In the Browse for Folder dialog box, choose the Color folder for CorelDraw and click OK.

   ▲ Choose Download Profiles to fetch profiles from the Internet. After several minutes, a dialog box appears (**Figure 10.19**). Specify your connection speed, select a device type, click the check boxes of the desired profiles, and click Download. After the profiles have downloaded, click Cancel. The new profiles can then be selected from the relevant device's drop-down list.

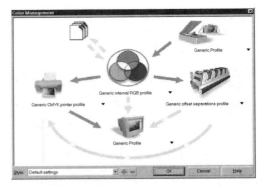

Figure 10.18 Set input and output device profiles in the Color Management dialog box.

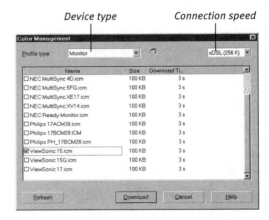

Figure 10.19 With an active Internet connection, you can download additional device profiles.

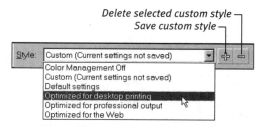

Delete selected custom style ⌐
Save custom style ⌐

Figure 10.20 If you don't want to install hardware profiles, you can choose one of the basic color management setups from the Style menu.

5. Repeat Steps 3 and 4 for any additional devices you want to configure.

6. Click the plus (+) button at the bottom of the dialog box, name the configuration in the Save Color Management Style dialog box that appears, and click OK.

7. Click OK to dismiss the Color Management dialog box.

✔ Tips

■ While there are some hardware profiles on Corel's Web site and on the CD, don't be too surprised if you don't find the ones you need. Check the software that came with your printer, scanner, monitor, or digital camera. If you still don't find an appropriate profile, contact the manufacturer.

■ For noncritical work, you may prefer to select one of the options from the Style drop-down list at the bottom of the Color Management dialog box (**Figure 10.20**). Note, however, that while these choices may suffice for desktop printing or for the Web, if you intend to get your output from a service bureau, it's highly recommended that you create your own hardware-specific profile. Contact the service bureau for the recommended choices for their equipment.

■ You can click on many of the icons in the Color Management dialog box to set additional options and view settings.

■ To delete a color management style that you no longer need, select it from the Style drop down-list (**Figure 10.20**) and click the minus (-) button.

Color Matching Systems

Designers use color matching systems to tell commercial printers exactly what colors to use for a print job. A matching system assigns a different number to every color. You can buy swatch books that show these colors at art supply stores. Suppose, for example, that you want to use a *fire engine red* in a brochure illustration. You'd look through a swatch book to find the exact shade of red you have in mind and then tell the printer its color number. Pantone, Spectramaster, Trumatch, and Toyo are examples of popular color matching systems.

Creating Fountain Fills

A *fountain fill* is a gradual blend between two or more colors across a closed path object. (Some programs call this a *gradient fill.*) There are four types of fountain fills (**Figure 10.21**):

◆ **Linear.** The blend of colors moves in a straight line.

◆ **Radial.** The blend of colors moves in concentric circles from the center.

◆ **Conical.** The blend of colors moves in a circular path, radiating from the center.

◆ **Square.** The blend of colors moves in a series of concentric squares that radiate from the center.

You can create a fountain fill with these tools:

◆ **Fill Tool (Fountain Fill Dialog).** Create a fountain fill by setting options in a dialog box.

◆ **Interactive Fill Tool.** Create a fountain fill by setting property bar options and then clicking and dragging within the object you want to fill.

To create a fountain fill with the Fountain Fill Dialog:

1. Select an object with a closed path.

2. From the Fill Tool flyout in the toolbox, select the Fountain Fill Dialog (**Figure 10.22**) or press F11.
   The Fountain Fill dialog box appears (**Figure 10.23**).

3. Select a fill type from the Type list.

4. Set other options, such as the start and end colors, the angle, and the midpoint.

5. Click OK.
   The fountain fill is applied to the object (**Figure 10.24**).

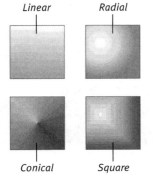

Linear *Radial*

Conical *Square*

Figure 10.21 These are the four kinds of fountain fills.

Fountain Fill Dialog (F11)

Figure 10.22 Select the Fountain Fill Dialog from the Fill Tool flyout.

Fill type *Fill preview*

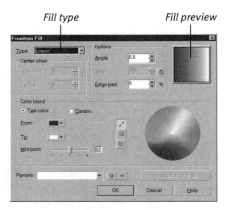

Figure 10.23 Set options in the Fountain Fill dialog box.

Figure 10.24 A carefully chosen radial fill can transform a flat circle into a realistic ball.

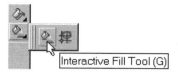

Figure 10.25 Select the Interactive Fill Tool from the toolbox.

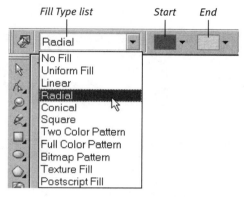

Figure 10.26 Select a fill type, start color, and end color from the property bar.

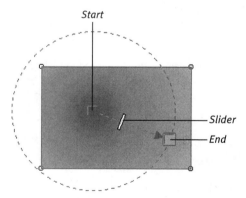

Figure 10.27 You can manually adjust the fill by dragging these three items.

✔ Tips

■ Rather than design a custom fountain fill, you may find what you're looking for in the Presets drop-down list. The radial fill in Figure 10.24 is an example of a preset fill.

■ After creating a custom fill you want to reuse, you can name and save it in the Presets list by clicking the plus (+) button. To delete a custom fill, select its name from the Presets list and click the minus (-).

To create a fountain fill with the Interactive Fill Tool:

1. Select the Interactive Fill Tool from the toolbox (**Figure 10.25**) or press G.

2. Click to select an object with a closed path.

3. On the property bar (**Figure 10.26**), pick a fill type from the Fill Type drop-down list.

4. Choose start and end colors from the property bar.

5. Adjust the fill by dragging the slider, start handle, and end handle (**Figure 10.27**) or by setting options on the property bar.

✔ Tips

■ You can put the start and end color squares anywhere inside or outside of the object.

■ You can freely switch from one type of fountain fill to another—as well as change the fill properties—by selecting the object with the Interactive Fill Tool again and choosing different options.

■ You can add intermediate colors to a fill by dragging them from an open color palette onto the dashed line between the handles. To remove an intermediate color, select the Interactive Fill Tool and right-click its color square in the object.

■ You can replace the start or end color by dragging a colored square onto it from an open color palette.

Adding Patterns to Objects

Patterns can add interesting effects to your graphics. There are three types of pattern fills: Two-color, Full color, and Bitmap. As was the case with fountain fills, there are two ways to add a pattern to an object: with the Fill Tool (Pattern Fill Dialog) or Interactive Fill Tool.

Figure 10.28 Select the Pattern Fill Dialog from the toolbox.

To add a pattern fill to an object with the Pattern Fill Dialog:

1. Select an object with a closed path.

2. From the Fill Tool flyout in the toolbox, select the Pattern Fill Dialog (**Figure 10.28**).

   The Pattern Fill dialog box appears (**Figure 10.29**).

3. Select a pattern type by clicking one of the three radio buttons.

4. Choose a pattern by clicking the down arrow beside the pattern box.

5. Click OK.

   The object fills with the selected pattern (**Figure 10.30**).

To add a pattern fill to an object with the Interactive Fill Tool:

1. Select a closed-path object with the Interactive Fill Tool.

2. Select one of the three pattern types from the Fill Type drop-down list on the property bar (see Figure 10.26).

   The object is filled with a default pattern of the chosen type.

3. To change the pattern, click the Pattern drop-down list on the property bar (**Figure 10.31**) and select another pattern.

   The object is filled with the new pattern.

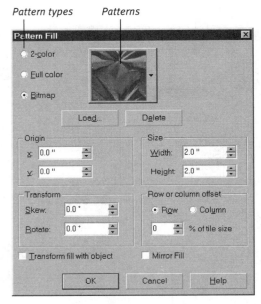

Figure 10.29 Select a pattern type and a specific pattern from this dialog box.

Figure 10.30 This is an example of a bitmap pattern created in the Pattern Fill dialog box.

Pattern types   Patterns   Front color   Back color   Sm   Md   Lg

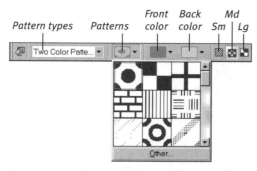

Figure 10.31 You can select a new pattern from those presented in this drop-down list. The property bar also contains icons you can click to modify the chosen pattern's colors and size.

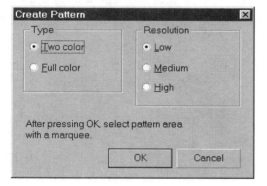

Figure 10.32 Select a pattern type and resolution from this dialog box.

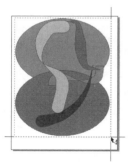

Figure 10.33 Using the guides as aids, drag to select the area from which the pattern will be created.

To create a custom pattern fill:

1. Create the object(s) you want to use as a pattern for the fill.

2. Choose Tools > Create > Pattern.

   The Create Pattern dialog box opens (**Figure 10.32**).

3. If the pattern objects contain two colors or less, click the Two color radio button and then select a resolution.

   or

   If the pattern objects contain many colors, click the Full color radio button.

4. Click OK.

   Vertical and horizontal guides appear, attached to the tip of the pointer.

5. Drag a marquee rectangle to select a pattern (**Figure 10.33**).

6. When you release the mouse button, CorelDraw asks you if you want to create a pattern from the selected area. Click OK.

7. If it is a two-color pattern, the pattern is added to the other two-color patterns in the Fill drop-down list on the property bar.

   or

   If it is a full-color pattern, you are asked to name and save it as a pattern (.pat) file.

✔ Tips

■ To fill an object with a custom two-color or full-color pattern, select the Interactive Fill Tool, click the object, choose Two Color Pattern or Full Color Pattern from the Fill Type list, and then choose a pattern from the Fill drop-down list.

continues on next page

ADDING PATTERNS TO OBJECTS

- To change the colors of a two-color pattern, choose colors from the Front Color and Back Color lists on the property bar (**Figure 10.34**).

- To make a pattern smaller or larger, click the Small (Sm), Medium (Md), or Large (Lg) icons on the property bar.

- To rotate or skew the object and the pattern along with it, click the Transform Fill With Object icon on the property bar. Otherwise, an applied pattern stays stationary while the object rotates.

- You can also create your own two-color patterns by clicking the Other button at the bottom of the Pattern drop-down list. The Two-Color Pattern Editor opens (**Figure 10.35**). Select a pattern size and a pen size by clicking radio buttons. To fill a square, left-click it; to empty a filled square, right-click it. When you click OK, the new pattern is added at the bottom of the Pattern list.

- If your computer has limited memory (RAM), it's possible to create and save full-color patterns that are too complex to later be applied to objects. Either keep such patterns simple or small, increase the amount of memory available to CorelDraw (in the Memory section of the Options dialog box), or install more memory.

- You can also use bitmap patterns as fills. Choose Bitmap Pattern from the Fill Type drop-down list. Then choose a pattern from the Fill drop-down list. To load a pattern or image from disk (such as a scan, photo, or artwork), click the Other button at the bottom of the Fill drop-down list.

Front color *Back color*

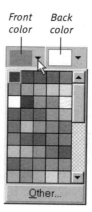

Figure 10.34 You can pick a different front or back color for a two-color pattern.

Drawing area *Grid and pen size*

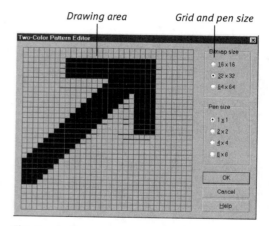

Figure 10.35 You can create your own two-color patterns by clicking and dragging in this window.

Figure 10.36 Pick a named PostScript texture from the list on the property bar.

Texture Library list —   — Fill list

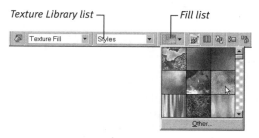

Figure 10.37 Pick a normal texture from the drop-down list on the property bar.

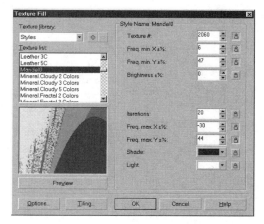

Figure 10.38 Using the Texture Fill dialog box, you can modify every setting for a texture. Click the Preview button to see the effects of your changes.

Adding a Texture Fill

In addition to colors and patterns, you can use texture fills to create decorative, visually interesting objects. CorelDraw 11 supports two types of textures: PostScript and normal.

To fill an object with a PostScript texture:

1. Select a closed-path object with the Interactive Fill Tool (see Figure 10.25).

2. Select PostScript Fill from the Fill Type drop-down list on the property bar.

3. Select a fill from the PostScript Fill Textures drop-down list (**Figure 10.36**) on the property bar.

To fill an object with a normal texture:

1. Select a closed-path object with the Interactive Fill Tool (see Figure 10.25).

2. Select Texture Fill from the Fill Type drop-down list on the property bar.

3. Select a texture from the Fill drop-down list (**Figure 10.37**) on the property bar.

✔ Tips

- CorelDraw 11 includes several libraries of textures. To view the contents of the various libraries, choose a folder name from the Texture Library drop-down list on the property bar (**Figure 10.37**).

- Like colors and patterns, you can also add texture and PostScript fills using a dialog box rather than picking options from the property bar. Click the Fill Tool in the toolbox, and then select Texture Fill Dialog or PostScript Fill Dialog. Using the Texture Fill Dialog (**Figure 10.38**) allows you to modify all texture colors and other settings. Use the PostScript Fill Dialog if you want to be able to preview the PostScript textures before applying them to an object.

Interactive Mesh Fill Tool

You can use the Interactive Mesh Fill Tool (**Figure 10.39**) to add gradual color or shading to objects.

The Interactive Mesh Fill Tool works by superimposing a grid on a selected object. The intersection points of this grid are joined with nodes that can be manipulated with the Shape Tool. You can add color to the grid that radiates out from a node or a *patch* (any discrete area of the grid).

To fill an object with color using the Interactive Mesh Fill Tool:

1. Select the Interactive Mesh Fill Tool from the Interactive Fill flyout in the toolbox (**Figure 10.39**) or press M.

2. Click the object you want to fill.
   A mesh is superimposed over the object (**Figure 10.40**).

3. *Optional:* If you wish, you can change the number of grid columns and/or rows by typing numbers into the Grid Size text boxes on the property bar.

4. To add color, *do one of the following:*

   ▲ Select a patch and then click a color in the color palette. The patch fills and the color diffuses out beyond the mesh surrounding the patch (**Figure 10.41**). (You can also drag a color onto a patch.)

   ▲ Select a node and then click a color in the color palette. The area under the node fills and the color blends outward into the surrounding patches (**Figure 10.42**). (You can also drag a color onto a node.)

   ▲ Select a node or a patch with the Interactive Mesh Fill Tool. Hold down Ctrl and click the color you want to add. With each click, the color gets darker. Keep clicking until you achieve the desired coloring (**Figure 10.43**).

Figure 10.39 Select the Interactive Mesh Fill Tool from the toolbox.

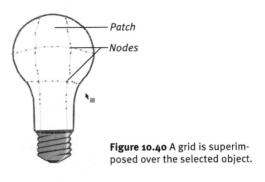

Figure 10.40 A grid is superimposed over the selected object.

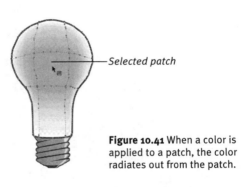

Figure 10.41 When a color is applied to a patch, the color radiates out from the patch.

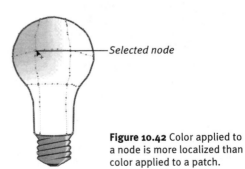

Figure 10.42 Color applied to a node is more localized than color applied to a patch.

Figure 10.43 You can Ctrl-click a color to gradually darken a selected node or patch.

Figure 10.44 By repositioning nodes, you can create some interesting effects, like this burned-out lightbulb.

✔ Tips

- If you don't like the effect of an added color, press Ctrl Z, choose Edit > Undo Mesh Fill, or click the Undo button on the property bar.

- You can select several nodes at once by using a marquee selection.

- You can affect how the colors are blended with the Interactive Mesh Fill Tool. Reshape the mesh by moving its nodes. When you fill the object, the colors will follow the contours of the manipulated mesh (**Figure 10.44**).

- You can add nodes, change their type, delete nodes, and manipulate them as described in Chapter 6, "Nodes and Paths."

INTERACTIVE MESH FILL TOOL

WORKING WITH TEXT

Pictures can be worth a thousand words, but sometimes you need *actual* words to convey a message. For instance, it's hard to imagine brochures or pamphlets without text.

There are two varieties of text in CorelDraw:

- *Artistic text* is generally used for single text lines (such as titles) or for text to which you want to add a special effect, such as fitting the text to a path.

- *Paragraph text* is used for blocks of text and text-intensive projects, such as ads, brochures, and newsletters.

Note that any text created in CorelDraw 11, whether artistic or paragraph, is a *text object*.

In this chapter, you'll learn how to perform the following text-related tasks:

- Add artistic and paragraph text to documents

- Format text by changing fonts and sizes

- Change the spacing between characters and lines

- Convert between artistic and paragraph text

- Import text into a document

- Make text flow between text frames, along a path, and into an object

- Add bullets to a list and create drop caps

CorelDraw Fonts

CorelDraw 11 Disc 1 (Fonts folder) and Disc 2 (Fonts and Extra Fonts folders) contain scores of additional TrueType and Type 1 (PostScript) fonts that you can use. To view the new fonts and load them into your PC, you can use the Bitstream Font Navigator application (choose Programs > Corel Graphics Suite 11 > Bitstream Font Navigator). Note, however, that Windows can only handle about 500 fonts at a time. The more fonts you install, the longer it will take Windows to boot.

Adding Text to a Document

The following sections explain how to add artistic and paragraph text to a document, convert from one text type to the other, and edit the text.

To add artistic text to a document:

1. Select the Text Tool (**Figure 11.1**) or press F8.

   The pointer changes to a cross-hair with a tiny "A" attached to it.

2. Click where you want the artistic text to start.

   A vertical line called the *insertion marker* appears where you click.

3. Type the text.

4. When you are finished typing or pause while typing, handles appear around the text object, showing that it is selected (**Figure 11.2**).

To add paragraph text:

1. Select the Text Tool (**Figure 11.1**) or press F8.

2. Click where you would like the text to start and drag diagonally to create a text frame (**Figure 11.3**).

   When you release the mouse button, an insertion marker appears inside the frame. Handles surround the frame, and there are text handles at the top and bottom.

3. Type the text (**Figure 11.4**).

4. When you're done typing, select the Pick Tool.

Text Tool (F8)

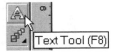

Figure 11.1 Select the Text Tool from the toolbox.

Sample text
Insertion marker
A
Cursor

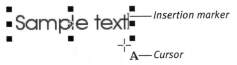

Figure 11.2 This is an example of an artistic text object.

A

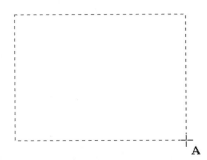

Figure 11.3 Click and drag to create a box that's the desired size for the text.

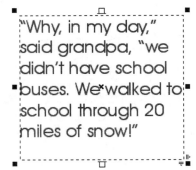

"Why, in my day,"
said grandpa, "we
didn't have school
buses. We walked to
school through 20
miles of snow!"

Figure 11.4 The text box works like a miniature word-processing window. Text automatically wraps as necessary.

Formatting toolbar

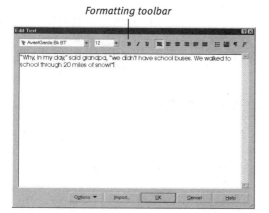

Figure 11.5 It's often more convenient to edit large text blocks in the Edit Text dialog box.

Suspect word

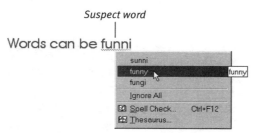

Figure 11.6 You can correct typos and misspellings by right-clicking them and choosing the correct spelling.

On-the-Fly Spell Checking

As you type, CorelDraw checks your spelling. If there's a squiggly red line beneath a word, it means that the word is spelled incorrectly or isn't in the spelling dictionary. To view suggested spellings, select the Text Tool and right-click the suspect word. A pop-up menu with spelling suggestions appears (**Figure 11.6**). Choose the correct word to replace the misspelled word in the text object or choose Ignore All.

To convert artistic to paragraph text:

1. Select the artistic text object with the Pick Tool.

2. Choose Text > Convert To Paragraph Text or press ⌈Ctrl⌉⌈F8⌉.

A paragraph text frame appears around the text.

To convert paragraph to artistic text:

1. Select the paragraph text object with the Pick Tool.

2. Choose Text > Convert To Artistic Text or press ⌈Ctrl⌉⌈F8⌉.

The paragraph frame disappears and the eight black handles remain.

To edit artistic or paragraph text:

◆ Set the insertion marker by clicking in the text block with the Text Tool. Edit the text.

or

◆ Select the text object with the Pick Tool. Choose Text > Edit Text or press ⌈Ctrl⌉⌈Shift⌉⌈T⌉.

The Edit Text dialog appears (**Figure 11.5**). Edit the text in the window and click OK.

✔ Tips

■ Another way to convert between artistic and paragraph text is to right-click the text object and choose the relevant command from the pop-up menu that appears.

■ You *must* use the Edit Text dialog box to edit artistic text that has had the Perspective, Envelope, or Extrude special effect applied to it. To learn about these special effects, see Chapter 15, "Special Effects."

■ You can convert a selected paragraph text block to editable curves by choosing Arrange > Convert To Curves or by pressing ⌈Ctrl⌉⌈Q⌉.

ADDING TEXT TO A DOCUMENT

129

Formatting Text

When you add text, CorelDraw uses a default font (AvantGarde), font size (24 points), justification (none), and character and line spacing (100 percent of character size). You can change any of these attributes by choosing new settings from the property bar or by opening the Format Text dialog box.

Character formatting

Character formatting refers to any formatting that can be applied on a character-by-character basis, such as font, style, and size.

To apply a new font to a text object:

1. Select the text object with the Pick Tool.

2. *Do one of the following:*
   ▲ Choose a font from the Font List on the property bar (**Figure 11.7**).
   ▲ Choose Text > Format Text, press ⌃Ctrl ⌃T, or click the Format Text icon on the property bar. The Format Text dialog box opens (**Figure 11.8**). On the Character tab, choose a font from the Font drop-down list and click OK.

   The text redraws in the new font. Note that the new font is assigned to every character and word in the text block.

To change the font size of a text object:

1. Select the text object with the Pick Tool.

2. *Do one of the following:*
   ▲ Choose or type a size in the Font Size List on the property bar (**Figure 11.7**). The default unit for type is *points*; there are 72 points per inch.
   ▲ Choose Text > Format Text, press ⌃Ctrl ⌃T, or click the Format Text icon on the property bar. The Format Text dialog box opens (**Figure 11.8**). On the Character tab, choose or type a size in the Size drop-down list and click OK.

Font List   Font Size List   Font preview

Figure 11.7 Select a font from this list. Recently used fonts (if any) are listed separately at the top of the list.

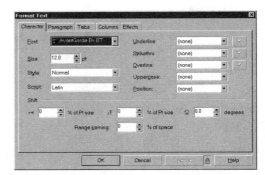

Figure 11.8 You can set the font, size, and/or style of a text block or selected text on the Character tab of the Format Text dialog box.

Formatting with Style

If you use text extensively in your projects, you may want to take advantage of CorelDraw's *style* support. You can define styles for artistic and paragraph text that incorporate your preferred font, size, and paragraph formatting. See *Creating, editing, and applying graphic or text styles* in Help.

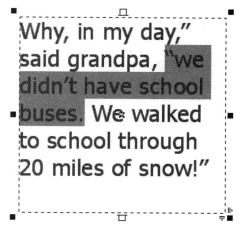

Figure 11.9 To format specific characters or words, select the text before applying the formatting. Unselected text will be unaffected.

More Formatting Options

Because CorelDraw 11 has such extensive text formatting and layout capabilities, you'll find that this chapter only scratches the surface of what you can do with text. You'll also want to explore some of the other formatting and layout options, such as adding indents and tabs (with or without leaders), creating multiple column layouts, and using the many writing tools (spell checker, grammar checker, thesaurus, and QuickCorrect).

✔ Tip

- Another way to change artistic or paragraph text size is to select the text object with the Pick Tool and, if you are resizing artistic text, drag the appropriate handle. If you are resizing paragraph text, hold down Alt and drag a corner handle. (If you drag without pressing Alt, you will change only the size of the text box, not the text size.)

To change the formatting of individual characters or words:

1. Select the Text Tool.

2. Select (highlight) the text that you want to format (**Figure 11.9**).

3. Choose new formatting options from the property bar.

   or

   Make the desired changes in the Character Tab of the Format Text dialog box and click OK.

✔ Tips

- To quickly select an individual word, double-click anywhere within the word. To select an entire text block, triple-click anywhere within it. To select multiple characters or words, click to set the insertion marker and drag.

- Another way to select a section of text (such as a paragraph, sentence, or several words) is to click to set the insertion marker, press and hold Shift, and press the appropriate arrow keys.

- Text can also be colored. To set the color for selected text or a text block, click a color well in any open color palette. To set an outline color for selected text or a text block, right-click a color well in any open color palette.

Paragraph formatting

Paragraph formatting is any type of format that affects an entire paragraph, such as alignment, the amount of space before and after the paragraph, and indents. While it makes most sense to apply paragraph formatting to paragraph text, it can also be applied to artistic text.

To change paragraph alignment:

1. To set the alignment for an entire text object, select the object with the Pick Tool.

   or

   To set the alignment for selected paragraphs, place the insertion marker within the text block and select the paragraphs that you wish to format.

2. *Do one of the following:*

   ▲ Click the Horizontal Alignment icon on the property bar and choose an alignment from the pop-up menu that appears (**Figure 11.10**).

   ▲ Choose Text > Format Text, press [Ctrl] [T], or click the Format Text icon on the property bar. The Format Text dialog box appears. Click the Paragraph tab (**Figure 11.11**), choose an alignment from the Alignment drop-down list, and click OK.

   The selected text changes to assume the chosen alignment style (**Figure 11.12**).

✔ Tip

■ When selecting paragraphs for formatting, it isn't necessary to select the *entire* paragraph. To select a single paragraph, it's sufficient to merely place the insertion marker in it. For multiple paragraphs, all you have to do is make certain that you've selected *part* of each paragraph.

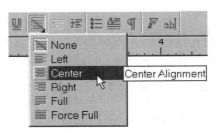

Figure 11.10 To set the alignment for selected paragraphs or a text block, you can choose an option from the Horizontal Alignment menu.

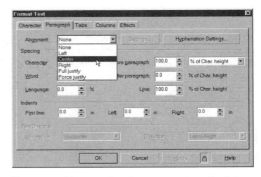

Figure 11.11 You can also choose a paragraph alignment from the Alignment drop-down list (found on the Paragraph tab of the Format Text dialog box).

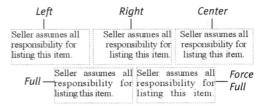

Figure 11.12 These paragraph samples show the differences between the various alignment options.

Words can be fun

Figure 11.13 To manually adjust the kerning, click and drag the arrow in the bottom-right corner.

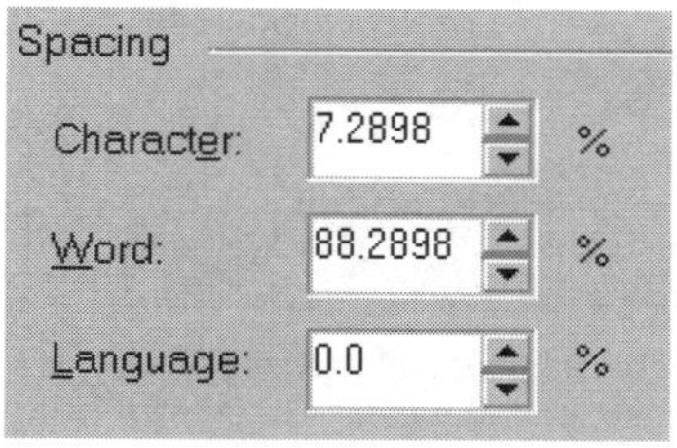

Spacing			
Character:	7.2898	▲▼	%
Word:	88.2898	▲▼	%
Language:	0.0	▲▼	%

Figure 11.14 For more precise kerning of a selected text block, enter a percentage in the Character text box.

Kerning and leading

The space between characters is called *kerning*. The distance from the bottom of one line of text to the bottom of the next line is called *leading*. These are common publishing and desktop publishing terms. There are several ways to change the kerning and leading.

To kern the space equally between all characters (via click-and-drag):

1. Click the text object with the Shape Tool to select it (**Figure 11.13**).

   Two arrows appear: one on the object's lower left pointing downward, and one on the lower right pointing to the right.

2. Click the arrow on the lower-right corner. Drag to the right to add space between letters, or drag to the left to decrease the space between letters.

To kern the space equally between all characters (via Format Text dialog box):

1. Select the text object with the Pick Tool.

2. Open the Format Text dialog box by choosing Text > Format Text, pressing Ctrl T, or clicking the Format Text icon on the property bar.

3. Click the Paragraph tab.

4. Type or choose a percentage in the Character text box (**Figure 11.14**).

   The number entered represents the percentage of the width of the space character.

5. Click OK.

✔ Tip

- You can also set spacing *between words* on the Paragraph tab of the Format Text dialog box. To change between-word spacing, type or choose a percentage in the Word text box.

To kern selected text:

1. Within a text block, select the text that you want to kern (**Figure 11.15**).

2. Open the Format Text dialog box by choosing Text > Format Text, pressing Ctrl T, or clicking the Format Text icon on the property bar.

3. Click the Character tab, and enter or choose a percentage in the Range kerning text box (**Figure 11.16**).

   As you make changes, you can see the kerning change for the selected text (**Figure 11.17**).

4. Click OK to dismiss the dialog box.

✔ Tips

■ Kerning selected words is frequently done to make copy fit, such as correcting a bad break at the end of a line. You may find—especially with some fonts—that certain letter pairs also need to be kerned because they are too close together or far apart.

■ Another way to make text fit within a frame is to choose Text > Fit Text To Frame. Type within the selected frame will be reduced to make all text visible.

To manually set leading for a text object:

1. If the object is artistic text, select it with the Shape Tool. If it is paragraph text, you can select it with any tool.

   Depending on the type of text and the tool with which it was selected, the down arrow will be in the bottom-left (see Figure 11.13) or bottom-right corner (**Figure 11.18**).

2. Click the down arrow and drag. (Drag down to add space between lines, or drag up to decrease the space between lines.)

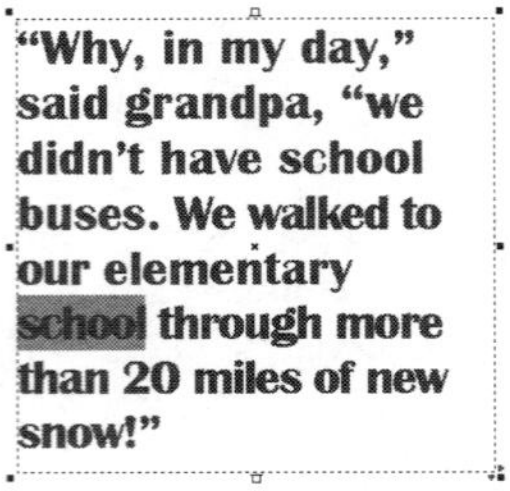

"Why, in my day," said grandpa, "we didn't have school buses. We walked to our elementary school through more than 20 miles of new snow!"

Figure 11.15 By reducing the kerning of the word "school," a bad break in the text can be eliminated.

Figure 11.16 To reduce between-letter spacing, enter a negative number. To increase it, enter a positive number.

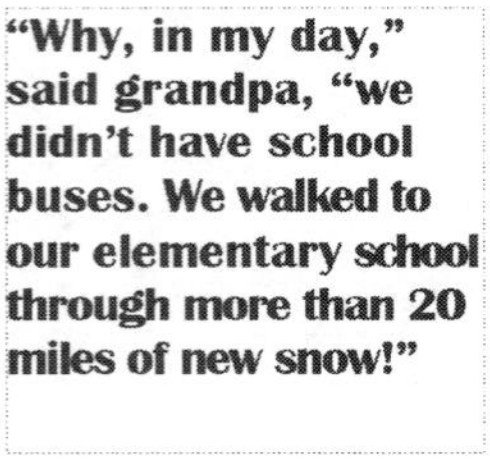

"Why, in my day," said grandpa, "we didn't have school buses. We walked to our elementary school through more than 20 miles of new snow!"

Figure 11.17 The text block now avoids the bad break.

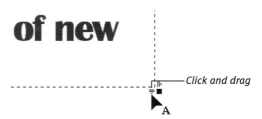

Figure 11.18 Drag up or down to change the leading for the current text block.

FORMATTING TEXT

Select an option

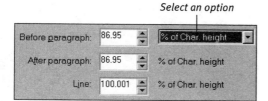

Before paragraph:	86.95	% of Char. height
After paragraph:	86.95	% of Char. height
Line:	100.001	% of Char. height

Figure 11.19 To set line spacing (leading), select an option from the drop-down list and enter a number in the Line text box.

To set leading for a text object using the Format Text dialog box:

1. Select the text object with the Pick Tool.

2. Choose Text > Format Text, press Ctrl T, or click the Format Text icon on the property bar.

3. In the Format Text dialog box, click the Paragraph tab, and enter a number in the Line text box (**Figure 11.19**).

You can base the line spacing on a percentage of the character height, a specific number of points, or a percentage of the point size (depending on the option chosen from the drop-down list).

4. Click OK.

Importing Text

If you already have the text for a brochure or newsletter saved as a word processing document, there's no need to retype it into a CorelDraw project. You can *import* it into the project as paragraph text and manipulate it just as if you were using a page layout program.

To import text into a project:

1. Choose File > Import or press Ctrl I. The Import dialog box appears.

2. Navigate to the drive and folder that contains the document that you want to import, and select its file name.

3. Click Import.
   If the file contains formatted text, the Importing/Pasting Text dialog box appears (**Figure 11.20**).

4. Click a radio button to select a formatting option and click OK.
   A special cursor appears (**Figure 11.21**).

5. Select the spot on the page that you want to serve as the upper-left corner of the paragraph text box and then click to place the text.
   The text appears in a large text frame (**Figure 11.22**). You can work with it like you can any paragraph text object.

✔ Tips

- When *pasting* formatted text, the dialog box shown in **Figure 11.20** also appears.

- If you don't select the Text Tool and set the insertion point before pasting copied text, the original fonts and formatting will automatically be retained. The Importing/Pasting Text dialog box will not appear.

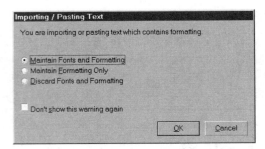

Figure 11.20 This dialog box appears when you import formatted text. You can retain all fonts and formatting, retain the formatting but use the default CorelDraw font, or discard all fonts and formatting.

autobiography add on.doc

Figure 11.21 This cursor indicates that CorelDraw is ready to import the named document.

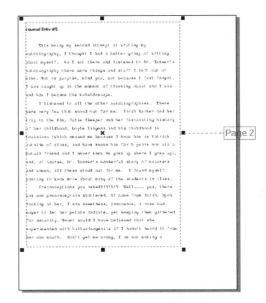

Figure 11.22 This is an example of placed text.

Text flow tab

Figure 11.23 To link the current text frame to a new frame, click the text flow tab and drag to draw the new frame.

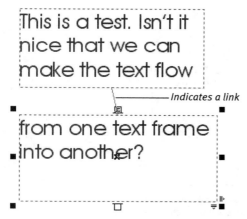

— *Indicates a link*

Figure 11.24 Additional text from the first frame flows into the second frame.

Text Layout

CorelDraw 11 has many features that are commonly found in page layout programs. For instance, you can have multiple linked text frames, enabling the text to flow from one to another. If you add or delete text from a linked paragraph text frame, the text will automatically adjust, flowing between the linked frames as necessary. This feature is commonly used in laying out multi-column newsletters, for example. You can also make text flow onto a path, into an object, or wrap around objects.

To flow text between paragraph text frames:

1. Create the paragraph text or import a text file, as explained previously.

2. Select the paragraph text object.

3. If you reshape the text object so all the text isn't displayed, the bottom text handle displays as a text flow tab (**Figure 11.23**).

4. Click the bottom text handle.
   The pointer changes to a page symbol.

5. Position the mouse where you want the paragraph text to continue. Click and drag a new frame to receive the additional text.
   When you release the mouse button, the extra text from the first text frame flows into the new text frame (**Figure 11.24**).

✔ Tips

- You can flow text between paragraph text frames on different pages.

- Another way to link text frames is to marquee select them and choose Text > Link.

- You can break the links between select frames, enabling each text frame to be edited individually. Marquee-select two or more linked text frames and then choose Text > Unlink.

Advanced text flow

In CorelDraw 11, you aren't restricted to merely flowing text from frame to frame. You can also flow paragraph text into a closed object (such as a circle or star), fit text to the path of an open object (such as a curved line), or make text wrap around an object.

To flow text into an object or onto an open path:

1. Create the paragraph text or import a text file, as explained previously.

2. Select the paragraph text object with the Pick Tool.

3. Resize the paragraph text frame so that a text flow tab appears at the bottom (see Figure 11.23).

4. Click the text flow tab, and then move the pointer over the closed object that will receive the text (**Figure 11.25**) or over the open path.

   The pointer changes to a large black arrow.

5. Click to flow the text into the object or onto the path (**Figure 11.26**).

To make text wrap around an object:

1. Make sure the object has a closed path.

2. Open the Object Properties docker by choosing Window > Dockers > Properties.

3. Select the object by clicking it or by pressing ⟨Tab⟩ (**Figure 11.27**).

4. Click the General tab in the Object Properties docker (**Figure 11.28**).

5. Select a wrap style from the Wrap paragraph text list, and enter an offset amount in the Text wrap offset box. (This is the distance the wrapped text will be offset from the object.)

   The text wraps around the object (**Figure 11.29**).

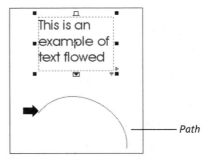

Figure 11.25 Move the cursor over the object or path that will receive the overflow text.

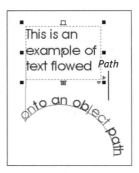

Figure 11.26 The overflow text is added to the object or path.

Selected object

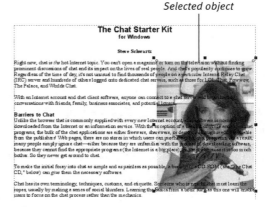

Figure 11.27 Click or press ⟨Tab⟩ to select the object.

TEXT LAYOUT

General tab

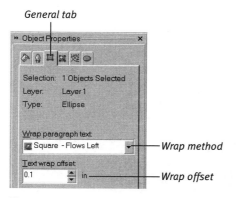

Figure 11.28 Set text wrap options for the object in the Object Properties docker.

Wrap method

Wrap offset

Figure 11.29 The text wraps around the object as you've specified.

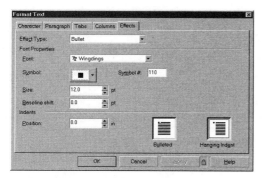

Figure 11.30 Choose bullet settings and click OK.

Embellishing Text

CorelDraw 11 provides many ways that you can embellish your text. Two of the more useful embellishments are the addition of bullets and drop caps.

To add bullets to paragraph text:

1. Using the Text Tool, highlight the paragraphs to which you want to add bullets.

2. Choose Text > Format Text, press Ctrl T, or click the Format Text icon on the property bar.

3. Click the Effects tab (**Figure 11.30**).

4. Select Bullet from the Effect Type drop-down list.

5. Choose a bullet style from the Symbol drop-down list. (You can also choose a different font from the Font drop-down list, if you like.)

6. Set a point size for the bullet in the Size text box.

7. To set a formatting style for the bullet paragraphs, click the Bulleted or Hanging Indent icon.

8. Enter a number in the Position text box to specify the distance that the bullet character will be indented from the text frame.

9. Click OK.

✔ Tip

■ You can also alter the distance between the bullets and the paragraph text. Click the Paragraph tab to display that page of the dialog box, and then enter new figures for the First line and Left indents.

To add a drop cap to paragraph text:

1. With the Text Tool, click to position the insertion marker at the beginning of the paragraph where you want to create the drop cap.
2. Choose Text > Format Text, press Ctrl T, or click the Format Text icon on the property bar.
3. Click the Effects tab (**Figure 11.31**).
4. Select Drop cap from the Effect Type drop-down list.
5. In the Dropped lines text box, set the number of lines of text that the cap will drop.
6. To set a style for the drop cap, click the Dropped or Hanging Indent icon.

   The icons show how the drop cap will be formatted in relation to the paragraph text.
7. Click OK (**Figure 11.32**).

✔ Tips

- Depending on the drop cap's font and particular character, you may find that it is too close to the normal paragraph text. To move it farther away, increase the number in the Distance from text box.
- You can change the drop cap's font by selecting the character with the Text Tool and then choosing a new font from the drop-down list on the property bar.

Drop cap styles
Format Text
Character
Paragraph
Tabs
Columns
Effects
Effect Type:
Drop cap
Dropped lines:
3
Indents
Distance from text:
0.0
in
Dropped
Hanging Indent
OK
Cancel
Apply
Help

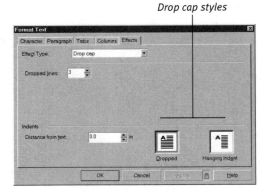

Figure 11.31 Set drop cap options on the Effects tab of the Format Text dialog box.

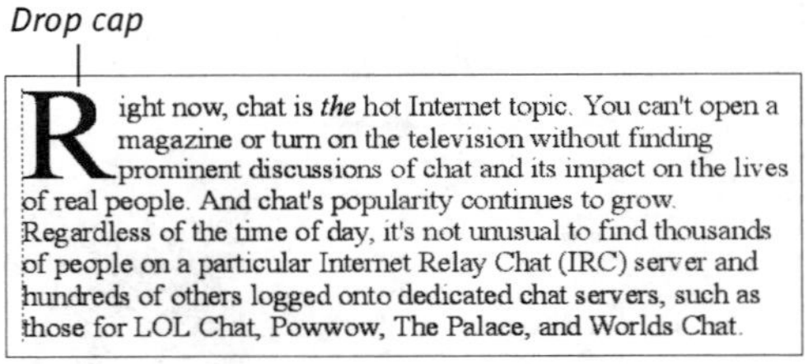

Drop cap
Right now, chat is *the* hot Internet topic. You can't open a magazine or turn on the television without finding prominent discussions of chat and its impact on the lives of real people. And chat's popularity continues to grow. Regardless of the time of day, it's not unusual to find thousands of people on a particular Internet Relay Chat (IRC) server and hundreds of others logged onto dedicated chat servers, such as those for LOL Chat, Powwow, The Palace, and Worlds Chat.

Figure 11.32 The paragraph now begins with an impressive-looking drop cap.

TEXT
SPECIAL EFFECTS

In Chapter 11, "Working with Text," you learned how to add and format text. This chapter shows you how to turn text into a design element. You'll learn how to do the following:

♦ Skew and rotate text objects

♦ Add a drop shadow to text

♦ Fit text to a path

♦ Extrude artistic text, and embellish it with bevels and lighting effects

♦ Create neon text

Skewing and Rotating Text

To *skew* an artistic text object, you slant it vertically or horizontally. To *rotate* an artistic text object, you spin it around a central point (called the *center of rotation marker*). There are two ways you can manually skew or rotate text (or any other selected object):

◆ Drag a skewing or rotation handle with the Pick Tool.

◆ Click and drag using the Free Skew Tool or the Free Rotation Tool.

Using the Pick Tool

The skewing and rotation handles become visible when you double-click any object with the Pick Tool. The *skewing handles* are the arrows in the center of each side of the object. The *rotation handles* are the curved arrows in the corners. Rotation and skewing are both measured in degrees.

To skew text:

1. Double-click an artistic text object with the Pick Tool.

   Skewing and rotation handles appear around the object (**Figure 12.1**).

2. To skew the text horizontally, drag the top or bottom skewing handle to the left or right (**Figure 12.2**).

   or

   To skew the text vertically, drag the left or right skewing handle up or down (**Figure 12.3**).

   As you drag, a blue outline of the text characters is displayed.

3. Release the mouse button to complete the skewing process.

Skewing handle   Skewing handle   Rotation handle

Figure 12.1 Double-click an artistic text object to display the skewing and rotation handles.

Figure 12.2 Drag the top or bottom skewing handle to skew the text horizontally.

Figure 12.3 Drag the left or right skewing handle to skew the text vertically.

SKEWING AND ROTATING TEXT

Figure 12.4 Double-click an artistic text object.

Figure 12.5 You can rotate artistic text to any angle.

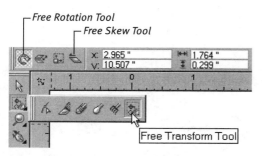

Figure 12.6 Select the Free Transform Tool from the toolbox. You must set a specific tool to be used in conjunction with it by clicking a property bar icon.

Figure 12.7 As you drag, you are shown an outline preview of the skewed text.

To rotate text:

1. Double-click the artistic text object with the Pick Tool.

   The rotation and skewing handles appear (**Figure 12.4**). At the center of the text object is a circle with a dot in its center. This is the center of rotation marker.

2. Drag a rotation handle clockwise or counterclockwise.

   As you drag, a blue outline of the text characters is displayed.

3. Release the mouse button to complete the rotation process (**Figure 12.5**).

✔ Tip

- Experiment with dragging the center of rotation marker to new positions. Then rotate the text object and note how it moves around the marker.

Using the Free Transform Tool

Another way to rotate and skew text is to use the Free Transform Tool (**Figure 12.6**). The Free Transform Tool works in conjunction with property bar icons to give you access to the Free Rotation, Free Angle Reflection, Free Scale, and Free Skew Tools (**Figure 12.6**).

To skew text with the Free Skew Tool:

1. Select the Free Transform Tool from the Shape Tool flyout (**Figure 12.6**).

2. Click the Free Skew Tool icon on the property bar (**Figure 12.6**).

3. Click the object to select it, and then drag left, right, up, and/or down (**Figure 12.7**).

4. When you attain the desired skew, release the mouse button.

To rotate text with the Free Rotation Tool:

1. Select the Free Transform Tool from the Shape Tool flyout (see Figure 12.6).

2. Click the Free Rotation Tool icon on the property bar (see Figure 12.6).

3. Click the object where you would like the center of rotation to be and drag in the direction you wish to rotate (**Figure 12.8**).

   A dashed blue line appears, showing the angle from the center of rotation. A blue outline version of the text rotates as you drag the mouse.

4. Release the mouse button when you are done rotating the text.

✔ Tip

■ If you know the precise angle you want for a skew or rotation, you can select the object and then enter the angle(s) in a property bar text box (**Figure 12.9**) or the appropriate section of the Transformation docker (**Figure 12.10**).

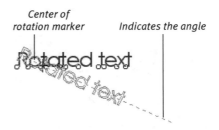

Figure 12.8 Click to select a center of rotation and then drag to set the angle.

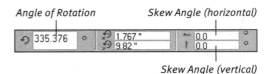

Figure 12.9 Rotation and skew angles for an object can also be entered in these property bar boxes.

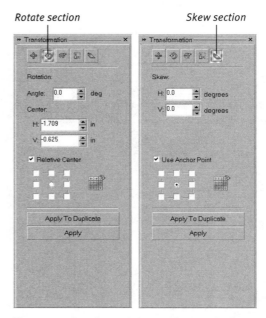

Figure 12.10 Rotation and skew angles can also be entered in the Transformation docker. To open the docker, choose Window > Dockers > Transformations, followed by Rotate or Skew.

Original   Duplicate

Artistic Text
Artistic Text

Figure 12.11 Duplicate the text and change the color of the original text to make it the shadow.

Artistic Text

Figure 12.12 Drag the duplicate onto the original, offsetting it slightly to create the shadow effect.

Creating Drop Shadows

Shadows give the impression of three dimensionality. There are many ways to create drop shadows with CorelDraw 11. The first method described here uses duplication to make shadows. The second method uses the Interactive Drop Shadow Tool and produces extremely realistic shadows.

To create text shadows via duplication:

1. Create some artistic text and format it with your favorite font.

2. Select the text object with the Pick Tool.

3. Make a copy of the text by choosing Edit > Duplicate or pressing Ctrl D.

    A duplicate appears, above and to the right of the original text object.

4. Change the color of the original text object by selecting it and left-clicking a color well in the color palette (**Figure 12.11**).

    Light gray is a good choice since this text will become the shadow.

5. Select the duplicate and drag so that it is slightly offset from the original (**Figure 12.12**).

    The amount and direction of the offset depend on the lighting effect you want to emulate.

To create shadows with the Interactive Drop Shadow Tool:

1. Select the Interactive Drop Shadow Tool from the Interactive Tool flyout in the toolbox (**Figure 12.13**).

2. Select the text or other object to which you want to add a drop shadow.

3. Click near the center of the object and drag in the direction you want the drop shadow to appear.

4. To change the drop shadow's visibility, move the slider bar on the drop shadow arrow (**Figure 12.14**). To change the direction or distance of the drop shadow from the text, drag the black box.

5. Release the mouse button.

✔ Tips

- The property bar provides a wealth of controls and options that you can use to modify a drop shadow (**Figure 12.15**). Select an existing drop shadow with the Interactive Drop Shadow Tool. As you try out different settings, the effect on the drop shadow is shown immediately.

- A quick way to create an impressive drop shadow is to select one from the Presets drop-down list (**Figure 12.16**).

- You can copy a drop shadow from one object to another. Select the destination object, choose Effects > Copy Effect > Copy Drop Shadow From. A large black arrow appears. Click the object whose drop shadow you want to copy.

- To remove a drop shadow, select the object with the Interactive Drop Shadow Tool and click the Clear Drop Shadow toolbar icon. To change the drop shadow's color, click the Color toolbar icon.

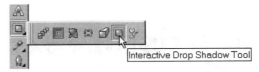

Figure 12.13 Select the Interactive Drop Shadow Tool.

Controls

Figure 12.14 To change the features of the drop shadow, you can manipulate the controls.

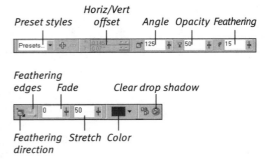

Figure 12.15 To precisely set the angle, opacity, offset, color, and other attributes of a drop shadow, you can use these property bar controls.

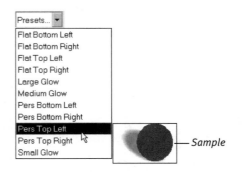

Figure 12.16 You can select a preset shadow style from this drop-down list on the property bar.

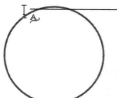

Figure 12.17 Click on the object's path to set the insertion marker.

Figure 12.18 As you type, the text wraps around the object.

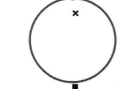

Figure 12.19 Select both objects.

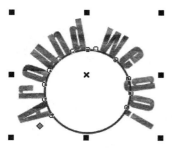

Figure 12.20 Choose the Text > Fit Text To Path command.

Fitting Text to a Path

Fitting text to a path refers to binding a line of text to the path of an object. As the text moves along the object's path, it assumes the shape of the path. You can fit text to a path interactively or choose a command from the Text menu.

To interactively fit artistic text to a path:

1. Using the Pick Tool, select the object to which you want to fit the text. The object must either have a closed path or be a line.

2. Position the Text Tool on the object's path. The cursor changes from the Text Tool's normal cross-hair to an I-beam.

3. Click to place the insertion marker at the desired starting point on the object or line (**Figure 12.17**).

4. Choose a font and size from the property bar drop-down lists. (In this example, the font is Bremen Bd BT, 48 point.)

5. Type the text.
   As you type, the text follows the object's outline (**Figure 12.18**).

To fit existing text to a path:

1. Create an object to which you want to fit the text.

2. Create some artistic text, choose a font, and set its color, pattern, or texture.

3. Select both objects either by [Shift]-clicking or by dragging a marquee with the Pick Tool (**Figure 12.19**).

4. Choose Text > Fit Text To Path.
   The text redraws, following the object's path (**Figure 12.20**).

continues on next page

FITTING TEXT TO A PATH

✔ Tips

- After placing the text, you can edit it to achieve the desired result. You can click the pink diamond with the Pick Tool and drag to change the text's starting point (**Figure 12.21**). You can also select the text with the Text Tool and alter its font, size, and so on by making choices from the property bar.

- You can make changes to the text's placement via the property bar (**Figure 12.22**). Click the text with the Pick Tool and the property bar will then allow you to set the following options (among others):

  ▲ **Text orientation.** Specifies how the text "stands," giving it an upright or sideways appearance, for example.

  ▲ **Vertical placement.** Specifies where the text sits on the path: on top of it, beneath it, and so on.

  ▲ **Text placement.** Specifies where the text is centered on the path: on the top, bottom, left, or right.

- You can also flow existing paragraph text onto a path, as explained in Chapter 11, "Working with Text."

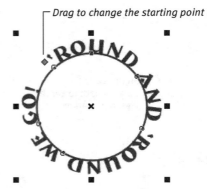

⌐ Drag to change the starting point

Figure 12.21 Even after placing the text, you can still modify it.

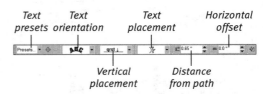

Text presets · Text orientation · Text placement · Horizontal offset · Vertical placement · Distance from path

Figure 12.22 To precisely specify how the text is to be placed, you can pick options from the property bar.

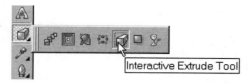

Figure 12.23 Select the Interactive Extrude Tool from the Interactive Tool flyout in the toolbox.

Figure 12.24 This is the original text object, changed to an outline.

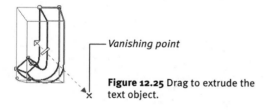

Vanishing point

Figure 12.25 Drag to extrude the text object.

Figure 12.26 This is the final extruded object with a bevel, fill, and lighting.

Extruding Text

Extruding gives a two-dimensional object the appearance of three dimensions. You use the Interactive Extrude Tool (**Figure 12.23**) to create extrusions.

An extrusion is created by projecting points from the edges of a two-dimensional object (**Figure 12.24**) and joining them to converge toward a vanishing point (**Figure 12.25**). The illusion of depth is created by the addition of objects on top of the original (or *control*) object. After creating an extrusion, bevels, fills and ambient lighting can be added to enhance the effect (**Figure 12.26**). The object can also be rotated in three dimensions, letting you view it from any side or angle.

✔ Tips

■ Although extrusions are illustrated in the following pages in relation to text objects, the techniques you'll read about can be applied to *any* kind of CorelDraw vector object.

■ Bitmap extrusions, a feature of CorelDraw 10, are no longer available in CorelDraw 11.

EXTRUDING TEXT

To create an extrusion:

1. Select the Interactive Extrude Tool from the toolbox (see Figure 12.23).

2. Choose an extrusion type from the drop-down list on the property bar (**Figure 12.27**).

3. Select the text object you want to extrude.

4. Position the mouse pointer near the center of the text object. Click and drag in the direction you want the extrusion to go (**Figure 12.28**).

5. Adjust the extrusion as needed by clicking and dragging the extrusion controls.

6. To complete the extrusion, click away from the object or select another tool (**Figure 12.29**).

✔ Tip

■ Changing the text to an outline will make the extrusion look better. Left-click the X (no fill) option in the color palette. To set the outline color, right-click a color well.

Embellishing an extrusion

You can embellish an extrusion with color, bevels, and lighting effects, and by rotating it.

To color the extruded portion of the text:

1. Select the extruded object with the Interactive Extrude Tool.

2. Click the Color icon on the property bar. The Color box appears (**Figure 12.30**).

3. Click one of the three color fill icons:

   ▲ **Use Object Fill.** Click to apply the original object's fill color to the extrusion.

   ▲ **Use Solid Color.** Click to select a solid fill color for the extrusion.

   ▲ **Use Color Shading.** Click to apply a two-color fountain fill to the extrusion. Choose the colors from the From and To drop-down palettes.

Extrusion type drop-down list

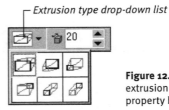

Figure 12.27 Choose an extrusion type from the property bar.

Figure 12.28 Drag to create the extrusion.

Figure 12.29 This is the extruded text.

Color property bar icon

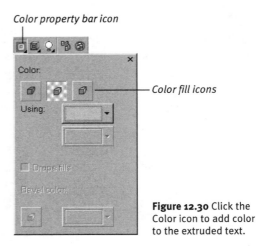

Color fill icons

Figure 12.30 Click the Color icon to add color to the extruded text.

Figure 12.31 This text had a fountain fill applied to the extrusion and a solid color (uniform fill) applied to its face.

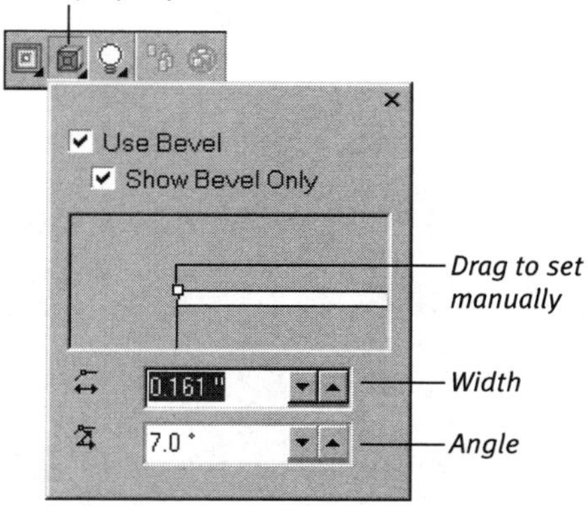

Bevel property bar icon

Drag to set manually

Width

Angle

Figure 12.32 Set bevel settings in this drop-down box.

Figure 12.33 An extruded object redraws with the specified bevel settings.

To add a color, pattern, or texture fill to the face of an extrusion:

1. Select the Interactive Fill Tool from the toolbox or press [G].

2. Select a fill type from the Fill Type drop-down list on the property bar.

3. Depending on the fill type chosen, follow the directions for applying the fill as explained in Chapter 10, "Color and Fills." After you make a selection, the face of the object fills with the color, pattern, or texture (**Figure 12.31**).

To bevel the face of an extrusion:

1. Select the extruded object with the Interactive Extrude Tool.

2. Click the Bevel icon on the property bar. The Bevel box appears (**Figure 12.32**).

3. Check the Use Bevel check box.

4. *Optional:* Since the bevel is only applied to an extruded object's face, you may want to check the Show Bevel Only check box.

5. Set the bevel's thickness and angle by entering numbers in the two text boxes or by clicking and dragging the dot in the preview box.

6. Close the Bevel box to complete the drawing (**Figure 12.33**).

✔ Tips

- To eliminate an applied bevel, select the object and uncheck the Use Bevel check box.

- To edit *any* attribute of an extruded object, select it first with the Interactive Extrude Tool.

EXTRUDING TEXT

To add lighting effects to an extrusion:

1. Select the extruded object with the Inter-active Extrude Tool (**Figure 12.34**).

2. Click the Lighting icon on the property bar. The Lighting drop-down box appears (**Figure 12.35**).

3. Click the bulb #1 icon to turn that light on. A black dot with a "1" in its center appears in the preview area.

4. Drag the dot to the position on the grid where you want the light.

   As you make changes to the lighting, the extrusion's lighting changes.

5. Move the Intensity slider bar to set the light's brightness.

6. To add more lighting, click the other light-bulb icons and repeat Steps 4 and 5.

7. When you are satisfied with the lighting, close the Lighting box (**Figure 12.36**).

✔ Tip

■ If you want to export an extrusion, you have to group it first. To learn how to group objects, refer to Chapter 14, "Object Arrangement."

Figure 12.34 Begin by selecting the extruded object with the Interactive Extrude Tool.

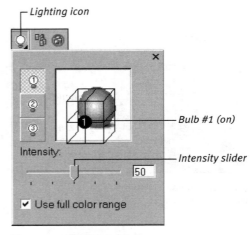

Figure 12.35 Specify lighting settings in this drop-down box.

Figure 12.36 Lighting can produce dramatic effects.

Rotation cursor

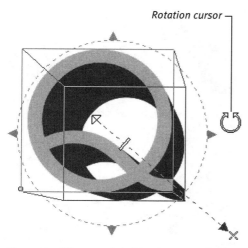

Figure 12.37 The extruded object is surrounded by a green circle, indicating that it is ready to be rotated.

Figure 12.38 Rotating an extruded object can produce a very different visual effect.

To rotate an extruded object:

1. Select the extruded object with the Interactive Extrude Tool.

2. Double-click the extrusion.

   A green circle with triangular handles surrounds the object (**Figure 12.37**).

3. Move the pointer over the circle.

4. Click and drag in any direction to rotate the object (**Figure 12.38**).

The Neon Effect

Highlighting text with a bright neon effect is a great way to grab attention. The effect consists solely of different color outlines that have been blended together. The following steps show how to create this effect.

To create the neon effect:

1. Create some artistic text and change it to a favorite font in a large point size (**Figure 12.39**). Zoom as necessary to see the text clearly (200–400 percent, for example).

2. Convert the text to curves (**Figure 12.40**) by pressing Ctrl Q or choosing Arrange > Convert To Curves.

3. Select the Outline Pen Dialog from the Outline Tool flyout menu or press F12.

4. As shown in **Figure 12.41**, set the following options:
   ▲ Set the Width to 0.056 inches.
   ▲ Change the Color to Red.
   ▲ In the Corners section, select the rounded corner.
   ▲ In the Line caps section, select the rounded cap.
   ▲ Check the Scale with image check box.

5. Click OK to dismiss the dialog box (**Figure 12.42**).

6. With the text object selected, press Ctrl C or choose Edit > Copy.

   A copy of the text object is transferred to the Clipboard.

7. Press Ctrl V or choose Edit > Paste.

   A copy of the text object is pasted directly on top of the original.

8. On the color palette, left-click the color well with the X in it to remove the fill color from the copy.

Figure 12.39 We'll use 72-point Harlow Solid Italic as the font.

Figure 12.40 After conversion, the text has nodes.

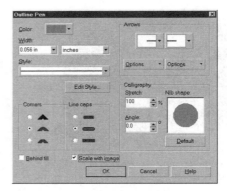

Figure 12.41 Set these outline properties for the copy of the text object.

Figure 12.42 This is what the text looks like after changing its outline properties.

Figure 12.43 This is what the copy looks like after changing its outline properties. The original text shows through from beneath.

Figure 12.44 This is the finished neon text.

Figure 12.45 If you shift the copy up and to the right before performing the blend, you get this startling effect.

9. Open the Outline Pen dialog box and set the following options:
   - ▲ Set Color to White.
   - ▲ Set Width to 0.014 inches.

10. Click OK to close the dialog box (**Figure 12.43**).

11. Select the Interactive Blend Tool from the Interactive Tool flyout.

12. Position the pointer over the center of the text objects. Click and drag about one inch to the right, and then release the mouse button.

    The outlines of the text objects blend together, creating the neon effect (**Figure 12.44**).

✔ **Tip**

- ■ Variations of this technique can produce equally stunning results. You might wish to stop after Step 10, for example, and skip the blend. Or try moving the copy slightly up and to the right before creating the blend to produce a very different effect (**Figure 12.45**).

Converting Text to Curves

After text has been converted to curves, you can no longer edit it with the Text Tool. The reason for this is that CorelDraw sees it only as closed-path shapes, rather than as text.

STACKING AND LAYERS

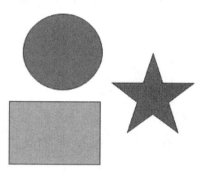

Figure 13.1 When objects don't overlap, the stacking order isn't apparent.

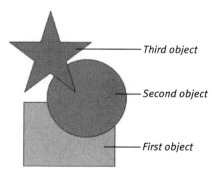

Third object

Second object

First object

Figure 13.2 Now that the objects have been moved so that they overlap, you can see the stacking order.

When two objects are drawn, CorelDraw 11 automatically stacks the second object on the first. When a third object is drawn, it is stacked on the second, and so on. This positioning is called the *stacking order*. If the objects don't overlap, the stacking order isn't apparent (**Figure 13.1**). But a stacking order is always present—even when you can't see it.

You've probably noticed messages such as "Rectangle on Layer 1" on the status bar. By default, CorelDraw 11 places all objects on one layer. For instance, **Figures 13.1** and **13.2** are single-layer drawings. *Layers* are invisible planes that stack vertically, one on top of the other. Layers help keep a drawing's distinct elements separate. For example, when creating an ad or a birthday announcement, you might want to place the graphic elements on one layer and put all of the text on a second layer. This can simplify the drawing process. You can add as many layers to a drawing as you need.

✔ Notes

- Stacking order and layers are two distinct concepts. There is always a separate stacking order on each layer of a drawing, but there is no requirement that a drawing have multiple layers.

- When you add a layer, it is added to *all* pages of the document.

Changing the Stacking Order

To change an object's position in the stacking order, choose commands from the Arrange > Order submenu (**Figure 13.3**).

To move an object forward in the stacking order:

1. Select the object you want to move.

2. *Do one of the following:*

   ▲ To move an object to the front of the stacking order, press [Shift][Pg Up] or choose Arrange > Order > To Front.

   ▲ To move an object forward one place in the stacking order, press [Ctrl][Pg Up] or choose Arrange > Order > Forward One.

   ▲ To move a selected object in front of another object, choose Arrange > Order > In Front Of. The pointer changes to a black right-arrow. Click the object that will be behind the selected object (**Figures 13.4** and **13.5**).

To move an object backward in the stacking order:

1. Select the object you want to move.

2. *Do one of the following:*

   ▲ To move an object to the back of the stacking order, press [Shift][Pg Dn] or choose Arrange > Order > To Back.

   ▲ To move an object backward one object in the stacking order, press [Ctrl][Pg Dn] or choose Arrange > Order > Back One.

   ▲ To move a selected object behind another object, choose Arrange > Order > Behind. The pointer changes to a black right-arrow. Click the object that will be in front of the selected object.

✔ Tip

■ To swap the order of two or more selected objects, choose Arrange > Order > Reverse Order.

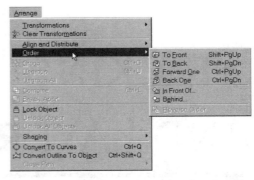

Figure 13.3 To alter the stacking order of a selected object, choose a command from the Order submenu.

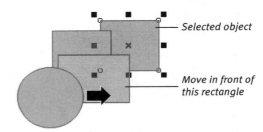

Figure 13.4 Click the rectangle to move the selected object in front of it.

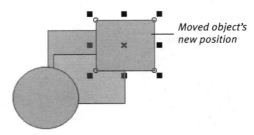

Figure 13.5 The object moves to its new position in the stacking order.

CHANGING THE STACKING ORDER

Layer manager view

Edit across layers

Active layer

Show object properties

Menu

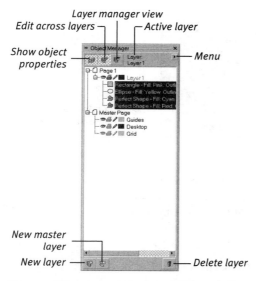

New master layer

New layer

Delete layer

Figure 13.6 You can create and arrange layers in the Object Manager docker.

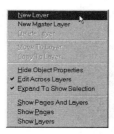

Figure 13.7 Choose New Layer from this pop-up menu.

New layer

Figure 13.8 You can name the new layer, if you wish.

Working with Layers

Using the Object Manager docker (**Figure 13.6**), you can create and work with layers. Each layer's settings determine whether it can be seen, printed, or drawn upon.

If you're creating a multi-page document, you can also designate *master layers*—where any contained graphics and text will appear in the same place on every page. For instance, if you were designing a company newsletter, you could place your logo on a master layer, rather than having to copy it to each page.

To open the Object Manager docker:

Do one of the following:

◆ Choose Tools > Object Manager.

◆ Choose Window > Dockers > Object Manager.

To create a new layer:

1. *Do one of the following:*

   ▲ Click the New Layer button at the bottom of the docker.

   ▲ Click the arrow at the top of the Object Manager docker. Choose New Layer from the pop-up menu that appears (**Figure 13.7**).

   The new layer appears above the previous topmost layer (**Figure 13.8**).

2. Name the layer (or accept the default name of "Layer *x*") and then press (Enter).

   The new layer is displayed in red type to show that it is currently active.

To work in a different layer:

◆ Click the name of the layer that you want to make current or active.

   The layer name is displayed in red to show that it is active. Any new objects you create will be added to that layer.

WORKING WITH LAYERS

To change a layer's settings:

Do one of the following:

◆ Right-click the layer's name and choose the setting you want to change from the pop-up menu (**Figure 13.9**). A checkmark indicates that the setting is enabled.

◆ Click the relevant icon to enable or disable a level's property (**Figure 13.10**). If the icon is grayed out, the setting is disabled.

To reorder the layers:

1. Click the name of the layer you want to move and drag it up or down in the list.

   A black bar appears as you drag, indicating the layer's destination position.

2. Release the mouse button to place the layer.

   The layer moves to the new position and become the active layer.

To move an object to a different layer:

1. Click the object in the Object Manager docker and drag it into the destination layer's section.

   Note that the order in which objects are listed in each layer is the stacking order. Higher objects are closer to the front.

2. Release the mouse button.

   The object moves to the destination layer.

To copy or move an object to a layer:

1. Select the object in the Object Manager docker or in the drawing window.

2. Click the triangle in the upper-right corner of the Object Manager docker, and choose Move To Layer or Copy To Layer from the pop-up menu that appears (**Figure 13.11**).

3. Click the name of the destination layer in the Object Manager docker.

   The object moves or is copied to the destination layer.

Figure 13.9 You can set the current properties for a level with this pop-up menu.

Visible   Editable

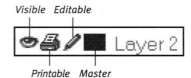

Printable   Master

Figure 13.10 Or you can click an icon to enable or disable a property.

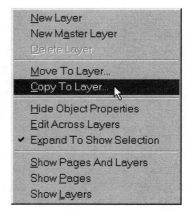

Figure 13.11 Copy To Layer duplicates the object into a layer. Move To Layer transfers the object between layers.

To change a layer from normal to master (or vice versa):

Do one of the following:

◆ Right-click the layer name and choose Master from the pop-up menu that appears (see Figure 13.9).

◆ In the Object Manager docker, click the Master icon (see Figure 13.10).

◆ Drag the layer into or out from the Master Page section.

To delete a layer:

◆ Right-click the layer and choose Delete from the pop-up menu that appears (see Figure 13.9).

✔ Tips

■ The status bar will always tell you which layer a selected object is on.

■ You can select an object by clicking it in the Object Manager docker. You can change a selected object's stacking order within a layer by dragging it up or down.

■ If you're done with a layer and don't want to inadvertently move or alter any of its objects, click the Pencil icon to make the layer uneditable.

■ If Edit Across Layers isn't enabled, you won't be allowed to move an object from an inactive layer to the active layer.

■ In a complex drawing, it's sometimes easier to work with layers individually. You can temporarily hide other layers by disabling their Visible property.

■ You can create or designate *multiple* master layers, if you like. Click the triangle in the upper-right corner of the Object Manager docker. Choose New Master Layer from the pop-up menu that appears (see Figure 13.11).

Using Layers to Create Plans

Layers can be very helpful when creating technical plans for items such as buildings, gardens, and cars. For instance, when making a house plan, you could create separate plumbing, electrical, and framing layers. Drawings of pipes would be placed on the plumbing layer, wiring diagrams on the electrical layer, and window layouts on the framing layer.

When it comes time to print the plans, you can print the composite drawing, as well as separate pages for each layer. In that way, you could give each contractor a page for his or her specialty.

WORKING WITH LAYERS

OBJECT ARRANGEMENT

It's amazing what you can do with a few mouse clicks. Many of the commands in the Arrange menu (Group, Combine, Lock Object, Transformations, and Shaping) are among the most powerful and easy to use tools in CorelDraw.

In this chapter, you'll learn about these important Arrange commands, as well as how to accomplish many key object transformations using the Transformation docker.

✔ Tips

- To learn about the commands in the Arrange > Order submenu, as well as the Align and Distribute command, refer to Chapter 9, "Tools for Precision."

- Any of the transformations discussed in this chapter (such as grouping, rotating, and sizing) can also be performed on multiple objects or groups. Select the objects you want to change, and then follow the steps listed in this chapter.

- Remember that text blocks and strings are objects, too. Text can also be manipulated with the commands in the Arrange menu.

Grouping Objects

Grouping objects binds them together so you can manipulate them as a unit. For instance, if you want to move several objects yet keep them in the same positions relative to each other, you could group the objects and then move them as a unit.

Formatting applied to a group also affects all objects in the group. You could add a blue fill to all objects in a group by selecting the group and clicking a blue shade on the color palette. If you later need to work with the individual objects that make up the group, you can simply *ungroup* them.

To group objects:

1. Using the Pick Tool, select two or more objects.

   To select multiple objects, you can hold down Shift while clicking the objects, or you can drag a marquee around the objects (**Figure 14.1**).

2. Choose Arrange > Group or press Ctrl G.

   The next time you select the grouped objects, you'll notice that the handles now appear around the group rather than the individual objects (**Figure 14.2**).

To ungroup objects:

1. Using the Pick Tool, select the grouped objects.

2. Choose Arrange > Ungroup or press Ctrl U.

✔ Tips

- To ungroup all objects on a page, choose Arrange > Ungroup All.

- You can select an individual object within a group by pressing Ctrl as you click.

Figure 14.1 One way to select objects for grouping is to drag a selection rectangle (called a *marquee*) around them.

Figure 14.2 When you select a group, it is surrounded by a single set of handles.

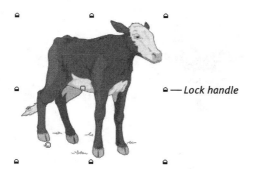

—Lock handle

Figure 14.3 When you select a locked object, the normal black handles are replaced by padlocks.

Locking Objects

Locking an object prevents it from being moved or altered in any way. This feature is especially handy when used in conjunction with a complex drawing. The objects that you've completed or don't want to alter by mistake can be locked, leaving the remaining objects available for selection and editing.

To lock an object:

1. Use the Pick Tool to select the object(s) that you wish to lock.

2. Choose Arrange > Lock Object.
   The handles of the object(s) change to tiny padlocks (**Figure 14.3**).

If you want to modify a locked object, you must first unlock it.

To unlock an object:

1. Select the locked object by right-clicking it with the Pick Tool.

2. Choose Unlock Object from the pop-up menu that appears or choose Arrange > Unlock Object.

✔ Tips

- You can lock *every* type of object in CorelDraw—any single object, several selected objects, a group, or a set of groups.

- You can simultaneously unlock all locked objects on a page by choosing Arrange > Unlock All Objects.

Combining and Breaking Objects Apart

When you *combine* objects, lines and shapes fuse to create new shapes. Any overlapping areas are removed, creating *clipping holes* that let you see what's underneath. You can use the Combine command to create a graphic effect in which half the drawing is white on black and the other half is black on white.

To create a black/white graphic:

1. Create a closed-path object and fill it with black (**Figure 14.4**).

2. Use the Rectangle Tool to draw a rectangle that covers the right half of the graphic (**Figure 14.5**).

3. Copy the selected rectangle by choosing Edit > Copy or pressing Ctrl C.

4. Fill the rectangle with black.
   The rectangle obscures the graphic beneath.

5. Select both objects, and choose Arrange > Combine (or press Ctrl L).
   The half of the graphic covered by the rectangle becomes a cutout (**Figure 14.6**).

6. Paste a copy of the rectangle by choosing Edit > Paste or pressing Ctrl V, drag it so it covers the left half of the image, send it to the back (press Shift Pg Dn), and fill it with white (**Figure 14.7**).

✔ Tips

- To add an interesting effect to the drawing, create a large square that completely covers the objects. Send the square to the back and then fill it with a color or a texture. The cutout (created by the combined objects) lets the large square's fill or texture shine through (**Figure 14.8**).

- You can use this technique on text, too (**Figure 14.9**).

Figure 14.4 Create a closed path object.

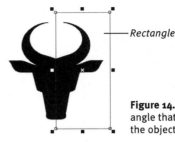

Rectangle

Figure 14.5 Draw a rectangle that covers half of the object.

Figure 14.6 Apply Combine so that the half covered by the rectangle becomes a cutout.

Rectangle

Figure 14.7 To complete the drawing, fill a second rectangle with white and send it to the back.

Figure 14.8 A textured square placed behind the drawing adds visual interest.

Figure 14.9 You can also use the black/white technique to create interesting text effects.

Breaking objects apart

Just as there are commands to reverse the effects of Group and Lock, you can use the Break Apart command to separate objects that have been fused with Combine.

To break objects apart:

1. Select the combined objects.

2. Choose Arrange > Break Apart or press Ctrl K.
   The objects resume their original shape, and you can now work with them as separate objects.

✔ Tip

■ Depending on what is selected, the command may be worded as Break Curve Apart, rather than Break Apart.

Working with Clip Art Images

Many clip art images are created by grouping and/or combining several objects. By ungrouping or breaking these graphics apart, you can modify clip art to suit your needs and taste. Once you've made changes, you can regroup or recombine the graphics.

You can determine if an object has been combined or grouped by selecting it and then opening the Arrange menu. If the Ungroup or Break Apart command is available, then the graphic has been grouped or combined.

Transforming Objects

The Transformation docker (**Figure 14.10**) has sections for setting the position, rotation angle, scale, size, and skew of objects. These transformations can also be performed using the Transform toolbar (**Figure 14.11**).

To open the Transformation docker, choose Window > Dockers > Transformations, followed by any of the five section names, such as Position. Or you can open it by choosing a command from the Arrange > Transformations submenu (**Figure 14.12**). The docker opens to the chosen section.

To open the Transform toolbar, choose Window > Toolbars > Transform. The Transform toolbar floats and can be dragged by its title bar to any onscreen location.

Positioning an object

In the Position section of the Transformation docker (**Figure 14.10**), you can set a selected object's exact screen position or move it relative to its current position. You can optionally create and move a *duplicate* of the selected object, rather than the original.

To set an object's new screen position:

1. Select the object you wish to move.

2. To change the object's position to match the ruler coordinates, remove the Relative Position checkmark and enter new (H) horizontal and/or (V) vertical coordinates.

   or

   To move the object relative to its current position, check the Relative Position check box and enter the (H) horizontal and/or (V) vertical distance you want to move the object

3. Click Apply to move the object to the new position, or click Apply to Duplicate to move a copy of the selected object to the new position.

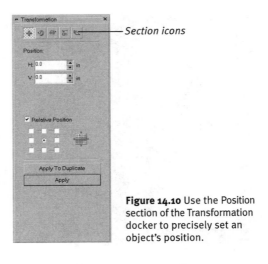

Figure 14.10 Use the Position section of the Transformation docker to precisely set an object's position.

Apply to Duplicate

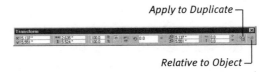

Relative to Object

Figure 14.11 You can also use the Transform toolbar.

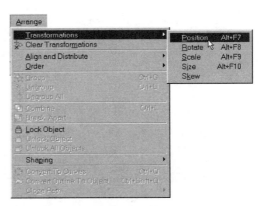

Figure 14.12 Or you can use the Transformations submenu.

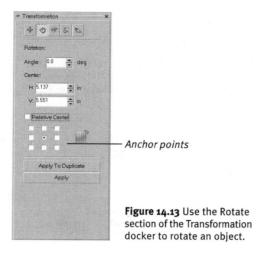

Figure 14.13 Use the Rotate section of the Transformation docker to rotate an object.

— Anchor points

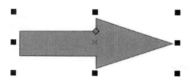

Figure 14.14 Select an object to rotate.

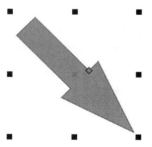

Figure 14.15 The object has been rotated -45 degrees (clockwise).

✔ Tip

■ To set a selected object's screen position using the Transform toolbar, enter new horizontal and vertical data in the X and Y text boxes. Whether the move is to an absolute position or relative to the current position depends on the status of the Relative to Object icon at the right end of the toolbar (see Figure 14.11).

Rotating an object

In Chapter 12, you learned how to use the rotation handles and the Free Transform Tool to rotate a text object. You can use the same techniques on any object or group of objects in conjunction with the Rotate section of the Transformation docker (**Figure 14.13**).

To rotate an object:

1. Select the object to be rotated (**Figure 14.14**).

2. In the Angle text box, enter the number of degrees you want to rotate the object. (Negative numbers rotate clockwise; positive numbers rotate counterclockwise.)

3. If you want to use one of the object's handles as the *anchor point* around which the object will be rotated (rather than rotating it around the object's center), click the check box that corresponds to the new anchor point.

4. Click Apply to rotate the selected object (**Figure 14.15**), or click Apply To Duplicate to rotate a copy of the selected object.

✔ Tip

■ You can also rotate an object by typing an angle in the Angle of Rotation text box on the Transform toolbar or the property bar. To apply the rotation to a copy of the object rather than to the original, click the Apply to Duplicate icon near the end of the Transform toolbar (see Figure 14.11).

Scaling an object

Scaling an object makes its vertical, horizontal, or both dimensions larger or smaller. In Chapter 4, "Select, Move, Copy, and Size," you learned how to scale an object by dragging a handle. However, you can use the Scale and Mirror section of the Transformation docker (**Figure 14.16**) to scale objects with greater accuracy.

To scale an object:

1. Select the object you want to scale (**Figure 14.17**).

2. In the H and V text boxes, enter the horizontal and/or vertical percentages by which you want to scale the object.

   An entry of 100 represents the object's current size, 50 would be half, and 200 would be double.

3. To proportionately change the object's horizontal and vertical scale, remove the checkmark from the Non-proportional check box.

4. *Do one of the following:*
   ▲ Click Apply to scale the selected object (**Figure 14.18**).
   ▲ Click Apply To Duplicate to scale a copy of the selected object.

✔ Tip

■ Subsequent entries in the H and V text boxes refer to the object's *current* size, not its *original* size. For example, if you originally scaled the horizontal dimension to 50 percent of the object's original size, clicking Apply a second time will further reduce it to half its current width.

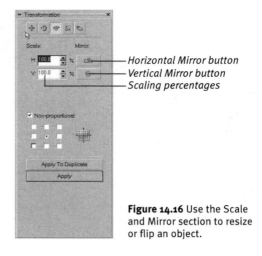

Figure 14.16 Use the Scale and Mirror section to resize or flip an object.

Horizontal Mirror button
Vertical Mirror button
Scaling percentages

Figure 14.17 Select an object to scale.

Figure 14.18 The object has been scaled by 200 percent.

Drag this handle to the left

Figure 14.19 By dragging the right-center handle to the left ...

Figure 14.20 ... you can flip an image horizontally.

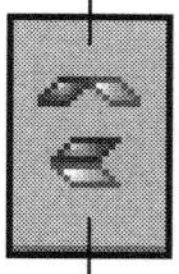

Flip horizontally

Figure 14.21 Mirror buttons can also be found on the Transform toolbar and the property bar.

Flip vertically

Mirroring an object

Mirroring an object flips it vertically, horizontally, or in both directions. You can mirror objects by dragging a center handle or using the Scale and Mirror section of the Transformation docker (see Figure 14.16).

To mirror an object manually:

1. Using the Pick Tool, select the object to be mirrored.

   Eight black handles appear around the object (**Figure 14.19**).

2. Press Ctrl while dragging the left-center or right-center handle in the opposite direction. (Drag the left handle to the right or the right handle to the left.) The object will flip horizontally (**Figure 14.20**).

   or

   Press Ctrl while dragging the top-center or bottom-center handle in the opposite direction. (Drag the top handle downward or the bottom handle upward.) The object will flip vertically.

To mirror an object using the Transformation docker:

1. Using the Pick Tool, select the object to be mirrored.

2. Click the Horizontal Mirror button and/or the Vertical Mirror button.

3. Click Apply to mirror the original object, or click Apply To Duplicate to mirror a copy of the object.

✔ Tips

- Mirror buttons are also available on the property bar and the Transform toolbar (**Figure 14.21**).

- You can easily create a decorative border by rotating and mirroring duplicates of original objects.

TRANSFORMING OBJECTS

Sizing an object

Sizing an object is similar to scaling it. But rather than changing dimensions by percentages, you enter *exact* dimensions for the object (for example, 6.5" x 4.75") in the Size section of the Transformation docker (**Figure 14.22**). You can set the horizontal and vertical dimensions independently or force the new dimensions to be proportional to each other.

To set the size of an object:

1. Select the object to be resized.

2. To resize the object *proportionately*, remove the checkmark from the Non-proportional check box and then enter the H (horizontal) or V (vertical) dimension. The unentered dimension is automatically increased or decreased proportionately.

   or

   To resize the object *non-proportionately* (where each dimension is independent of the other), check the Non-proportional check box and enter the H (horizontal), V (vertical), or both dimensions.

3. Click Apply to resize the selected object, or click Apply To Duplicate to resize a copy of the object.

✔ Tip

■ You can also resize or scale an object by selecting it, entering the new dimensions or percentages in the appropriate text boxes on the property bar or Transform toolbar (**Figure 14.23**), and then pressing ⎆Enter⎆. To resize or scale proportionately, the padlock icon should be raised. When the padlock icon is depressed, you can resize or scale non-proportionately.

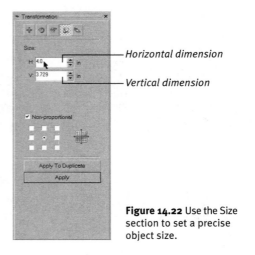

Horizontal dimension

Vertical dimension

Figure 14.22 Use the Size section to set a precise object size.

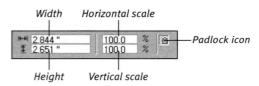

Width   Horizontal scale

Padlock icon

Height   Vertical scale

Figure 14.23 You can also resize or scale an object via the property bar or the Transform toolbar.

TRANSFORMING OBJECTS

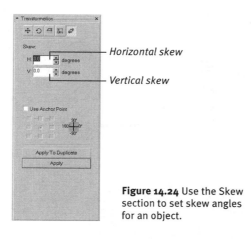

Figure 14.24 Use the Skew section to set skew angles for an object.

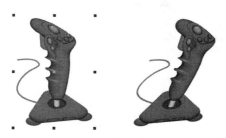

Figure 14.25 Here are normal and skewed versions of the same object.

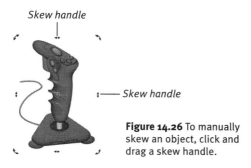

Figure 14.26 To manually skew an object, click and drag a skew handle.

Skewing an object

To *skew* an object means to tilt or slant it. You can skew an object by entering the desired horizontal and vertical angles in the Skew section of the Transformation docker (**Figure 14.24**) or by clicking and dragging a skew handle.

To skew an object using the Transformation docker:

1. Select the object to be skewed.

2. In the H (horizontal) and/or V (vertical) text boxes, enter the number of degrees you wish to skew the object. (Negative numbers skew clockwise; positive numbers skew counterclockwise.)

3. Click Apply to skew the selected object (**Figure 14.25**), or click Apply To Duplicate to skew a copy of the object.

To skew an object manually:

1. Select the object to be skewed and then click it a second time.

   Rotation and skew handles appear (**Figure 14.26**).

2. Click and drag one of the four skew handles.

3. When the desired skew has been achieved, release the mouse button.

✔ Tip

■ You can also skew an object by entering the number of horizontal and/or vertical degrees in the Skew Angle text boxes at the right end of the Transform toolbar.

TRANSFORMING OBJECTS

Shaping Objects

To open the Shaping docker, choose Window > Dockers > Shaping or Arrange > Shaping > Shaping. By choosing commands from the drop-down list at the top of the docker (**Figure 14.27**), you can combine objects in the following useful ways:

◆ **Weld.** Merge multiple objects into a single object.

◆ **Intersect.** Create new objects from the areas of overlap between objects.

◆ **Trim.** Cut out overlapping areas of multiple objects.

◆ **Simplify.** A variation of Trim in which the overlapping areas of the topmost objects are automatically cut out of the objects that they cover.

◆ **Front Minus Back** and **Back Minus Front.** Variations of Trim in which the back object is removed from the front object or the front object is removed from the back object, respectively.

Welding objects together

Welding lets you connect several objects to create one object. If you weld objects together that overlap, they bind together, creating an object with one outline. If you weld objects together that do not overlap, they create a weld group that looks like separate objects but acts like a single object. When welding, one object (called the *target object*) is used as the anchor to which the other objects (called the *source objects*) are welded.

To weld objects together:

1. Select the source objects that you want to weld to the target object (**Figure 14.28**).

2. Choose Weld from the drop-down list at the top of the Shaping docker.

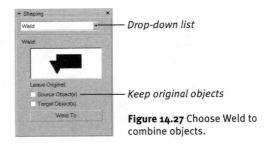

Drop-down list

Keep original objects

Figure 14.27 Choose Weld to combine objects.

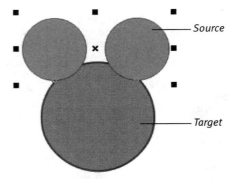

Source

Target

Figure 14.28 Select the source object(s). Note the difference in outline and fill from the target object.

Figure 14.29 The resulting welded object has a single outline. It assumes the fill and outline of the target object.

Figure 14.30 Use Trim to cut out intersecting parts of objects.

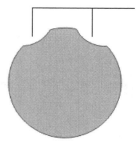

Trimmed areas

Figure 14.31 Trimming the two top circles from the large bottom circle leaves this toilet seat shape as the result.

3. *Optional:* To retain a copy of the target object, check the Target Object(s) check box. To retain copies of the source objects, check the Source Object(s) check box.

4. Click the Weld To button.

5. Click the target object.

   The selected objects weld themselves to the target object. The resulting object takes on the fill and outline of the target object (**Figure 14.29**).

✔ Tip

- If you don't need copies of the source or target options, you can perform a weld by selecting all the objects and then clicking the Weld property bar button. Note that the topmost items will automatically weld to the lower items. Thus, the lower items will determine the fill color, outline, and other properties of the resulting object.

Trimming objects

Use the Trim section of the Shaping docker (**Figure 14.30**) to cut out the intersecting parts of source object(s) from a target object.

To trim an object:

1. Select the source object(s) whose intersection(s) you want to trim from the target object (see Figure 14.28).

2. Choose Trim from the drop-down list at the top of the Shaping docker.

3. *Optional:* If you want to keep the target object, check the Target Object(s) check box. If you want to keep the source objects, check the Source Object(s) check box.

4. Click the Trim button.

5. Click the target object.

   The intersection(s) of the source objects are trimmed from the target object (**Figure 14.31**).

   continues on next page

SHAPING OBJECTS

✔ Tips

- To trim a source object from multiple target objects, check the Source Object(s) check box. After performing the initial trim, you can re-select the source object and then trim it from the second object.

- Familiarize yourself with the Simplify, Front Minus Back, and Back Minus Front choices in the Shaping docker's drop-down list. The difference between these procedures and a Trim is that you select *all* objects to which you want to apply the command, and then click the button. CorelDraw determines which objects are the source and target by their stacking order.

Intersecting objects

You can think of Intersect as the opposite of Trim. That is, rather than trim the intersections from the target, all that is left are the intersections.

To intersect objects:

1. Select the source object(s) (see Figure 14.28).

2. Select Intersect from the drop-down list at the top of the Shaping docker (**Figure 14.32**).

3. *Optional:* If you want to keep the target object, check the Target Object(s) check box. If you want to keep the source objects, check the Source Object(s) check box.

4. Click the Intersect With button.

5. Click the target object.
   The intersection(s) are created as a new object (**Figure 14.33**).

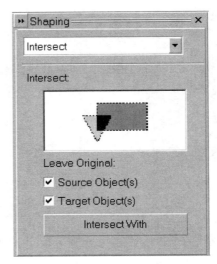

Figure 14.32 Intersect eliminates everything but the overlapping sections of a set of objects.

Figure 14.33 This new object is the intersection of the circles.

SPECIAL EFFECTS

Previous chapters showed you how to transform objects by duplicating, skewing, grouping, blending, and filling them with patterns and color. This chapter shows you how to use what you've learned in combination with some new tools to create exciting special effects.

You'll learn how to create the following effects:

- Use the Interactive Envelope Tool to create envelopes that distort an object's shape

- Use the Interactive Blend Tool to morph one object into another

- Add perspective to objects

- Use the Interactive Extrude Tool to create impressive 3D objects

- Use the PowerClip command to insert one object into another

- Use the Interactive Transparency Tool to make objects you can see through

- Use the Interactive Distortion Tool to stretch and reshape objects

- Use the new Roughen and Smudge Brushes to modify the edges of objects

- Use the Interactive Contour Tool to add contour lines to an object

- Use an object as a special-effects lens when placed over another object

- Copy and clone effects between objects

Using Envelopes

Envelopes are used to distort the shape of objects. An envelope is like a container placed around an object. The object takes the shape of the container, becoming distorted in the process. You can shape an envelope with the Shape Tool, the Interactive Envelope Tool, and the nodes that appear around the envelope. The Interactive Envelope Tool works in conjunction with property bar modes and options.

To use the Interactive Envelope Tool to shape an object:

1. Select the Interactive Envelope Tool from the Interactive Tool flyout (**Figure 15.1**).

2. Select the object you want to shape.

   A red-dashed rectangle appears around the selected object.

3. Select an envelope mode by clicking one of the following property bar icons (**Figures 15.2** and **15.3**):

   ▲ **Straight-line.** A straight line is maintained between each of the corner nodes.

   ▲ **Single-arc.** A curved line is allowed between each pair of corner nodes.

   ▲ **Double-arc.** A wavy line is allowed between each pair of corner nodes.

   ▲ **Unconstrained.** You can edit the envelope path—dragging nodes and control points—as if it were an outline drawn with the Freehand or Bézier Tool.

4. Drag the nodes with the Interactive Envelope Tool until the envelope is the desired shape.

Figure 15.1 The Interactive Envelope Tool is found on the Interactive Tool flyout.

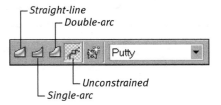

Figure 15.2 Set the mode for the envelope by clicking one of these property bar icons.

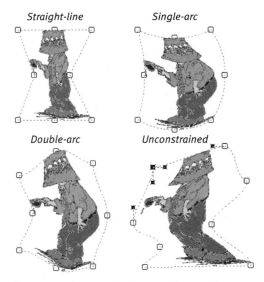

Figure 15.3 These are the four envelope modes.

Figure 15.4 An illustration (left) was placed inside of a heart outline and shaped with the Interactive Envelope Tool to match the shape of the outline (right).

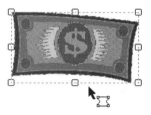

Figure 15.5 Select the object with the Interactive Envelope Tool.

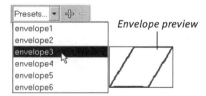

Figure 15.6 Choose an envelope shape from the Add Preset drop-down list on the property bar.

Figure 15.7 The object reshapes itself to match the envelope preset.

✔ Tips

■ If you want to put several objects in an envelope, you must group them first.

■ When working in unconstrained mode, you can add nodes, change node types, and manipulate the envelope's outline like any ordinary path by using the Shape Tool and the property bar. To learn about nodes, see Chapter 6, "Nodes and Paths."

■ You can also create envelopes that mimic a shape. In **Figure 15.4**, a heart outline was placed behind an illustration. The illustration was selected and an unconstrained mode envelope added around it. Finally, the envelope and illustration were shaped using the heart as a guide.

■ An envelope effect—like other special effects—can be copied from one object to another. See "Copying and cloning effects" at the end of this chapter for details.

Envelope presets

You can choose a *preset* to quickly apply a specific envelope shape to an object. Presets also help teach you how to create your own envelopes.

To apply a preset envelope to an object:

1. Select the Interactive Envelope Tool from the Interactive Tool flyout (see Figure 15.1).

2. Select the object to which you want to add a preset envelope shape (**Figure 15.5**).

   An envelope, represented by eight nodes connected by a dashed red line, appears around the object.

3. Choose a preset envelope shape from the Add Preset drop-down list on the property bar (**Figure 15.6**).

   The object redraws to match the envelope shape (**Figure 15.7**).

Envelope mapping mode

You may have noticed one additional drop-down list on the property bar: Mapping Mode. The chosen mapping mode affects the manner in which the object fits itself to the envelope.

To set a mapping mode for an envelope:

1. Using the Interactive Envelope Tool, select an object to which an envelope has previously been applied (**Figure 15.8**).

2. Select an option from the Mapping Mode drop-down list on the property bar (**Figure 15.9**).

3. Drag nodes to reshape the object as you wish (**Figure 15.10**).

   The object maps itself to the envelope based on the chosen mapping mode.

Figure 15.8 This object was mapped to fit into a heart.

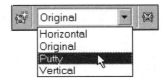

Figure 15.9 Choose a Mapping Mode setting from this drop-down list on the property bar.

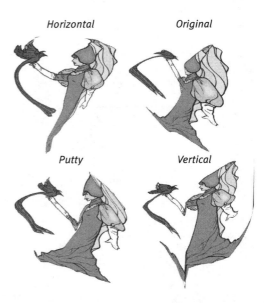

Figure 15.10 Here are the four mapping modes applied to the same object.

Figure 15.11 Select the two objects to be blended.

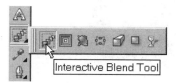

Figure 15.12 Select the Interactive Blend Tool from the toolbox.

Figure 15.13 When you release the mouse button, the objects blend.

Number of steps   *Rotation angle*

Figure 15.14 You can alter the number of blend steps or the angle by using these property bar controls.

Figure 15.15 You can also use the Interactive Blend Tool to create a series of evenly spaced copies of a single object.

Using Blends

Blends create a specific number of intermediate objects (or steps) between two selected objects. You can use a blend to quickly create multiple copies of the same object or to blend two objects together to create a morph. Blends can also be blended together to create multiple blends. Using multiple blends, you can create highlights and make objects sparkle.

To blend two objects together:

1. Use the Pick Tool to select the two objects you want to blend (**Figure 15.11**).

2. Select the Interactive Blend Tool from the Interactive Tool flyout in the toolbox (**Figure 15.12**).

3. Click the first object and drag over to the second object.
   A dashed line separated by two white boxes appears.

4. Release the mouse button.
   The blend steps appear between the two objects (**Figure 15.13**).

✔ Tips

- Using the property bar, you can increase or decrease the number of blend steps and specify whether the blend will rotate at an angle (**Figure 15.14**).

- To create a series of evenly distributed copies of an object, copy the object and then place the copy at a distance from the original. Finally, create a multistep blend between the two objects (**Figure 15.15**).

Multiple blends

When creating a multiple blend, you'll first need to draw all the objects you intend to blend. The objects can be filled with colors of your choice and then blended together one by one. This example creates a gorgeous star that has depth.

To create a multiple blend:

1. Create the objects you want to use in the multiple blend.

   In this example, four copies of a star were made. The duplicates were scaled down so they would fit inside each other.

2. Fill the objects with the colors you want to use and position them where the blends will start and end (**Figure 15.16**).

   Starting from the outermost star, the stars were filled with white, black, 50 percent black, and white, and aligned to their centers using the Align and Distribute dialog box. (See Chapter 9, "Tools for Precision," for instructions.)

3. Create blends by dragging from one star to another until you achieve the desired effect (**Figure 15.17**).

✔ Tip

■ After you have created a multiple blend, you can still change the number of steps for each individual blend. Select one of the original objects with the Pick Tool and enter a new number in the Number of Steps text box on the property bar (see Figure 15.14).

Figure 15.16 Four stars were colored and placed inside of each other.

Figure 15.17 The final object consists of three blends.

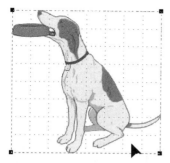

Figure 15.18 Select the object and choose Effects > Add Perspective. A grid appears over the object.

Figure 15.19 Drag one or more handles to set the perspective.

Figure 15.20 Select the Pick Tool to view the object's new perspective.

Adding Perspective

Setting an object's perspective lets you add the illusion of distance and depth.

To add perspective to an object:

1. Select the object with the Pick Tool.

2. Choose Effects > Add Perspective.
   A red, dotted grid with four handles appears (**Figure 15.18**).

3. Click and drag one or more handles to change the shape of the grid.
   As you drag, the perspective changes (**Figure 15.19**).

4. When you're done, select the Pick Tool or press (Spacebar) to see the effect (**Figure 15.20**).

✔ Tips

■ As you drag, an X will appear somewhere on the drawing page. This is the *vanishing point*. You can also drag the X to change the perspective.

■ You can simultaneously add perspective to as many objects as you want. Just group the objects before selecting them.

■ To restore an object to its original shape, select the object and choose Effects > Clear Perspective.

Extruding Objects

Rather than just changing your viewing angle of an object as the Add Perspective command does, the Interactive Extrude Tool adds dimensionality to an otherwise flat object.

To extrude an object:

1. Select the Interactive Extrude Tool from the toolbox (**Figure 15.21**).

2. Select an extrusion type from the drop-down list on the property bar (**Figure 15.22**).

   If the Extrusion Type drop-down list isn't available, make sure that no object is currently selected. (Click an empty area in the drawing window, if necessary.)

3. Select the object you want to extrude, and then click near the center of the object and drag (**Figure 15.23**).

4. Adjust the extrusion as needed by clicking and dragging the extrusion controls.

5. To complete the extrusion (**Figure 15.24**), click away from the object or select another tool.

To learn more about extruding objects, see Chapter 12, "Text Special Effects."

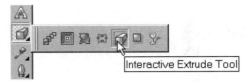

Figure 15.21 Select the Interactive Extrude Tool from the toolbox.

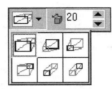

Figure 15.22 Select an extrusion type from this drop-down list on the property bar.

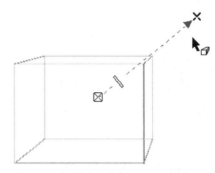

Figure 15.23 Click and drag to create the extrusion.

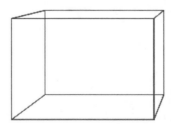

Figure 15.24 The rectangle is now a three-dimensional box.

184

Figure 15.25 We can place this bitmap image into a CorelDraw heart.

Figure 15.26 When you click the container object (heart), the contents (photo) is redrawn inside of it.

Figure 15.27 Large text can be an excellent container.

The PowerClip Command

With the PowerClip command, you can put one object inside another. One object acts as a container, while the other serves as the contents. Any part of the contents that doesn't fit within the container's path is discarded.

To PowerClip two objects:

1. Use the Pick Tool to select the object you want to use as the contents (**Figure 15.25**).

2. Choose Effects > PowerClip > Place Inside Container.

   The pointer changes to a large black arrow.

3. Click the container object.

   The contents object redraws inside the container object (**Figure 15.26**).

✔ Tips

- The container object can be any closed-path object created in CorelDraw, such as a star, polygon, or artistic text (**Figure 15.27**). The contents object can be any object created with CorelDraw or an imported object, such as a bitmap image or clip art.

- After using the PowerClip command, it's not unusual to find that the contents object is improperly centered or the wrong size. To modify the contents, select the container with the Pick Tool and choose Effects > PowerClip > Edit Contents. Make the desired changes to the contents and then click the Finish Editing Symbol button at the bottom of the drawing window.

Creating Shadowed Objects

Shadows can make drawings look more realistic, as if they were three dimensional. By following the technique described below, you can create a shadowed object filled with the same color as the background (**Figure 15.28**).

Figure 15.28 This shadowing technique creates 3D objects.

To create an object defined by its shadow:

1. Right-click a ruler and choose Ruler Setup from the pop-up menu that appears.

   The Options dialog box appears, open to the Rulers section.

2. Change the value in the Nudge text box to 0.01 inch (**Figure 15.29**) and click OK.

3. Use the Pick Tool to select the object you want to shadow (**Figure 15.30**).

4. To fill the object with color, click the desired color in the color palette. Then right-click the color well with the X in it to remove the object's outline (**Figure 15.31**).

   This example uses 30 percent black for the background and object fill.

5. Choose Edit > Copy or press Ctrl C to copy the object to the Windows Clipboard.

6. Right-click the object, and drag down and to the right. Release the mouse button when you've dragged the copy to the position where you want the outer edge of the shadow to be.

7. Choose Copy Here from the pop-up menu that appears.

8. Choose Arrange > Order > Back One.

   The copy moves behind the original object.

9. Select the original object with the Pick Tool.

Figure 15.29 Change the Nudge value to 0.01 inch.

Figure 15.30 Select the base object with the Pick Tool.

Figure 15.31 Fill the object and remove its outline.

CREATING SHADOWED OBJECTS

Figure 15.32 Set the original object's color to a few shades darker than the background.

Figure 15.33 The 40-step blend will be the shadow.

Figure 15.34 Choosing Edit > Paste creates another copy of the original object.

10. Set the original object's fill color a few shades darker than the original color (**Figure 15.32**).

This example uses a 60 percent black fill.

11. To select both objects, use the Pick Tool to drag a marquee around them.

12. Select the Interactive Blend Tool from the Interactive Tool flyout (see Figure 15.12).

13. On the property bar, set the number of steps to 40 (see Figure 15.14).

14. Click the original object, drag the pointer onto the copy, and release the mouse button.

The two objects blend together (**Figure 15.33**).

15. Select the Pick Tool, and choose Edit > Paste or press Ctrl V.

A copy of the original object appears and is selected.

16. Click the white color in the color palette to fill the copy with white.

17. Press ↑ once and then ← once to nudge the white-filled copy up and to the left to create a highlight.

Since each nudge is only 0.01 inch, you may not even notice the object move.

18. Choose Edit > Paste or press Ctrl V.

Another copy of the original object appears (**Figure 15.34**).

19. Use the Rectangle Tool to draw a rectangle that will serve as the background bounding box around the objects.

20. Fill the rectangle with the fill color you chose in Step 4.

21. Choose Arrange > Order > To Back.

22. To finish the drawing, adjust the bounding box's position as necessary (see Figure 15.28).

The Interactive Transparency Tool

You use the Interactive Transparency Tool to create transparent objects. If you place a transparent object on top of another object, the object beneath remains visible, though its appearance is changed by the see-through quality of the overlying transparency.

The Interactive Transparency Tool works like the Interactive Fill Tool (see Chapter 10), adding transparent uniform, fountain, pattern, and texture fills to objects. The fills are actually grayscale masks. A *mask* covers part of an object and restricts changes to that part.

To create a transparency:

1. Select the Interactive Transparency Tool from the toolbox (**Figure 15.35**).

2. Click the object that you want to make transparent.

3. Click where you want the transparency to start and drag to where you want it to end (**Figure 15.36**).

4. Release the mouse button.

5. As needed, adjust the transparency by moving the three control elements.

To see the effects of the transparent object, drag it over another object (**Figure 15.37**).

✔ Tips

■ The simplest way to get the desired transparency effect is to create and adjust it with the objects in place over one another.

■ Depending on the order in which the objects were created, you may have to use the Arrange > Order submenu to move the transparent object to the front.

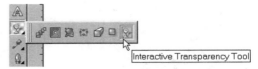

Figure 15.35 Select the Interactive Transparency Tool from the toolbox.

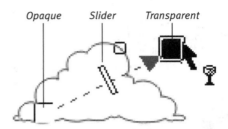

Figure 15.36 Drag the Interactive Transparency Tool to make the selected object transparent.

Figure 15.37 When placed in front of another object, the cloud's transparency becomes apparent.

THE INTERACTIVE TRANSPARENCY TOOL

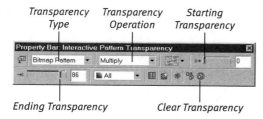

Transparency Type   *Transparency Operation*   *Starting Transparency*

Ending Transparency   *Clear Transparency*

Figure 15.38 You can choose settings from the property bar to alter the transparency. Some controls may differ, depending on the selected transparency type.

Transparency types

When you select the Interactive Transparency Tool, you can use the property bar to specify a transparency type (**Figure 15.38**). There are four transparency types from which to choose:

♦ **Uniform.** An even transparency covers the object.

♦ **Fountain.** The transparency gradually increases across the object. The types of fountain fills are linear, radial, conical, and square.

♦ **Pattern.** A transparent pattern covers the object. The types of pattern fills are two-color, full-color, and bitmap.

♦ **Texture.** A transparent texture covers the object.

Using the property bar, you can also set how a transparency's colors interact with the colors of the objects beneath the transparency.

✔ Tips

■ Experiment with the transparency types to see what kinds of effects you can create. Many types will give you a more realistic effect than the default fountain fill.

■ If you create a transparency that you don't like, click the Clear Transparency icon to start over. (Note that you can even clear the transparency of an object in a drawing that you've previously saved and reopened.)

■ For more information on the four types of fills, see Chapter 10.

THE INTERACTIVE TRANSPARENCY TOOL

Interactive Distortion Tool

You can use the Interactive Distortion Tool (**Figure 15.39**) to quickly add amazing effects to objects. There are three types of distortions: Push/Pull, Zipper, and Twister. Distortions can be applied to any CorelDraw object and to artistic text. Just like the other interactive tools, property bar options can be used to modify the distortion effects (**Figure 15.40**).

To create a push or pull distortion:

1. Select the Interactive Distortion Tool from the Interactive Tool flyout (**Figure 15.39**). A rumpled icon is attached to the pointer.

2. Click the Push/Pull Distortion icon on the property bar (**Figure 15.40**).

3. Click near the center of the object you want to distort (**Figure 15.41**) and then drag. Drag to the right to create a push distortion or drag to the left to create a pull distortion (**Figure 15.42**).

4. Release the mouse button when you are satisfied with the results.

✔ Tips

- To create a zipper or twister distortion (**Figure 15.43**), follow the same procedure, but click the appropriate icon in Step 2.

- When creating a twister distortion, drag in a clockwise or counterclockwise direction.

- As is the case with many of the interactive tools, the property bar contains a selection of preset distortions that you can apply by choosing them from the Preset List.

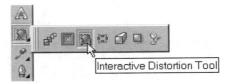

Figure 15.39 Select the Interactive Distortion Tool from the toolbox.

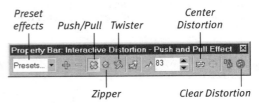

Figure 15.40 Select a distortion type and set options using the property bar.

Figure 15.41 Move the Interactive Distortion Tool over the object you want to distort.

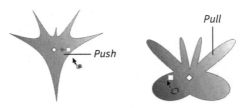

Figure 15.42 Drag to the right to create a push distortion or to the left to create a pull distortion.

Figure 15.43 Zipper (left) and twister (right) examples.

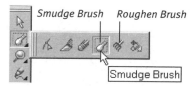

Figure 15.44 Select the Smudge Brush or Roughen Brush from the toolbox.

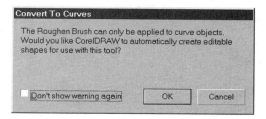

Figure 15.45 The Smudge and Roughen Brushes can only be applied to curve objects.

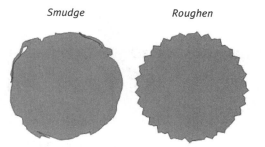

Smudge   *Roughen*

Figure 15.46 These examples show the results of applying the Smudge and Roughen Brushes to a circle.

Using the Smudge and Roughen Brushes

Tired of shapes with perfectly smooth edges? The new Smudge and Roughen Brushes enable you to add some imperfections to object outlines. Either tool can be used with a mouse or a drawing tablet.

To smudge or roughen a line or outline:

1. Select the Smudge Brush or the Roughen Brush from the Shape Edit flyout on the toolbox (**Figure 15.44**).

2. Set the size of the tool in the Nib Size text box on the property bar.

    The larger the nib size, the greater the distortion created.

3. Click the line or object that you want to distort.

4. If the selected object isn't a curve object, the Convert To Curves dialog box appears (**Figure 15.45**). Click OK to convert the object to curves.

5. Drag the tool around the object's edges.

    The object is distorted (**Figure 15.46**).

✔ Tip

- When you're using a drawing tablet, both tools respond to differences in pressure and the angle at which the pen is held. These and other settings can be modified by choosing property bar options (even if you're using a mouse). For instructions, refer to these Help topics: "To smudge an object" and "To roughen an object."

The Interactive Contour Tool

When you add contours to an object with the Interactive Contour Tool, CorelDraw uses the object's outline to create *contour lines*. You can set the offset, color, and direction of the contours. The three types of contours are to the center, inside, and outside of the object (**Figure 15.47**).

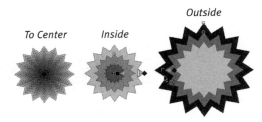

Figure 15.47 These are the three types of contours—all created from the same original object.

To add contours to an object:

1. Select the Interactive Contour Tool from the Interactive Tool flyout (**Figure 15.48**).

2. Click the object.

3. Click one of the three contour effect type icons on the property bar (**Figure 15.49**).

   or

   Drag towards the center of the object to create an inside contour or away from the object to create an outside contour.

4. *Optional:* Drag the control slider (within the object) to change the number of steps.

Figure 15.48 Select the Interactive Contour Tool from the toolbox.

Property bar settings

When you select the Contour Tool, the property bar changes to show contour options. After selecting the contoured object with the Pick Tool or the Interactive Contour Tool, you can do the following:

- Specify a different contour offset in the Contour Offset text box.

- Choose contour fill and outline colors.

- Change the number of steps for an inside or outside contour by typing a number in the Contour Steps text box.

- Alter the object or color acceleration for a contour (**Figure 15.50**).

- Choose pre-designed contours from the Preset List.

- Remove the contour effect by clicking the Clear Contour icon.

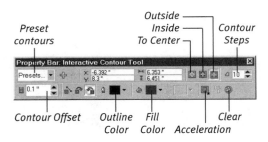

Figure 15.49 You can pick a contour type and adjust other contour settings on the property bar.

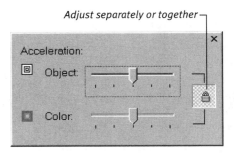

Figure 15.50 You can adjust the acceleration of the object and/or the color in the drop-down Acceleration box.

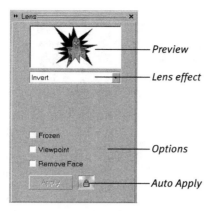

Figure 15.51 The Lens docker.

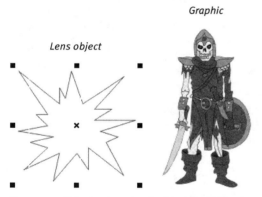

Figure 15.52 Select a closed-path object that will act as the lens.

Figure 15.53 This is an example of the Invert lens effect.

The Lens Docker

The Lens docker lets you simulate camera lens effects, such as fish-eye, magnify, brightening, and transparency. You can select any closed-path object (such as a square, star, or artistic text object) to be used as the lens. When the lens object is moved over any other image, you see its effect.

To add a lens effect to a graphic:

1. To open the Lens docker (**Figure 15.51**), choose Window > Dockers > Lens, choose Effects > Lens, or press Alt F3 .

2. Using the Pick Tool, select the object that is going to become the lens (**Figure 15.52**) and drag it onto the graphic that will be viewed through it.

3. Select a lens effect from the drop-down list on the Lens docker.

4. Click Apply.
   The lens graphic redraws, showing the visual effect on the graphic beneath it (**Figure 15.53**).

✔ Tip

■ If the Auto Apply button is in the down position, each lens effect is applied the moment you choose it. There's no need to click the Apply button—it's grayed out.

Copying and Cloning Effects

If you've struggled to get just the right effect for an object, you'll be happy to learn that you can easily transfer that effect to other objects in your drawing by copying or cloning it.

Copying an effect simply applies it to the second object. *Cloning* has the same result but creates a link between the object to which the effect is applied and the original (or master) object. Effects that can be copied are perspective, envelope, blend, extrude, contour, lens, PowerClip, drop shadow, and distortion. The effects that can be cloned are blend, extrude, contour, and drop shadow.

To copy or clone an effect:

1. Using the Pick Tool, select the destination object (**Figure 15.54**).

2. Choose Effects > Copy Effect or Effects > Clone Effect, followed by the specific property you want to copy or clone (such as Contour From).

   A large black arrow appears (**Figure 15.55**).

3. Click the object whose effect you want to copy or clone.

   The effect is applied to the destination object (**Figure 15.56**).

✔ Tip

■ The effects listed in the Copy Effect and Clone Effect submenus are limited to the ones that are in use by objects in the current drawing.

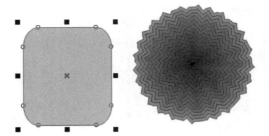

Figure 15.54 Select the object that will receive the copied or cloned effect (the round rectangle, in this instance).

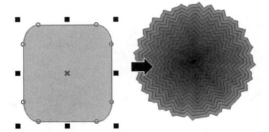

Figure 15.55 Click the object whose effect will be copied or cloned.

Figure 15.56 The effect is copied or cloned to the destination object.

SYMBOLS, CLIP ART, & BITMAPS

In this chapter, you'll learn how to perform the following tasks:

- ◆ Insert symbol characters (such as foreign characters, bullets, and Dingbats) into text, place symbols as independent objects, and create symbols from your own objects

- ◆ Use the Scrapbook docker to insert clip art, photos, and bitmap images into your documents

- ◆ Convert vector objects into bitmaps and vice versa

- ◆ Embellish bitmap images using filters and correct them using a variety of controls

- ◆ Acquire bitmap images from connected external sources, such as digital cameras, desktop video cameras, and scanners

Characters and Symbols

CorelDraw 11 changes the way you'll deal with characters and symbols, separating the two. To work with characters (whether they are text, numbers, or Dingbat-style objects), you'll use the new Insert Text docker. Reusable symbols are now stored and organized in document-specific collections in the Library docker. (Note that text characters can *still* be stored as symbols.)

Working with Symbols

In CorelDraw, you can add symbol characters to your documents from fonts such as Wingdings and Zapf Dingbats. And you can take any graphic that you've created and store it in a library for reuse.

Inserting symbol characters into a document

There are two ways that a symbol character—or any other text character, such as a number or foreign language character—can be added to a document: embedded within artistic or paragraph text or placed as a separate object. Within text, symbols can be colored and formatted with the same commands used for other text characters. When placed as objects, symbols can be colored, resized, skewed, and manipulated like any other object.

To insert symbol characters:

1. Choose Text > Insert Character or press Ctrl F11.

   The Insert Character docker opens (**Figure 16.1**).

2. Select a font from the drop-down list.

3. Scroll down until you find the symbol you want. Select a symbol.

4. To add a symbol to your document as a separate graphic object, click the symbol and drag it into the drawing area (**Figure 16.2**) or click the Insert button.

   or

   To add a symbol as text to an existing text string, position the insertion marker within the text string and double-click the symbol in the docker window (**Figure 16.3**) or click the Insert button.

✔ Tip

- You can set the size of a symbol using the Character Size text box.

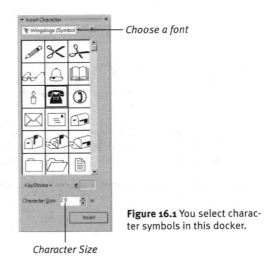
Choose a font

Character Size

Figure 16.1 You select character symbols in this docker.

Figure 16.2 When symbols are placed as objects, you can embellish them by adding a drop shadow, a texture, or color, for example.

You can freely add symbols (such as ♦, ☎, and ●) within any normal text.

Figure 16.3 You can embed symbols within artistic or paragraph text.

Figure 16.4 You can preview and install additional fonts using the included Bitstream Font Navigator.

Selected object   *Library docker*

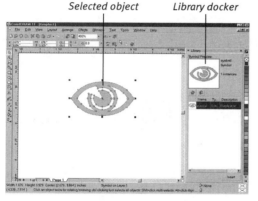

Figure 16.5 Select an object in the drawing window and then add it to the document's library.

More Symbol Fonts

You can find many additional symbol fonts in the Extra Fonts\Symbols folder on Disc 2. To examine or install these fonts, use the Bitstream Font Navigator program (**Figure 16.4**).

Creating your own symbols

If a drawing uses the same object repeatedly, you can reduce the document's size by storing the object as a reusable symbol. Any changes made to a stored symbol are automatically reflected in all instances of the symbol.

All instances of a symbol need not be identical; you can alter an instance's size, skew, rotation, or mirroring, for example. And although each document has its own unique symbol library, you can copy symbols between documents.

To store an object as a symbol:

1. Open the document's symbol library by choosing Edit > Symbol > Library.

2. Use the Pick Tool to select the object that you want to turn into a symbol.

3. *Do one of the following:*

   ▲ Choose Edit > Symbol > New Symbol.

   ▲ Right-click the object and choose Symbol > New Symbol from the pop-up menu.

   ▲ Drag the object into the Library docker.
   The object is added as a new symbol (**Figure 16.5**).

4. *Optional:* You can add a name and/or a description for the symbol. Click in the appropriate text box, type the name or description, and press (Enter).

✔ Tips

■ Virtually any object—as well as multiple objects—can be stored as a symbol. For a list of ineligible objects, refer to "symbols: unsupported object types" in Help.

■ To add a symbol instance to a drawing, drag the symbol into the drawing area, or select the symbol in the Library and click Insert.

WORKING WITH SYMBOLS

To edit a stored symbol:

1. Select the symbol in the Library docker (**Figure 16.6**).

2. Click the Edit Symbol button above the symbol list.

3. Make any desired changes to the symbol.

4. Click the Finish Editing Symbol button at the bottom of the document window.

   All instances of the symbol change to match the edited symbol.

✔ Tips

■ If you want to change a property of a symbol instance that normally isn't allowed (such as its color), right-click the instance and choose Revert to Objects from the pop-up menu. Or select the instance and choose Edit > Symbol > Revert to Objects.

■ To delete an unneeded symbol, select it in the Library docker and click the Delete Symbol button above the symbol list.

To copy a symbol between documents:

1. Open the CorelDraw document that contains the symbol you want to copy.

2. Open the document's symbol library by choosing Edit > Symbol > Library.

3. Select the symbol in the Library and choose Edit > Copy (or press Ctrl C). You can also right-click the symbol and choose Copy from the pop-up menu.

4. Paste the symbol into the drawing window of the destination document.

   An instance of the symbol appears in the drawing, and it is automatically added to the document's Library.

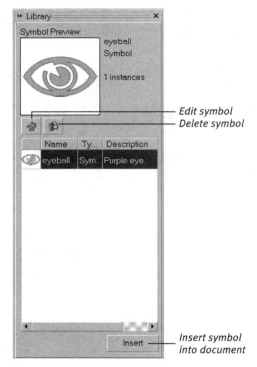

Edit symbol
Delete symbol

Insert symbol
into document

Figure 16.6 The Library docker.

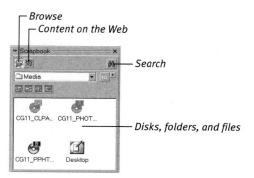

Browse
Content on the Web
Search
Disks, folders, and files

Figure 16.7 Select a file to insert from the Scrapbook docker.

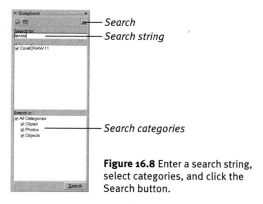

Search
Search string
Search categories

Figure 16.8 Enter a search string, select categories, and click the Search button.

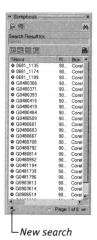

New search

Figure 16.9 Use the Search function to find a particular type of image.

Using the Scrapbook Docker

You can use the Scrapbook docker to insert clip art, photos, and other bitmap images from the CorelDraw 11 CDs or your hard disk into your documents.

To insert clip art or bitmap images:

1. Insert Disc 3, 4, or 5 into your CD-ROM drive, if necessary.

2. Choose Tools > Scrapbook > Browse or Window > Dockers > Scrapbook > Browse. The Scrapbook docker opens (**Figure 16.7**).

3. Use the file window the same way you would Windows Explorer. Double-click the drive and folder icons until you find the desired clip art, photo, or other image.

4. When you find an image that you want to use, drag it into your document and release the mouse button.

✔ Tips

- Clip art inserted in this fashion is grouped. To work with it, you'll usually want to ungroup it first.

- You can search for art on the CorelDraw 11 CDs. Click the Search icon at the top of the Scrapbook (**Figure 16.8**), enter search text (such as "coffee"), and click the Search button. The name and CD for each matching image are displayed (**Figure 16.9**). In Details view, a green circle preceding a file name means that the correct CD is already in the drive. A red circle means that you'll be prompted to insert the correct CD if you attempt to import the image.

- To find images, you can also flip through the new *Digital Content Manual*.

- To view and download clip art from Corel's Web site, click the Content on the Web icon at the top of the Scrapbook docker (**Figure 16.7**).

Working with Bitmap Images

In the real world, all images begin as bitmaps. Whether they are scans or digital photos, images are composed of dots (called *pixels*). While CorelDraw will let you insert bitmap images into your vector drawings—treating them as large, complex objects—you can use CorelDraw tools to freely convert bitmaps to objects or objects to bitmap images.

To convert a vector object to a bitmap:

1. Select the object you want to convert.

2. Choose Bitmaps > Convert to Bitmap. The Convert to Bitmap dialog box opens (**Figure 16.10**).

3. Select a color model and a resolution from the drop-down lists.

4. Check the Anti-aliasing check box and the Dithered check box (if available).

   For a smoother look, *anti-aliasing* blends pixels at the boundaries between colors. In drawings that contain blends or fountain fills, *dithering* smooths the transition between colors.

5. If the bitmap will be set on a background that you want to shine through, click the Transparent Background check box.

6. Click OK to convert the object to a bitmap (**Figure 16.11**).

✔ Tips

- The converted image may be of lesser quality than the original. Lines may look "dotty," for example. If this is unacceptable, try another resolution or color model.

- When choosing a color model and resolution, note that the higher the settings, the larger the file will be when it's saved.

- If you think you'll need the vector, save a copy of it before converting to a bitmap or use the Undo docker to recover it.

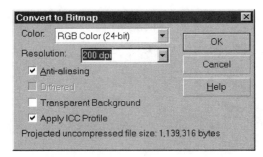

Figure 16.10 Select output settings in the Convert to Bitmap dialog box.

Figure 16.11 Differences in line quality can be noticeable since the lines in a bitmap are created with pixels. Look at the newspaper, for instance.

Color Model and Resolution

Your choices of color model and resolution depend on what you intend to do with the resulting image. If you're not sure of the best choices, choose CMYK for color printing, RGB for onscreen display, and Grayscale for non-color printing. For onscreen display on a Macintosh, set the resolution to 72 dpi; for Windows display, use 96 dpi. For printed output, use a setting between 150 and 300 dpi, depending on your printer's capabilities and the quality you desire or need.

Figure 16.12 Bitmaps with areas of high contrast convert best.

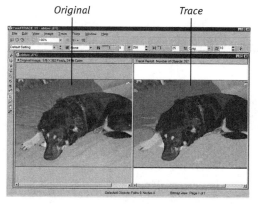

Original   *Trace*

Figure 16.13 CorelTrace 11 displays the original bitmap on the left and the resulting trace on the right.

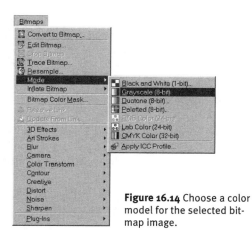

Figure 16.14 Choose a color model for the selected bitmap image.

To convert a bitmap to vector objects:

1. Select the bitmap image (**Figure 16.12**) with the Pick Tool.

2. Choose Bitmaps > Trace Bitmap. CorelTrace 11 launches and opens a copy of the selected bitmap image (**Figure 16.13**).

3. Select a tracing method from the Trace menu. If you want to use a Centerline method, you must first convert the image by choosing Image > Mode > Black and White.

4. Quit CorelTrace, or choose File > Close.

5. When prompted, click Yes to save the changes. When you return to CorelDraw, a grouped set of objects from the tracing appears on top of the original bitmap. To work with the resulting trace, you can drag it off the bitmap and/or ungroup the objects.

Choosing a color model

Many filters on the Bitmaps menu aren't available unless the selected bitmap is converted to a color model. (Color models are discussed in Chapter 10, "Color and Fills.") As explained previously in this chapter, the color model you choose depends on what you want to do with the image.

To convert a bitmap image from one color model to another:

1. Select the bitmap with the Pick Tool.

2. Choose Bitmaps > Mode, followed by your choice of color model (**Figure 16.14**).

WORKING WITH BITMAP IMAGES

Using bitmap filters

Bitmap filters enable you to create special effects, such as blurring and distortions. All you need to do is choose a filter from the Bitmaps menu and move the controls in the dialog box that appears. To get you started, three examples are presented: imposing a spherical or fish-eye effect, adding noise to make a bitmap resemble a photo taken with high-speed film, and creating a photo vignette.

To add a spherical effect to a bitmap:

1. Select a bitmap with the Pick Tool.

2. Choose Bitmaps > 3D Effects > Sphere. The Sphere dialog box appears (**Figure 16.15**).

3. Click an Optimize radio button and drag the Percentage slider to create the effect. (Drag to the right for a fish-eye effect; drag to the left for an inverse sphere effect.)

4. Click the Preview button.

5. If you like the effect, click OK (**Figure 16.16**); otherwise, click Reset to restore the bitmap to its original form.

Show/hide preview in dialog box
Quality setting

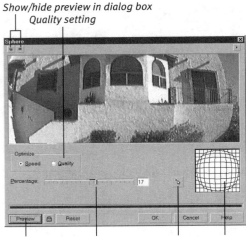

Create preview   Slider   Set center point   Shape

Figure 16.15 Experiment with and preview the effects in the Sphere dialog box.

Figure 16.16 The image shows the effect of increasing the sphere, producing a fish-eye effect.

WORKING WITH BITMAP IMAGES

Original   Preview

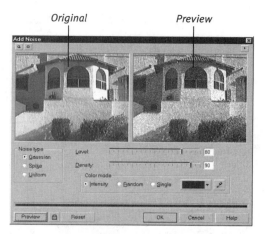

Figure 16.17 If you click the buttons in the top-left corner of the dialog box, you can view just the original or both the original and preview.

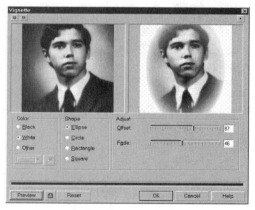

Figure 16.18 The vignette (right) is a popular way to present photos.

To add noise to a bitmap:

1. Select a bitmap with the Pick Tool.

2. Choose Bitmaps > Noise > Add Noise. The Add Noise dialog box opens (**Figure 16.17**).

3. Set the amount of noise by dragging the Level and Density sliders.

4. Select a noise type: Gaussian, Spike, or Uniform. Each of these mathematical noise formulas generates a different type of dot pattern.

5. Click the Preview button.

6. If you like the effect, click OK; otherwise, click Reset to restore the bitmap to its original form.

To create a vignette:

1. Select a bitmap with the Pick Tool.

2. Choose Bitmaps > Creative > Vignette. The Vignette dialog box opens (**Figure 16.18**).

3. Set the color and shape of the vignette by clicking the appropriate radio buttons.

4. Adjust the Offset and Fade sliders to set the amount of image that is visible and the amount that the edges fade.

5. Click the Preview button.

6. If you like the effect, click OK; otherwise, click Reset to restore the bitmap to its original form.

Acquiring Images

CorelDraw 11 can acquire images directly from a connected scanner, digital camera, or desktop video camera. The images are placed directly into the drawing window, ready for you to add personal touches and effects. However, before you can download (or *acquire*) images, you'll need to install your image source's software and tell CorelDraw what device you have.

To configure CorelDraw to use a connected image source:

1. Make sure that the camera or scanner is correctly connected to your computer and then turn on the device.

2. Choose File > Acquire Image > Select Source. The Select Source dialog box appears, listing all properly connected and configured video capture sources (**Figure 16.19**).

3. Select your device from the Sources list and click OK.

To acquire an image from your device:

1. Turn on the device, if it has an external switch. (Many devices are controlled directly by your computer.)

2. Choose File > Acquire Image > Acquire. A dialog box specific to the capabilities of your device appears (**Figure 16.20**).

3. Make any necessary adjustments by clicking buttons or using any other presented controls.

4. Click the button to acquire the image. (The button's name may vary according to the chosen device.)

The dialog box closes and the picture appears in the drawing window. You can now export the image for use in another program or on the Web, or add special effects and enhancements using the various bitmap filters.

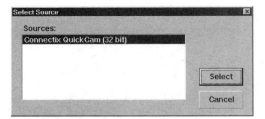

Figure 16.19 Select the appropriate image source from the Sources list and click OK.

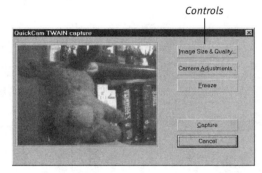

Figure 16.20 Make any desired adjustments by clicking buttons, and then click the button to acquire the image.

ACQUIRING IMAGES

Figure 16.21 Adjust the three sliders and click the Preview button to see the effects of your changes.

Touching up an acquired image

Once an image has been acquired or imported into CorelDraw, you can improve its quality by adjusting its brightness, contrast, hue, and saturation. Here's what these terms mean:

◆ *Brightness* refers to a photo's lightness or darkness.

◆ *Contrast* is the amount of difference between the light and dark areas.

◆ *Hue* is a color in a photo, such as red, green, or blue.

◆ *Saturation* refers to a hue's strength or purity. For instance, a lightly saturated red appears pink, whereas full saturation appears red.

To adjust the brightness or contrast:

1. Use the Pick Tool to select the image you want to adjust.

2. Choose Effects > Adjust > Brightness-Contrast-Intensity.

   The Brightness-Contrast-Intensity dialog box appears (**Figure 16.21**).

3. Use the three sliders to modify the settings.

4. Click Preview to see the effects of your changes.

   A preview of the effects is shown in the drawing window or in the dialog box.

5. When you are satisfied with the adjustments, click OK to close the dialog box.

   continues on next page

✔ Tips

- Adjusting an image's hue, saturation, and lightness is done in the same fashion using a very similar dialog box (**Figure 16.22**). In the Channels section of the dialog box, click the radio button for the color you want to adjust. To adjust all colors at the same time, click the Master radio button.

- Certain types of images (especially scans) can also benefit from being sharpened. CorelDraw has several sharpening tools with which you can experiment in the Bitmaps > Sharpen submenu.

- If you don't feel comfortable making the kinds of adjustments suggested in these procedures, you may want to try the Effects > Adjust > Auto Equalize command.

- To really fine-tune an image's contrast, choose the Effects > Adjust > Contrast Enhancement command (**Figure 16.23**). If you've used Adobe Photoshop, you may notice the similarity to its Levels command.

- While these commands are frequently used with acquired images, they can also be used to adjust *any* bitmap image.

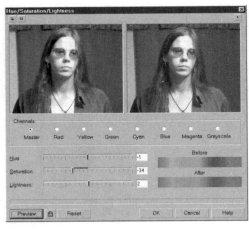

Figure 16.22 Hue, saturation, and lightness adjustments can be made color-by-color or for all colors at the same time (Master).

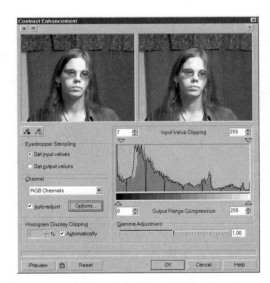

Figure 16.23 Although the Contrast Enhancement dialog box is one of the more complex ones in CorelDraw, it provides excellent tools for correcting contrast problems.

CORELDRAW AND THE WEB

17

The World Wide Web is a train with stops at every house that has a phone line or cable, modem, and computer. More people catch the Internet express every day, surfing and creating Web pages. With CorelDraw 11 and its Internet tools, you can jump on board and create your own Web site. There's no need for a separate Web design program.

This chapter will take you through the basics of creating a Web page. You'll learn how to do the following:

- Change the default ruler and resolution settings and load browser color palettes in preparation for creating a Web page
- Add text and graphics to a Web page
- Create rollover graphics
- Optimize graphics for display on the Web
- Add bookmarks and hyperlinks
- Convert your CorelDraw document pages into Web pages

World Wide Web Terms

Here are a handful of Internet/Web terms you should know:

alternate text Text that appears in the position where a graphic will be while the graphic loads. Normally, it identifies the graphic, such as *Assassination of Kennedy*. Because some Web graphics can be very large, providing alternate text enables users to decide whether to wait for the image to load.

browser A program that decodes the information for the Web pages you see on your monitor. The dominant browsers are Microsoft Internet Explorer (**Figure 17.1**) and Netscape Navigator.

HTML (HyperText Markup Language) The language in which Web pages are created.

link (hyperlink) Words or graphics on a Web page that—when clicked—transport you to another Web site, another page in the current Web site, or to another spot on the same page (**Figure 17.2**).

map A URL assigned to a graphic or text string, creating a link to another site or page.

URL (Uniform Resource Locator) An address for a Web page. An example of a URL is *http://www.peachpit.com*. To view a Web page, you can type its URL in your browser's Address box (**Figure 17.3**).

Web server A computer connected to the Web that *serves* Web pages to the computer users who wish to view the pages. When you click a link for a Web page that's available on a particular server, the data is transmitted from the server over the Internet to your computer.

World Wide Web An international system for linking text, graphics, and multimedia documents on the Internet.

Figure 17.1 Modern browsers can display the text, graphics, and multimedia from the World Wide Web.

Figure 17.2 When you move the cursor over a text or graphic link, it changes to a pointing hand to let you know that you can click it.

Figure 17.3 Whether you type, paste, or click a link for a URL, it appears in the browser's Address box.

Help with Internet Explorer

For help using and configuring Internet Explorer 5, check out *Internet Explorer 5 for Windows: Visual QuickStart Guide*. The book also provides extensive coverage of Outlook Express, Microsoft's companion email program.

WORLD WIDE WEB TERMS

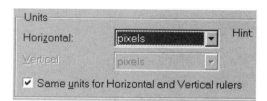

Figure 17.4 Set pixels as the unit for both the horizontal and vertical rulers.

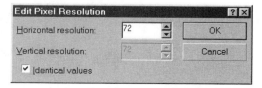

Figure 17.5 Set the horizontal and vertical resolution to 72 dpi or 96 dpi.

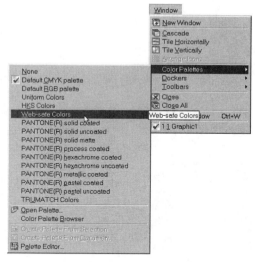

Figure 17.6 To ensure that the colors users see on your Web pages are true to your choices, use the Web-safe Colors color palette.

CorelDraw Web Settings

Since the Web is a visual medium, CorelDraw's settings should be based on a Web browser displayed on a computer monitor rather than a printed page. A monitor uses pixels as its unit of measure and a screen resolution of 72 or 96 dpi (dots per inch). (A dot equals a pixel.) It is equally important to restrict yourself to Web-safe colors that browsers can display well.

To change the rulers to pixels and set the resolution:

1. Right-click a ruler and choose Ruler Setup from the pop-up menu that appears.
   The Options dialog box opens with the Rulers heading selected.

2. In the Units section of the dialog box (**Figure 17.4**), select pixels from the Horizontal drop-down list.

3. Check the Same units for Horizontal and Vertical rulers check box.

4. Click the Resolution button.
   The Edit Pixel Resolution dialog box appears (**Figure 17.5**).

5. Set the Horizontal resolution to 72 or 96, and be sure that the Identical values check box is checked.

6. Click OK to return to the Options dialog box.

7. Click OK.
   The rulers change to show pixels.

To open the Web-safe Colors palette:

◆ Choose Window > Color Palettes > Web-safe Colors (**Figure 17.6**).

✔ Tip

■ While designing Web pages, you might want to temporarily close any other color palettes to avoid using them by mistake.

Adding a Page Background

A good place to start when designing a Web page is to add a background color or image. Images used as backgrounds on a Web page are usually *tiled*, meaning that the image is repeated seamlessly across and down the page.

To set a color or tiled image as the page background:

1. Choose Tools > Options or press `Ctrl` `J`. The Options dialog box opens.

2. Expand the categories to allow you to select the Document > Page > Background heading.

3. Click the Print and Export Background check box.

4. To use a solid color as the background, click the Solid radio button and pick a color from the drop-down palette (**Figure 17.7**).

   or

   To use a tiled image as the background, click the Bitmap radio button and then click Browse. In the Import dialog box (**Figure 17.8**), navigate to the drive/folder that contains the image you want to use, select the image, and click Import. In the Source area of the Options > Background dialog box, click the Embedded radio button.

5. Click OK to close the Options dialog box. The solid color or tiled image you chose appears on the page (**Figure 17.9**).

✔ Tip

■ If you decide to use an image as the background, pick an uncluttered one that won't prevent people from reading the text on the page. As **Figure 17.9** shows, you can use *any* compatible image as a page background. Some, however, work better than others (depending on what material you intend to place on the background).

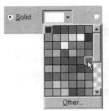

Figure 17.7 Select a solid color from this drop-down palette, or click Other to pick a custom color.

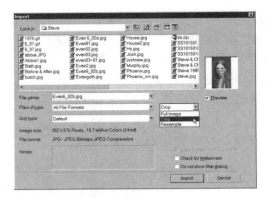

Figure 17.8 Select a background pattern from your hard disk or a CD. You can crop or *resample* (resize or change the resolution) of the image by choosing an option from the pull-down menu.

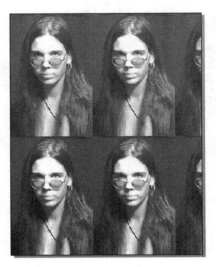

Figure 17.9 The selected background appears on your page.

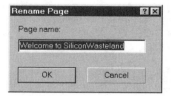

Figure 17.10 The title that you give your Web page will be displayed in the browser's title bar when the page is viewed.

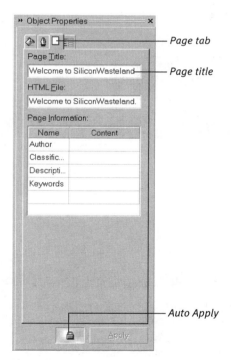

Figure 17.11 The fastest way to name or rename a Web page is to use the Rename Page dialog box.

Page tab

Page title

Auto Apply

Figure 17.12 You can also name a Web page on the Page tab of the Object Properties docker.

Naming a Web Page

Besides its file name, every Web page should also have a title. When the page is viewed in a browser, the title appears in the title bar (**Figure 17.10**).

To give a title to a Web page:

1. Move to the page to which you want to assign a title.

2. Choose Layout > Rename Page.
   The Rename Page dialog box appears (**Figure 17.11**).

3. Type the title in the Page name text box.

4. Click OK to close the dialog box.

✔ Tips

■ Because Web page titles are so prominent, you should choose them carefully.

■ You can also name/rename a page in the Object Properties docker. Right-click the document page and select Properties from the pop-up menu that appears. The Object Properties docker opens. Click the Page tab (**Figure 17.12**), and type the title in the Page Title text box.

   If Auto Apply is enabled, the page will automatically be named or renamed when you press (Enter) or when you tab or click out of the text box. Otherwise, click the Apply button to name or rename the page.

NAMING A WEB PAGE

Adding Text to a Web Page

To add text to your Web page, select the Text Tool, drag a paragraph text frame, and then type. (Creating paragraph text is discussed in Chapter 11, "Working with Text.") In order for text to export to the Web correctly, it must be both paragraph text *and* HTML compatible.

To make text HTML compatible:

◆ Use the Pick Tool to select the paragraph text frame. Choose Text > Make Text Web Compatible.

◆ Right-click the paragraph text frame, and select Make Text Web Compatible from the pop-up menu (**Figure 17.13**).

   or

◆ Choose Tools > Options and select the Workspace > Text > Paragraph heading. Check the option to Make all new paragraph text frames Web compatible.

✔ Tips

■ The size of Web text isn't measured in points. HTML text sizes range from 1 (smallest) to 7 (largest). After making a block of text HTML compatible, you'll note a new drop-down list on the property bar—the HTML Font Size List (**Figure 17.14**). To set the size for selected text, choose a size from this drop-down list.

■ You can format text using any fonts in your computer. However, if a person viewing the page doesn't also have that font installed, the text will appear in a default font (such as Times-Roman).

■ HTML also supports boldface, italic, underlined, and colored text.

■ Any text block that hasn't been designated as Web compatible will be stored on the Web page as a graphic. While this assures that the text will appear as you intended, it also increases the page's download time.

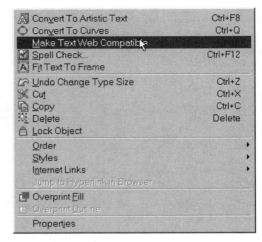

Figure 17.13 To ensure that proper fonts, sizing, and formatting are applied to the selected text block, choose Make Text Web Compatible.

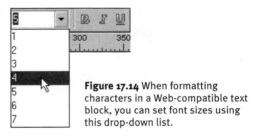

Figure 17.14 When formatting characters in a Web-compatible text block, you can set font sizes using this drop-down list.

Visit the Web Without a Browser

If there's a piece of information you need, but you don't feel like launching a browser, you can use the Web Connector docker to connect to the Internet and view Web pages. Just type a URL into the docker's text box and press [Enter] to fetch the Web page. Because the docker window is tiny, you may wish to undock it and expand the window.

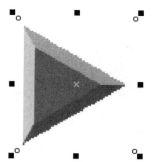

Figure 17.15 Select the image that you want to convert into a rollover graphic.

Adding Graphics to a Page

Graphics make Web pages visually interesting while helping to convey your message. With CorelDraw, you can create your own images, use ones from the included clip art library, or import images from other sources.

Normally, Web graphics must either be in GIF, JPEG, or PNG format. However, CorelDraw automatically converts other types of images to these formats when you convert your document to Web pages. So feel free to add images regardless of their file format.

If you want to use CorelDraw 11 to create graphics for use in other Web page editors (such as Adobe GoLive), you can export the images as GIF, JPEG, or PNG files. (For instruction on exporting files, see Chapter 2.)

To add a graphic to a Web page, use normal CorelDraw techniques, such as creating your own image, inserting images from the Scrapbook docker, or importing them via the File > Import command.

Creating Rollover Graphics

You've probably seen those nifty buttons that light up or display text when the cursor passes over them. These objects are called *rollover graphics*, and you can create them entirely within CorelDraw 11.

Each rollover has three states: *normal* (when no mouse activity is associated with the button); *over* (when the cursor passes over the button); and *down* (when the button is clicked).

To create a rollover graphic:

1. Create, import, or insert an object that will serve as the button (**Figure 17.15**).

2. Select the object and choose Effects > Rollover > Create Rollover.
   CorelDraw 11 transforms the object into a three-state rollover.

continues on next page

Web Graphic File Formats

Both JPEG and GIF are compressed file formats that represent images with minimal loss of detail. The *JPEG* format is ideal for photographs. When you export a graphic as a JPEG, you can set the graphic's compression. Less compression results in a larger file and longer load times. Keep the compression as high as possible (without sacrificing image quality) to minimize the file size.

The *GIF* format is typically used for black-and-white art, line drawings, and images with 256 or fewer colors. A special feature of this format is that you can create interlaced images. An *interlaced GIF* is displayed in the browser in chunks, similar to the way a vertical blind closes. You can also make *transparent GIFs*, where certain areas of the image let the background pattern or color show through.

PNG (Portable Network Graphics) is a relatively new "lossless" graphic format that offers high compression, 24-bit color, transparent backgrounds, and interlacing.

ADDING GRAPHICS TO A PAGE

3. Choose Effects > Rollover > Edit Rollover.

The drawing window changes as shown in **Figure 17.16.**

4. Click the Over tab and make the necessary changes to represent what the user should see when the cursor is passed over the button (**Figure 17.17**).

5. Click the Down tab and make the necessary changes to represent what the user should see when the button is clicked (**Figure 17.17**).

6. When you're done, click the Finish editing Rollover tab.

7. To preview the rollover, choose View > Enable Rollover. Test the rollover by moving the cursor over it and clicking it. Choose View > Enable Rollover again when you're through testing.

Exporting the rollover graphic

To use the rollover in a Web page, you must export it as an HTML or Flash object. Note that HTML has greater compatibility, since Flash objects only work if the person has the Flash plug-in installed for his or her browser.

To publish a rollover as an HTML object:

1. Select the rollover graphic and choose File > Publish To The Web > HTML.

The Publish To The Web dialog box appears (**Figure 17.18**). No Issues should be listed.

2. In the Export Range section of the General tab, click the Selection radio button.

3. *Optional:* To make sure that the rollover works properly, click the Browser Preview button to test the button in your browser.

4. In the Destination box, select a folder in which to store the HTML/JavaScript file. (The three button state images will be stored in an Images subfolder.)

5. Click OK to export the rollover as HTML.

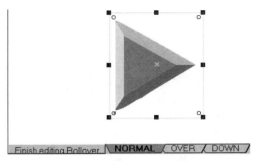

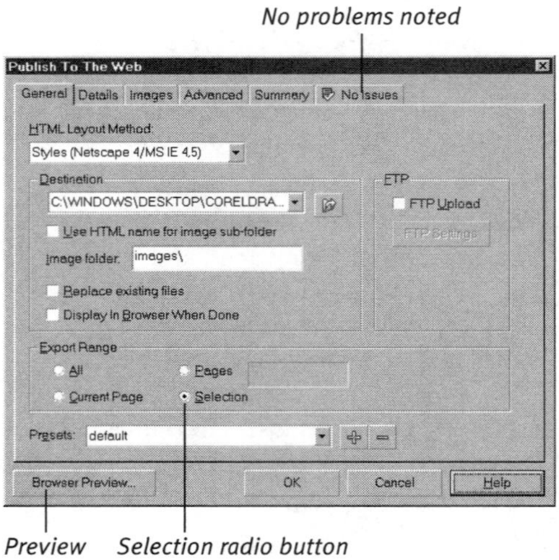

Figure 17.16 Each of the three tabs on the right represents one of the button states.

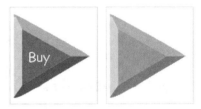

Figure 17.17 These images show the over (left) and down (right) states.

No problems noted

Figure 17.18 Use the Publish To The Web dialog box to export rollover to HTML with embedded JavaScript code.

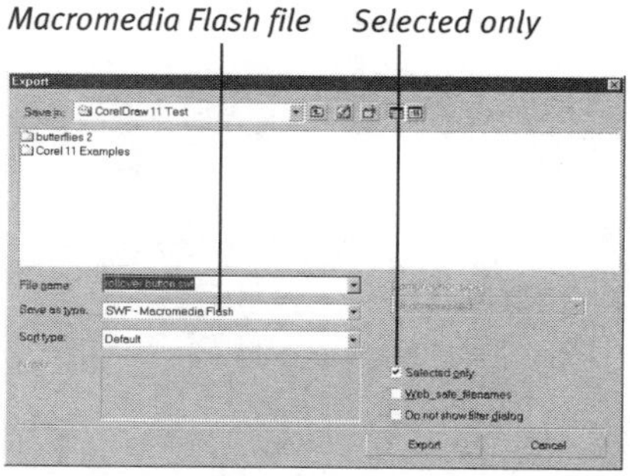

Macromedia Flash file   Selected only

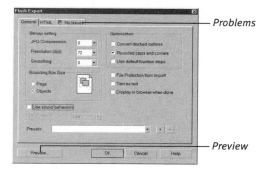

Figure 17.19 Name the resulting rollover file and pick a location in which to save it.

—— Problems

—— Preview

Figure 17.20 In the Flash Export dialog box, you can preview the effect or just click OK to create the file.

Original   Modem speed   Zoom   Preview

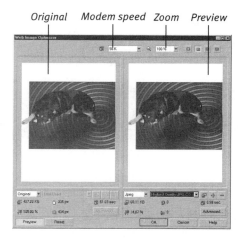

Figure 17.21 Use the Web Image Optimizer to reduce an image's size.

To publish a rollover as a Flash object:

1. Choose File > Publish To The Web > Flash embedded in HTML.

   The Export dialog box appears (**Figure 17.19**).

2. Name the object file, click the Selected only check box, and click Export.

   The Flash Export dialog box appears (**Figure 17.20**).

3. No Issues should be noted on the right-most tab. If you want to make sure that the rollover works properly, click the Preview button.

   The button is loaded into your browser.

4. Click OK to complete the export process.

   Two files are generated: an HTML (.htm) file and a Flash (.swf) file of the same name.

Optimizing images for the Web

The more images you place on a Web page and the larger their file sizes, the longer it will take the page to load in a person's browser. And although 56K and faster modems are the standard, some people still access the Internet with older, slower modems. As a result, it's important to balance image quality and size when preparing graphics for the Web. To handle this, CorelDraw 11 provides the Web Image Optimizer.

To optimize an image for the Web:

1. Open the image file in CorelDraw.

2. Choose File > Publish To The Web > Web Image Optimizer.

   The Web Image Optimizer dialog box appears (**Figure 17.21**).

3. Click a button in the upper-right corner to display two windows: one for the original and one for a preview of the revised image.

continues on next page

4. Select the modem speed for which you want to optimize from the drop-down list at the top of the dialog box.

5. In the first window, select the image's current file type from the drop-down list. (If the file is still in native CorelDraw format, choose Original.)

6. In the second window, select the image's destination file type from the drop-down list, and select a setting from the second drop-down list.

7. To set other options for the destination file, click the Advanced button.

A dialog box specific to the selected file type appears (**Figure 17.22**).

8. Set options as desired and click OK.

9. Click the Preview button to calculate the file's new size and its approximate transmission time, as well as to preview it in the second window.

10. To view results for other file types, repeat Steps 6–9. Otherwise, click OK.

A standard Save dialog box appears.

11. Name the file, choose a location on disk in which to save it, and click Save.

The file is saved in the specified format.

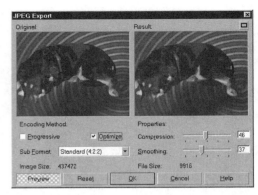

Figure 17.22 A dialog box specific to the selected output file format appears. Choose settings, preview the image (if you like), and click OK.

✔ Tips

■ You can move the image around to zero in on a particular area. Move the pointer into the left (original) image window. When the pointer changes to a hand, you can click and drag the image. The image in the second window moves to match.

■ If you select a *progressive JPEG* as the output format, the image downloads in a series of passes that get progressively clearer. Otherwise, the image downloads from its top to its bottom.

Figure 17.23 You can drag the Internet toolbar to any convenient position in the drawing window.

Internet tab

Figure 17.24 You can also set Internet options on the Internet tab of the Object Properties docker.

Hyperlinks and Bookmarks

When clicked in a Web browser, a *hyperlink* (or link) causes the user to jump from the current Web page to another in the same site, to a completely different site, or to another spot on the current Web page. *Bookmarks* (or anchors) are points on a given Web page that have been set as the target of a hyperlink. Bookmarks and hyperlinks can be assigned to either text or images. When assigned to an image, the area that the user can click is called a *hotspot*.

You can create bookmarks, hyperlinks, and hotspots using controls on the Internet toolbar (**Figure 17.23**) or the Object Properties docker (**Figure 17.24**).

To display the Internet toolbar, choose Window > Toolbars > Internet. To open the Object Properties docker, choose Window > Dockers > Properties. (You can also open this docker by selecting the Pick Tool, right-clicking an image or paragraph text object, and choosing Properties from the pop-up menu that appears.)

Creating bookmarks and links

Here's how bookmarks and links work. First, assign a bookmark to the text or graphic object to which you want the user to jump. Then select the text or graphic object that the user will click to trigger the jump, linking it to the bookmarked object.

To create a bookmark:

1. Display the Internet toolbar (**Figure 17.23**) or the Internet tab of the Object Properties docker (**Figure 17.24**).

2. With the Pick Tool, select the text object or image to which you want to assign the bookmark.

continues on next page

3. On the Internet toolbar (**Figure 17.25**) or the Internet tab of the Object Properties docker (**Figure 17.26**), select Bookmark from the Behavior drop-down list, type a name for the bookmark in the Internet Bookmark text box, and press (Enter).

The bookmark is assigned to the object. Whenever you select that object in the drawing window, the assigned bookmark name will be displayed in the Internet Bookmark text box

To create a link to a bookmark:

◆ Use the Pick Tool to select the trigger object, and—on the Internet toolbar or the Object Properties docker—select URL as the Behavior. Select the bookmark from the Internet Address drop-down list.

or

◆ Right-click the trigger object and choose the bookmark from the Internet Links submenu (**Figure 17.27**).

✔ Tip

■ The bookmark's document page name or number precedes its name in the URL box, such as *_PAGE 2#CDROM image.*

To create a link to a Web page:

1. Using the Pick Tool, select the text or graphic object that—when clicked—will serve as the link's trigger.

2. Select URL as the Behavior in the Internet toolbar or the Object Properties docker.

3. Type the URL in the Internet Address text box (**Figure 17.28**), or select a recently used URL from the drop-down list.

Behavior   *Bookmark name*

Figure 17.25 Using the Internet toolbar, select Bookmark as the Behavior and name the bookmark in the text box.

Internet tab

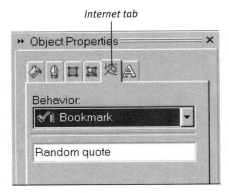

Figure 17.26 Creating a bookmark using the Object Properties docker is accomplished in the same manner as with the Internet toolbar.

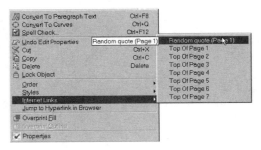

Figure 17.27 A simple way to establish a link to a bookmark is to right-click the trigger object and choose the bookmark name from this pop-up menu.

Behavior   *URL (address)*

Figure 17.28 Set URL as the Behavior and type the address of the Web page into the Internet Address text box.

Visit my Web site (Silicon Wasteland)
to learn more about my recent books.

Figure 17.29 Using the Text Tool, select the text that will serve as the hyperlink.

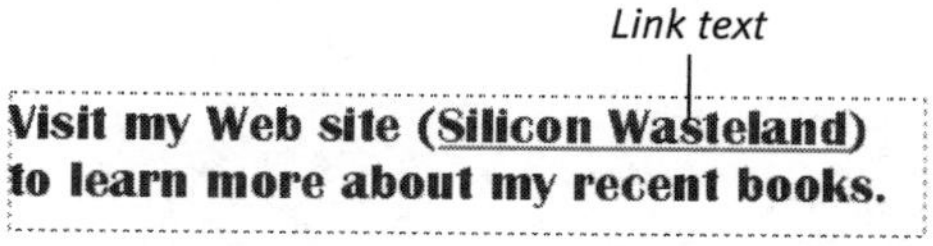

Link text

Visit my Web site (Silicon Wasteland)
to learn more about my recent books.

Figure 17.30 After creating the hyperlink, the link text is shown as underlined.

To link specific text to a Web page:

1. Select the text frame and make sure that the Text > Make Text Web Compatible command is preceded by a checkmark.

2. Within the text frame, use the Text Tool to select the words that will serve as the link (**Figure 17.29**).

3. Select URL as the Behavior in the Internet toolbar or the Object Properties docker.

4. Type, paste, or select the URL in the Internet Address list box on the Internet toolbar or the Object Properties docker.

    The selected text will be shown as underlined (**Figure 17.30**). The underlining indicates to anyone who views the page that the text is a clickable link.

✔ Tip

■ Typing a lengthy URL introduces the possibility of error. To make sure that the URL is correct, visit the target Web page in your browser, select the URL in the browser's Address box, copy it (Ctrl C), and then paste it (Ctrl V) into the Internet Address text box.

Too Many Bookmarks?

If a CorelDraw document contains more than a handful of bookmarks, you might want to open the Internet Bookmarks Manager docker. To quickly jump to any bookmark, click its name in the docker window and then click the Select button.

Converting Documents to Web Pages

After you've finished designing your Web pages, it's time to convert them into HTML and image files that can be read by Web browsers. Each document page will be converted to a separate Web page, and a folder will be created to store all the images on the pages. As part of the process, the pages are automatically checked for HTML conflicts and errors.

To convert a document to Web pages:

1. Be sure that your CorelDraw document has been saved normally.

2. Choose File > Publish To The Web > HTML.

    The Publish To The Web dialog box appears, open to the General tab (**Figure 17.31**).

3. Check the right-most tab to see if any issues are noted. If so, click the tab to read about them.

    Many issues can be corrected during the conversion process. If you'd rather fix them manually, click the Cancel button, make the necessary corrections, and begin again with Step 1.

4. On the General tab, choose a layout style from the HTML Layout Method drop-down list.

5. Enter a folder name for the HTML output in the Destination text box, or select a folder by clicking the folder icon.

6. In the Image folder text box, enter a name for the subfolder in which the images will be stored, or accept the default name.

7. If you've exported these pages previously and want to retain only the newest copies, click the Replace existing files check box.

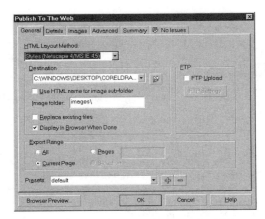

Figure 17.31 Most of the critical settings for HTML output can be found on the General tab.

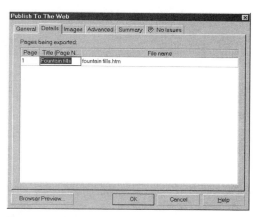

Figure 17.32 You can assign or change the display titles for your Web pages on the Details tab.

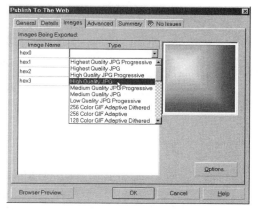

Figure 17.33 You can rename or change file type and compression settings for images on the Images tab.

Figure 17.34 The output consists of one or more HTML files and a folder that contains the images.

8. To automatically open the new pages in your browser following the conversion, click the Display In Browser When Done check box.

9. In the Export Range area, indicate whether you want to generate HTML files for all pages in the document, only the current page, or a range of pages.

10. On the Details tab (**Figure 17.32**), you can enter/edit the title and file name for each page. (The title is the text that will appear in a browser's title bar when the page is viewed.)

11. On the Images tab (**Figure 17.33**), you can view or alter the file and compression settings for the images on your Web pages.

12. Click OK to export the Web pages and close the dialog box (**Figure 17.34**).

✔ Tips

■ On the General tab, there's an FTP (*File Transfer Protocol*) section. By checking the FTP Upload check box, clicking the FTP Settings button, and entering the necessary log-on information, you can upload your Web pages and images to a server from CorelDraw. Contact the server administrator for the correct settings information.

■ Check the Summary tab to see how long it will take to download your exported pages at various modem speeds. If it will take too long, you may want to consider using a higher compression setting for images on the pages.

■ You can view the Web output by opening any of the resulting HTML files. Your browser will launch and display the selected Web page.

PRINTING

CorelDraw 11 stores vector drawings as mathematical equations and bitmap images as pixels, but both types of graphics are rendered as dots when they're printed. The quality of the printed page depends on the resolution of the output device. The higher the resolution, the finer and sharper the output will be.

Each time you print, you'll start by opening the Print dialog box (**Figure 18.1**). This tabbed dialog box provides access to all of CorelDraw's print services.

Specify what gets printed   *Selected printer*   *Set or view printer properties*   *Mini-preview*

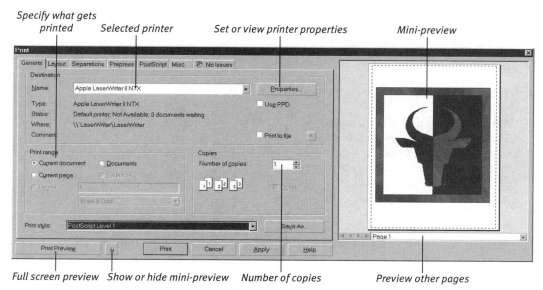

Full screen preview   *Show or hide mini-preview*   *Number of copies*   *Preview other pages*

Figure 18.1 The Print dialog box offers a generous assortment of print options.

Basic Printing

Printing most documents doesn't require you to set a multitude of confusing print options. All you may have to do is click a button or two.

To print one copy of a document:

1. Choose File > Print, press Ctrl P, or click the Print icon on the Standard toolbar.

   The Print dialog box opens to the General tab with your default printer selected (see Figure 18.1).

2. To accept the default printer and the current print settings, click the Print button.

✔ Tip

■ Always save your document before printing.

To print multiple copies of a document:

1. Choose File > Print, press Ctrl P, or click the Print icon on the Standard toolbar.

2. In the Copies area of the Print dialog box (**Figure 18.2**), type a number in the Number of copies text box or click the arrows to set the number.

3. To accept the remaining print settings, click the Print button.

✔ Tip

■ If your document has more than one page, the Collate check box will be available (**Figure 18.2**). Normally, when you request a printout of a three-page document, the printer prints all page ones, all page twos, and then all page threes. If you check the Collate check box, you'll receive the printouts in sorted order.

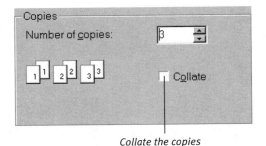

Collate the copies

Figure 18.2 Specify the number of copies desired.

BASIC PRINTING

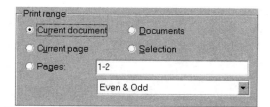

Figure 18.3 In the Print range area, specify what you want to print.

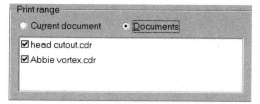

Figure 18.4 If you click the Documents radio button, you can indicate which open documents will print.

To print specific pages or objects:

1. Choose File > Print, press Ctrl P, or click the Print icon on the Standard toolbar.

2. Click one of the following radio buttons in the Print range area (**Figure 18.3**):

   ▲ **Current document**. Print the entire document that was active when you chose the Print command.

   ▲ **Documents**. If you have several documents open, this option lets you select the ones to be printed (**Figure 18.4**).

   ▲ **Current page**. Print only the currently active page in the active document.

   ▲ **Selection**. If you selected objects before opening the Print dialog box, only those objects will be printed.

   ▲ **Pages**. Print only specific pages of the current document. Use the text box to specify the page numbers or range to print. Using the drop-down list, specify whether even and odd, only even, or only odd pages in the range will print.

3. Click the Print button.

✔ Tips

■ If you use the Pages option, you can print a range of pages by separating them with a hyphen (1-5); individual, nonconsecutive pages by separating them with commas (1, 5, 7); or a combination of ranges and individual pages (1-3, 6, 8-10). If you enter a number followed only by a hyphen (such as 3-), the document will print from the specified page to the end of the document.

■ While working on a document, you can display the area of the page that will print by choosing View > Show > Printable Area.

Printing Oversized Drawings

If you create a drawing that is larger than can fit on a single page (such as a poster), you can use the Layout tab to *scale* the drawing to fit or you can *tile* the printout. Tiling splits the drawing onto several pages. After printing, you can tape the pages together to view the entire drawing at its true size.

To scale a printout:

1. Choose File > Print, press Ctrl P, or click the Print icon on the Standard toolbar.

2. Click the Print dialog box's Layout tab (**Figure 18.5**).

3. Click Fit to page to scale the drawing to the largest size that will fit on the paper.

   or

   Click Reposition images to, select a paper position from the drop-down list, and enter a scale factor, width, or height. To resize proportionately, depress the padlock icon.

4. Set additional options or click Print.

To tile a printout:

1. Choose File > Print, press Ctrl P, or click the Print icon on the Standard toolbar.

2. Click the Print dialog box's Layout tab (**Figure 18.5**).

3. Check the Print tiled pages check box in the Tiling area.

   Two text boxes appear beneath the check box (**Figure 18.6**).

4. For the Tile overlap, enter a specific distance (such as 0.51 inches) or a percentage of the page width.

5. *Optional*: To make it easier to tape the pages together, check the Tiling marks check box (**Figure 18.6**).

6. Set additional options or click Print.

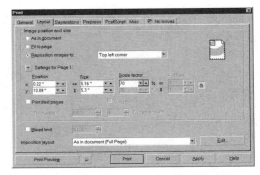

Figure 18.5 You can enable scaling and tiling in the Layout tab of the Print dialog box.

Figure 18.6 Set tiling options when printing an oversized drawing (such as a poster) on multiple pages.

Orientation — Paper size

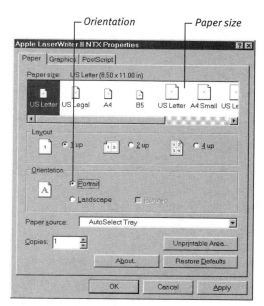

Figure 18.7 This is the Properties dialog box for an Apple LaserWriter IINTX.

PCL and PostScript Printers

There are many brands of printers and imagesetters that do an excellent job of printing vector drawings, but most use only two languages: PCL and PostScript. PCL (Printer Command Language), developed by Hewlett-Packard, is a printer-dependent language that operates only at the printer level. PostScript, developed by Adobe, is a programmable, device-independent language that can be used to *encapsulate* (contain) all the necessary information for printing a document.

The Hewlett-Packard DeskJet and LaserJet printers are popular PCL printers. Common PostScript output devices include the Linotronic imagesetters and Apple LaserWriters.

Alternate Printers and Paper Options

You may have access to more than one printer. Using the Print dialog box, you can select the specific printer you want to use and set its properties. Some of the properties include the size and orientation of the paper, the print resolution, and whether the printout will be color or black-and-white.

To select a different printer:

1. Choose File > Print, press Ctrl P, or click the Print icon on the Standard toolbar.

2. Click the Name drop-down list, and select the printer you want to use.

3. Set additional options or click Print.

To set a different paper size and orientation for a printer:

1. Choose File > Print, press Ctrl P, or click the Print icon on the Standard toolbar.

2. Click the Name drop-down list, and select the printer you want to use.

3. Click the Properties button.

   The Properties dialog box for the selected printer appears (**Figure 18.7**). The dialog box contains different options for different printers, depending on their capabilities.

4. Click the Paper tab (if it isn't selected).

5. Select a paper size from the scrolling list.

6. Select an orientation, indicating whether the page will be printed in *portrait* (normal) or *landscape* (sideways) mode.

7. Click OK to close the Properties dialog box.

8. Set additional options or click Print.

✔ Tip

■ You can also set properties for the current printer by choosing File > Print Setup.

Using a Service Bureau

When preparing files for a service bureau or print shop, you will probably need to generate PostScript (.ps) or Encapsulated PostScript (.eps) files, include crop marks, and provide information about the project and how you want it printed. If the project is color, you will need to prepare *color separations* (creating one sheet for each process and spot color) with registration marks.

Note that in order to generate a PostScript or Encapsulated PostScript file, you *must* print to a PostScript printer, such as one of the Apple LaserWriters. (If you don't actually *own* such a printer, you can always print to the Device-Independent PostScript File print driver or to the particular printer that is used by your service bureau. Contact them for help selecting an appropriate print driver.)

To add crop marks, registration marks, and file information:

1. Choose File > Print, press Ctrl P, or click the Print icon on the Standard toolbar.

2. Click the Misc. tab of the Print dialog box (**Figure 18.8**).

3. In the Proofing options area, check Fit printer's marks and layout to page.

4. To print an information sheet for the printer, check the Print job information sheet check box.

5. Click the Prepress tab (**Figure 18.9**).

6. Enter checkmarks for the items you wish to set.

7. Print the document or save it as a PostScript or Encapsulated PostScript print file (as explained on the following pages).

✔ Tip

■ Many prepress settings can be viewed in the mini-preview or in Print Preview mode.

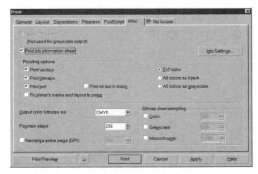

Figure 18.8 To ensure that the proofing marks will not appear outside the printer's printable area, check the option to Fit printer's marks and layout to page.

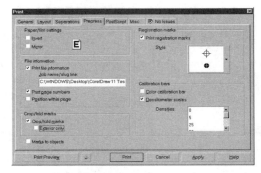

Figure 18.9 On the Prepress tab, you can set additional print options, such as crop marks. Check with your service bureau for their requirements.

Proofing Options

In the Proofing options area of the Misc. tab (**Figure 18.8**), you can specify the document elements that will appear when printed. By selectively checking items, you can make it easier to proof complex documents.

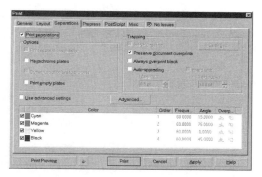

Figure 18.10 On the Separations tab, specify separation options, such as the individual colors to print.

PostScript printer
or print driver   View other options

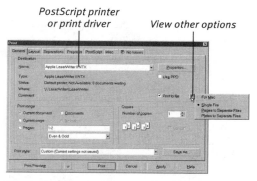

Figure 18.11 Choose a PostScript printer on which to base the print file.

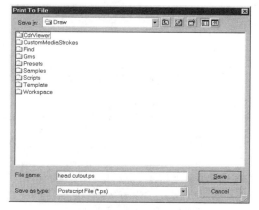

Figure 18.12 Specify a destination, file type (.ps), and file name in the Print To File dialog box.

To create color separations:

1. Choose File > Print, press Ctrl P, or click the Print icon on the Standard toolbar.

2. Click the Separations tab of the Print dialog box (**Figure 18.10**).

3. Check the Print separations check box.

4. Select the colors that you want printed as separations.

5. Click the Prepress tab (see Figure 18.9).

6. Check the Print file information check box to print the name of each color on its separation page.

7. Check the Position within page check box to print the file information on the page.

8. Check the Print registration marks check box.

9. Choose other printing options, click Print to print the separations, or print the file to disk for output at a service bureau.

To generate a PostScript (.ps) file:

1. Save your project by choosing File > Save or by pressing Ctrl S.

2. Choose File > Print, press Ctrl P, or click the Print icon on the Standard toolbar.

3. Select a PostScript printer (**Figure 18.11**).

4. Check the Print to file check box.

5. Click the Print button.
   The Print To File dialog box appears (**Figure 18.12**).

6. Navigate to the drive and folder where you want to save the print file.

7. Select *PostScript File (*.ps)* from the Save as type drop-down list.

8. Type a name in the File name text box.

9. Click the Save button.

USING A SERVICE BUREAU

229

To generate an Encapsulated PostScript (.eps) file:

1. Save your project by choosing File > Save or by pressing Ctrl S.

2. Choose File > Export or press Ctrl E. The Export dialog box appears (**Figure 18.13**).

3. Navigate to the drive and folder where you want to save the file.

4. Select *EPS–Encapsulated PostScript* from the Save as type drop-down list.

5. In the File name text box, enter a name for the export file.

6. Click the Export button. The EPS Export dialog box appears (**Figure 18.14**).

7. Set any desired options. (Check with the service bureau for the correct settings.)

8. Click OK to generate the EPS file.

✔ Tip

■ EPS files can also be imported into or opened in many graphics programs, such as Photoshop and CorelDraw 11. They can also be placed as images in desktop publishing layouts.

Choose EPS as the file type

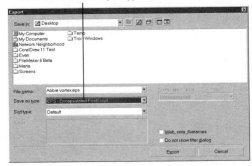

Figure 18.13 Specify a file type (EPS), location, and file name for the export file.

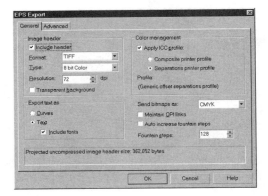

Figure 18.14 Set EPS export options and then click OK to generate the file.

The Service Bureau Wizard

If you aren't totally comfortable with preparing files for a service bureau and want to avoid costly mistakes, you can use the Service Bureau Wizard to step you through the process. It assembles the necessary files and even generates a PDF file that the service bureau can check against the job. To use the wizard, choose File > Prepare for Service Bureau.

USING A SERVICE BUREAU

Problems are listed on this tab

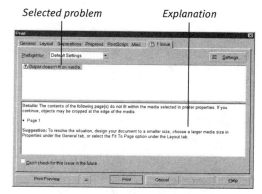

Figure 18.15 CorelDraw continuously performs preflight checks as you set print options.

Selected problem   Explanation

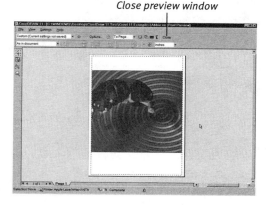

Figure 18.16 Select a listed problem for a detailed explanation, as well as suggestions for correcting it.

Close preview window

Figure 18.17 Use Print Preview mode to preview your printouts before committing them to paper or sending them to a service bureau.

Preflight and Print Preview

CorelDraw has two features that will help you determine if the printout will turn out as you expect—before committing it to paper or sending it to a service bureau. First, you can open the *Preflight tab* of the Print dialog box to view problems with the printout. Second, using the *Print Preview* feature, you can see exactly what the printout will look like. If you want to print a proof of a drawing but it is larger than the page or very small, you can scale the drawing in the Print Preview window.

To perform a preflight check:

1. When you open the Print dialog box, CorelDraw automatically does a preflight check on the current document. If there are problems, they are noted on the Preflight tab (**Figure 18.15**).

2. To view preflight problems (**Figure 18.16**), click the Preflight tab.

3. To see an explanation of a problem (along with suggested solutions), select a problem in the top part of the dialog box.

To open Print Preview:

Do one of the following:

◆ If you have the Print dialog box open, click the Print Preview button.

◆ Choose File > Print Preview.

  The Print Preview window opens (**Figure 18.17**). When you're ready to return to your drawing, click the Close button.

To resize a drawing in Print Preview:

1. Open the Print Preview window by clicking Print Preview in the Print dialog box or by choosing File > Print Preview.

2. Click on the drawing.

3. Drag a handle to resize the drawing.

continues on next page

PREFLIGHT AND PRINT PREVIEW

✔ Tips

- Scaling the drawing in Print Preview mode doesn't scale the actual drawing in your document. It only changes the size of the drawing when it's printed.

- You can drag the drawing to a new position on the page, if you wish. This is handy if the image is partially outside the page boundary, for example.

- While in Print Preview mode, you can zoom in or out to get different views of the drawing. Click the Zoom Tool in the Print Preview Toolbox (**Figure 18.18**). To zoom in, click in the Preview window or drag-select an area. To zoom out, press [Shift] as you click, press [F3], or right-click the drawing and choose Zoom Out from the pop-up menu that appears (**Figure 18.19**). For more precise zooming, you can also use the zoom tools in the toolbar (**Figure 18.20**).

- Are you wondering why your color drawing is previewing in grayscale? It's probably because you have a black-and-white or grayscale printer chosen. By default, preview mode uses the characteristics of the chosen printer to determine what should be displayed. To force a color or a grayscale preview, switch to Print Preview mode, and choose View > Preview Color > Color or View > Preview Color > Grayscale.

Figure 18.18 Use the Zoom Tool to change the magnification level.

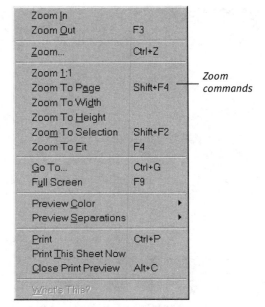

Figure 18.19 Right-click to choose any of these common Zoom settings.

Figure 18.20 When the Zoom Tool is active, you can also select Zoom commands from the toolbar.

Figure 18.21 Use Acrobat Reader to view PDF files.

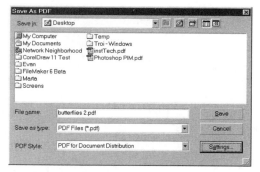

Figure 18.22 Specify an optimization option, disk location, and file name for the PDF file.

Creating a PDF File

Another useful print-to-disk or save option is CorelDraw's ability to create *PDF* (Portable Document Format) files from any document. PDF files are platform-independent and can be viewed or printed with Adobe Acrobat or Acrobat Reader (**Figure 18.21**), a free utility available from *www.adobe.com*. PDF files preserve the fonts, images, and formatting of the original document, making them ideal for general document distribution.

To create a PDF file:

1. Open the CorelDraw document from which you want to create a PDF file.

2. Choose File > Publish To PDF.
   The Save As PDF dialog box appears (**Figure 18.22**).

3. From the PDF Style list, choose one of the following formatting options:
   - ▲ **PDF for Document Distribution**. For distribution among members of a workgroup.
   - ▲ **PDF for Editing**. A document that can be edited with Adobe Acrobat.
   - ▲ **PDF for Prepress**. Suitable for being printed by a service bureau.
   - ▲ **PDF for the Web**. For inclusion on a Web page (Internet or intranet).
   - ▲ **PDF/X-1**. Another prepress format, using ZIP file compression rather than LZW (a popular format for compressing TIFF images).

4. In the File name text box, enter a name for the PDF file (or accept the proposed name).

5. Click the Save button.

continues on next page

✔ Tips

- To customize the settings of one of the PDF styles listed in Step 3 or to create your own, click the Settings button in the Save As PDF dialog box (see Figure 18.22). The Publish To PDF dialog box appears (**Figure 18.23**). Make any necessary changes and click OK.

- If a client or colleague needs to be able to see or print one of your CorelDraw documents (but not edit it), you might want to send him or her a PDF file instead. While few programs other than CorelDraw can open a native CorelDraw file, almost everyone has Acrobat Reader. (And if they don't, it's a free download from Adobe's Web site.)

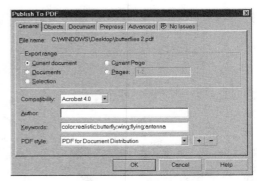

Figure 18.23 Make any desired changes and click OK.

CORELDRAW COMPONENTS

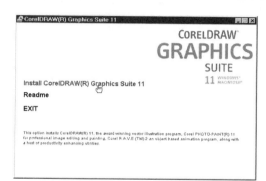

Figure A.1 When you insert Disc 1 into your CD-ROM drive, this splash screen appears. Click the first item to install CorelDraw Graphics Suite 11.

Suite vs. Stand-alone

CorelDraw 11 is available both as a suite of programs and as a separate (or *stand-alone*) application. The difference between the two is that CorelDraw Graphics Suite 11 includes Corel Photo-Paint 11, an image-editing application.

The locations of items mentioned in this appendix are specific to CorelDraw Graphics Suite 11. The arrangement of the discs, as well as the installation procedure, may be different for CorelDraw 11 (stand-alone).

CorelDraw Graphics Suite 11 comes with five CDs. The discs contain the following items, which you will learn about in this appendix:

- *1–Applications:* Main installation CD, containing the programs, fonts, and manuals (in Adobe Acrobat format)

- *2–Extras:* Installation CD for OmniPage SE, Acrobat Reader 5, QuickTime 5, and Microsoft VBA Web Service References Tool; also contains thousands of additional fonts in the Fonts and Extra Fonts folders

- *3–Clipart images:* Clip art, patterns, spray lists, frames, and tiles

- *4–Photos and objects:* Photographs, objects, brush textures, and sound files

- *5–Premium Photos:* Photographs (in TIFF format)

To install CorelDraw Graphics Suite 11, insert Disc 1 and—when the splash screen shown in **Figure A.1** appears—click the item labeled Install CorelDraw Graphics Suite 11.

When you have completed the basic installation, you can install ancillary utilities (such as Adobe Acrobat Reader and QuickTime) by inserting the 2–Extras CD and clicking items on the splash screen that appears.

Installed Programs

If you performed a Typical Installation, you installed CorelDraw 11, as well as the other primary CorelDraw Graphics Suite 11 programs and components (**Figure A.2**). Here's a rundown of the installed items:

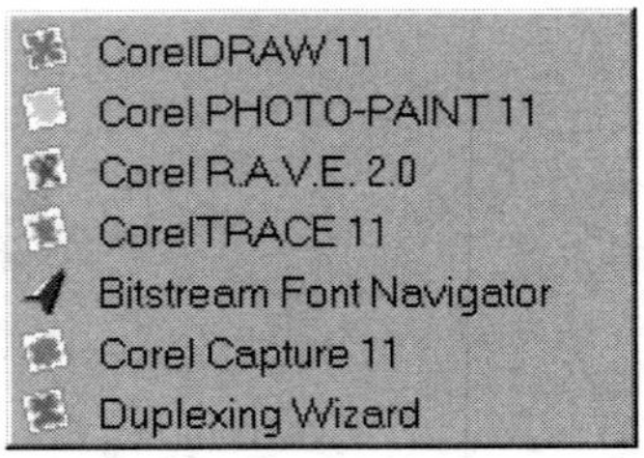

◆ **CorelDraw 11.** This drawing program is the subject of this book.

◆ **Corel Photo-Paint 11.** Clean up and embellish scans, photos, and other bitmap images with this image-editing program.

◆ **Corel R.A.V.E. 2.0.** Create object-based animations suitable for inclusion in Web pages with this program.

◆ **CorelTrace 11.** Trace bitmap artwork, photos, and scanned images and convert them into draw/vector objects.

◆ **Bitstream Font Navigator.** Create font groups, view and print font samples, and install new fonts with this font management utility.

◆ **Corel Capture 11.** Take snapshots of dialog boxes, menus, windows, and selected areas of the screen with this capture utility. It can also record onscreen actions as animations.

◆ **Duplexing Wizard.** Print documents on both sides of the paper.

✔ Tips

■ Many of the utilities have no documentation. Launch the programs and then read the associated Help file to learn how they work.

■ To reset the workspace for any of the major application to its default settings, hold down ⌊F8⌋ as the application launches.

Figure A.2 These items can be found in the Corel Graphics Suite 11 folder in the Programs menu.

- CorelDRAW 11
- Corel PHOTO-PAINT 11
- Corel R.A.V.E. 2.0
- CorelTRACE 11
- Bitstream Font Navigator
- Corel Capture 11
- Duplexing Wizard

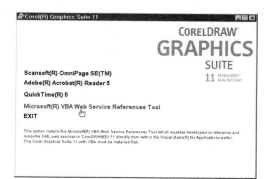

Figure A.3 Insert CD 2–Extras to install the optional utilities.

Clickable table of contents entries

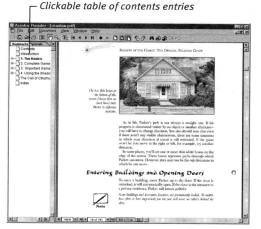

Figure A.4 Acrobat Reader can display any PDF file (such as this full-length book) on a PC or Mac.

Additional Utilities

From the Disc 2–Extras splash screen (**Figure A.3**), you can install these additional utilities:

◆ **Scansoft OmniPage SE.** OCR (Optical Character Recognition) utility that can convert scanned text documents into editable text files.

◆ **QuickTime 5.** System software that enables you to view video files (static or streaming) and graphic images in many popular formats.

◆ **Adobe Acrobat Reader 5.** View and print PDF (Portable Document Format) files with this free utility (**Figure A.4**). This format is very popular for creating platform-independent documents and is often used to produce software manuals and similar materials.

◆ **Microsoft VBA Web Service References Tool.** Enables developers to integrate XML *(eXtensible Markup Language)* Web services into CorelDraw 11.

✔ Tips

■ QuickTime *(www.apple.com/quicktime)* and Acrobat Reader *(www.adobe.com)* are regularly updated. Check their Web sites for the most current versions, updates, and upgrade options.

■ During the development of CorelDraw 11, QuickTime 6.0 was released. Unless you really want the older QuickTime 5.0 that's on Disc 2–Extras, visit Apple's Web site and download the most current version. QuickTime Player is free; QuickTime Pro (for developers) is an inexpensive upgrade.

■ If you want to test QuickTime, you can find plenty of sample movie clips at *www.apple.com/trailers*.

INDEX

WWW.PEACHPIT.COM

Quality How-to Computer Books

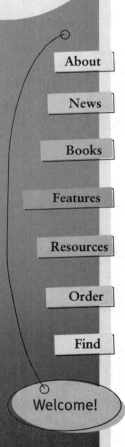

About

News

Books

Features

Resources

Order

Find

Welcome!

Visit Peachpit Press on the Web at www.peachpit.com

- Check out new feature articles each Monday: excerpts, interviews, tips, and plenty of how-tos

- Find any Peachpit book by title, series, author, or topic on the Books page

- See what our authors are up to on the News page: signings, chats, appearances, and more

- Meet the Peachpit staff and authors in the About section: bios, profiles, and candid shots

- Use Resources to reach our academic, sales, customer service, and tech support areas and find out how to become a Peachpit author

Peachpit.com is also the place to:

- Chat with our authors online
- Take advantage of special Web-only offers
- Get the latest info on new books